PASSPORT READING
JOURNEYS™ II

Expanded Learning
Voyager

PHOTO AND ART CREDITS

Expedition 1: 1, AP Images/Ellis Neel; 2, AP Images/John Terhune; 4, Michael Newman/PhotoEdit; 5, AP Images/Brad Ferris; 6, AP Images/Mike Deter; 9, AP Images/D.J. Peters; 10, AP Images/David Zalubowski; 12(t), AP Images/Kent Gilbert, (l), AP Images/Mike Lucia; 15(t), AP Images/Clay Jackson, (b), AP Images/Kathy Willens; 16, AP Images/Ramin Talaie

Expedition 2: 17, AP Images/Marco Ugarte; 18, AP Images; 21, AP Images; 23, AP Images/Derik Holtman; 28, AP Images/PA; 29, AP Images; 31, AP Images/Dean Hoffmeyer; 32, AP Images/Dave Bowman

Expedition 3: 33, 34, Photodisc, Inc.; 35, NASA; 36, ESA; 37, NASA; 38, ESA; 41, AP Images/Jim Campbell, Pool; 43, Jeff Greenberg/PhotoEdit; 44, ESA-S CORVAJA; 45, ESA-P Duque; 47, NASA; 48, NASA

Expedition 4: 49, SuperStock; 50, AP Images/Pete Leabo; 51(t), Eric Risberg, (b), AP Images/Deither Endicher; 52, AP Images/Roh Frehm; 53, Bob Daemmrich\PhotoEdit; 55, Michael Newman\PhotoEdit; 56, AP Images/Scott Audette; 58, Robert Brenner/PhotoEdit; 61(b), SuperStock; 63, SuperStock; 65, AP Images/NASA

Expedition 5: 67, AP Images/Jack Smith; 68, NASA; 69, FEMA; 71, Jonathan Ley; 74, SuperStock; 75, Corbis; 77, NASA; 82, FEMA

Expedition 6: 97, AP Images/Damian Dovarganes; 101, istockphoto; 102, AP Images/Ben Margot; 103, istockphoto

Expedition 7: 105, istockphoto; 106, AP Images/Steven Senne; 109-111, istockphoto; 113(t,b), AP Images/Doug Mills; 116, AP Images/Katsumi Kasahara; 117, AP Images/Jennifer Graylock; 120, AP Images; 121, istockphoto; 122, AP Images/Jack Plunkett; 123, AP Images/Mark Foley; 124, AP Images/Chris Pizzello

Expedition 8: 125, 126, 129-132, 137, 138, 141, istockphoto; 142, Fotosearch

Expedition 9: 145-146, 148(t), 149(t, bl), istockphoto; 149(br), Leslie Kell; 150, 152, 154, 156, istockphoto; 158, 159, AP Images/Erik S. Lesser; 160, AP Images/Fort Collins Coloradoan, V. Richard Varo; 161, AP Images/John Bazemore; 162, istockphoto

Expedition 10: 165, istockphoto; 166(l), AP Images/DAB, (r), istockphoto; 167-168, istockphoto; 169, AP Images/Daily News-Sun, Gregory Harris; 170, AP Images/Vanessa Allen Pool; 171, AP Images; 172, AP Images; 173, AIP Emilio Segrè Visual Archives, gift of James West; 175-177, istockphoto; 181, AP Images/Jeff Roberson; 182, AP Images/Eric Risberg; 183, AP Images/The Town Talk, Douglas Collier; 184, AP Images

Expedition 11: 186, AP Images; 189, Fotosearch; 201, AP Images; 185, 190, 193-197, istockphoto

Expedition 12: 213, AP Images; 216, Russell Moore; 217, Corbis; 205, 206, 209, 218, istockphoto

Expedition 13: 221, 222, 224, istockphoto; 225, AP Images; 226-228, istockphoto; 229, AP Images; 230, AP Images; 236, AP Images; 237, istockphoto; 240, Corbis; 241, AP Images

Expedition 14: 245, istockphoto; 246, AP Images; 249, 250 courtesy of David Brimner; 251, AP Images; 255, istockphoto; 257, David Alford; 258, 260, 263, 266, 270, AP Images; 267, courtesy DaimlerChrysler

Expedition 15: 271, 286, SuperStock; 274, Photo © copyright by Bill Eichner. Reprinted by permission of Susan Bergholz Literary Services, New York. All rights reserved; 272, 275, 288, 291, istockphoto; 277, *The Daily Pennsylvanian;* 278-281, AP Images; 283, istockphoto; 287, AP Images

LITERATURE CREDITS

From "Learning English: My New Found Land" by Julia Alvarez. Copyright © 1993 by Julia Alvarez. Published in *Newsday*, February 1993. Reprinted by permission of Susan Bergholz Literary Services, New York. All rights reserved.

From *Gig* edited by John Bowe, Marisa Bowe, and Sabin Streeter, copyright © 2000, 2001 by John Bowe, Marisa Bowe, and Sabin Streeter. Used by permission of Crown Publishers, a division of Random House, Inc.

From *A Migrant Family* by Larry Dane Brimner, 1992. Reprinted by permission of the Brimner/Gregg Trust. Text and photos copyright Larry Dane Brimner.

"Kipling and I" by Jesús Colón from *A Puerto Rican in New York, and Other Sketches,* 1993. Reprinted with permission of International Publishers/New York.

"The Loss of Love" by Countee Cullen. Reprinted by permission of GRM Associates Inc., Agents for the Estate of Ida M. Cullen. From the book *Copper Sun* by Countee Cullen. Copyright © 1927 by Harper & Brothers; copyright renewed 1955 by Ida M. Cullen.

From *Keeping the Moon* by Sarah Dessen. Copyright © 1999 by Sarah Dessen. Published by Viking, a division of the Penguin Group.

"How I Learned English" by Gregory Djanikian, from *Falling Deeply into America* (Carnegie Mellon). Reprinted with permission of Gregory Djanikian.

"I, Too," copyright © 1926 by Alfred A. Knopf, Inc. and renewed 1954 by Langston Hughes, from *Selected Poems of Langston Hughes* by Langston Hughes. Used by permission of Alfred A. Knopf, a division of Random House, Inc.

From *Holes* by Louis Sachar, Chapter 4, pages 11–15. Copyright © 1998 by Louis Sachar.

"Phizzog" from *Good Morning, America*, copyright 1928 and renewed 1956 by Carl Sandburg, reprinted by permission of Harcourt, Inc.

From *The Joy Luck Club* by Amy Tan, pages 23–25. Copyright © 1989 by Amy Tan.

ISBN 978-1-4168-0972-2

Copyright 2008 by Voyager Expanded Learning, L.P.

Printed in the United States of America

09 10 11 12 13 WEB 9 8 7 6 5 4 3

Table of Contents

Expedition 1
Connections

Expedition 2

Forensics
Digging into the Past

Expedition 3

Space
Traveling into the Unknown

Expedition 4

Your Health
Fit Minds, Fit Bodies

Expedition 5

Shockwaves
Earthquakes, Volcanoes, Tsunamis

Expedition 6
The Internet

Expedition 7
Money Matters

Expedition 8

The Environment

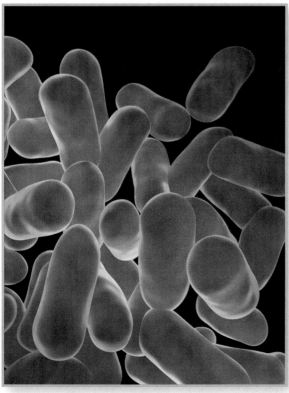

Expedition 9

Diseases

Expedition 10
Technology

Expedition 11

Expedition 12

Expedition 13

Expedition 1

CONNECTIONS

How We Fit Together

- *Why do people come to the United States to live?*
- *How have these immigrants helped to shape American culture?*
- *How do immigrants affect your daily life?*

Anything BUT Burgers!

¹"**I**'m hungry," Calla said, wiping off the soft drink machine.

²Ben stopped chopping onions. "So am I."

³Joy held up two hamburgers and offered them to Calla and Ben. She explained that a customer had changed her mind and didn't want them. But after working at the fast-food restaurant for two months, the teens were tired of hamburgers. The three decided to go out for dinner.

⁴When 7 p.m. arrived, the friends punched out on the time clock. Outside, the summer evening air was still **balmy**. They walked down the busy street, past a **variety** of restaurants. A Chinese take-out place stood on the corner. Next door was a Mexican restaurant. Across the street was an Italian café.

⁵"Stir-fried rice sounds good," Joy said.

⁶"No, I'm not in the mood for Chinese," Ben said. "How about burritos?"

⁷"We could get pasta," said Calla.

[8]Because they couldn't **agree**, they kept walking and passed a restaurant selling pita sandwiches. Calla asked what pita was, and Ben explained that it was a kind of bread that came from the Middle East. "It's good too," he said.

[9]Still, they had a **difficult** time deciding where to eat. Calla said it was because there were so many great ethnic restaurants. People from many different countries had come to their city to live. Each culture had brought its own special food and customs with it.

[10]The teens stopped at a red light and looked up a side street. The whole next block was closed to traffic for an outdoor world market. They decided to check it out.

[11]Under colorful umbrellas were booths filled with fresh fruits, candles, clothes, artworks, toys, trinkets, and every other thing you could imagine. Calla, Joy, and Ben stopped and clapped to the beat of conga drums played by a group of sidewalk musicians. Farther along, they watched a woman with a brush writing Japanese characters on a sheet of silky white paper. At the next table, a man was selling matzo ball soup.

[12]Ben pointed down the street. At the opening to the park, a large hanging sign read: *Foods from Around the World.*

[13]"Come on!" said Calla. "We can each **select** the food we want—all from one place."

[14]Each friend chose food from a different country. Then they shared with one another. It was an interesting and delicious feast!

Nachos

Pizza

Pita

Sushi

What's *Really* American?

¹If you were **stranded** on an island and could have only one kind of food to eat, what would it be? Maybe you'd **prefer** pizza or peanut butter. Perhaps you'd select a bagel, a taco, or a hamburger. Many of these foods are so common that you might think of them as American foods. But they, along with a variety of other foods, are from other countries. They were brought here by people coming to make the United States their home.

"American" Foods

[2]Pizza was brought to the United States by people from Italy in the late 1800s. At first, these new Americans made and ate their pizza at home. But in the early 1900s, Italian Americans started selling pizzas in grocery stores. Later, they opened pizza shops. Pizza soon became **popular** across the United States. Today, Americans eat about 400 slices of pizza every second.

[3]Peanuts probably first grew in South America. Explorers from Spain took peanuts back to their country in the 1500s. From there, traders carried them **throughout** Asia and Africa. When African people were enslaved and brought to America, peanuts came with them. Have you ever heard a peanut called a goober? That word comes from an African name for peanut—*nguba*. In the late 1800s, an American doctor smashed and ground peanuts to make peanut butter. He invented it as a health food. Now peanut butter is one of our country's favorite foods.

[4]Today you also can find bagel shops in many towns and cities. The first bagels probably were made by a Jewish baker in 1683. He made them to thank a king for helping protect the Jewish people from invaders. The king liked to ride horses, so the Jewish baker made the bagels in the shape of a stirrup. A stirrup was called a "bugel" in the Jewish baker's language. In the early 1900s, Jewish immigrants came to the United States. They brought bagels with them.

[5]Do you like tacos? Large numbers of Americans started eating Mexican tacos in the middle 1900s. They continue to enjoy **various** other Mexican foods, too, such as burritos and enchiladas.

[6]In the 1200s, fierce fighters rode their horses across Asia and conquered much of the land. While riding, they softened pieces of meat by placing them under their saddles. Eventually, some of these fighters moved into Russia. Later, in the 1600s, traders from Germany came into the area and learned how delicious ground meat could be. They took the idea back home. People there called the meat "Hamburg steak" after the city of Hamburg, Germany.

People who came to the United States from Germany brought Hamburg steak here. Sometime later, someone somewhere put the meat between two pieces of bread. It became known as a hamburger. Different people claim to be the inventor of the hamburger, but no one knows for sure who was. We do know for sure that many people love them.

"American" Words

[7]Food is not the only thing that other cultures bring to the United States. People also bring their languages. Some words are "borrowed" by Americans. When you speak English, you often use words from other countries.

[8]Have you ever gone to a carnival? Do you like piano music? *Carnival* and *piano* are words we borrowed from Italian.

[9]Did you ever swat a mosquito? Did you ever sit on a patio? Did you ever watch a rodeo? *Mosquito, patio,* and *rodeo* are words we borrowed from Spanish.

[10]Do you wear pajamas when you sleep? Do you like ketchup on your hot dogs? *Pajamas* is a word we borrowed from a language in India, and *ketchup* is from Chinese.

[11]We call these words "borrowed," but they are not really borrowed. We don't have to give them back. Now they are American words too. They are part of the American culture. That culture has been created by various groups of people from around the world.

A Juneteenth to Remember

¹**"W**hat exactly does your cousin look like?" Jill asked.

²Jill's friend Byron shrugged. "I'm not really sure. I haven't seen Keisha since her family moved up to Dallas. That was almost five years ago, when I was 10 and she was 13."

³"What did she say when she called you the other day?" asked Jill.

⁴"Just that she and a friend were driving here to Galveston for the **annual** Juneteenth festival," Byron replied. "So I said I'd meet them here after the parade." Juneteenth is one of Jill's favorite holidays. It **celebrates** the day the slaves of Texas were finally free.

⁵"Meet them where?" Jill asked.

⁶"We didn't say," Byron said. "I just said I'd look for her at the festival."

⁷Jill looked around the large park that already was filled with people. "In this big crowd?"

⁸Byron shrugged. "I guess I forgot how popular Juneteenth is."

⁹Jill and Byron walked past booths with games, treats, and homemade crafts. An enormous barbecue pit billowed smoke into the **humid** summer air. They headed across the lawn toward a crowd of people gathered in front of a stage set up at one end of the park.

¹⁰Jill was looking at faces in the crowd, not knowing what the face she was looking for looked like. "What else did Keisha say?"

¹¹"Nothing," Byron said. "except that she had some kind of surprise."

¹²"Yeah," Jill said. "The surprise is going to be us playing hide-and-seek with her!"

¹³A man on the stage was speaking about President Lincoln and the Emancipation Proclamation. He explained that unlike most people, who came to America of their own free will, the **ancestors** of African Americans had been brought from Africa to be enslaved in America. But in 1863, the government of the United States ruled that all the slaves must be set free. The crowd clapped when he said this.

¹⁴Jill glanced around at the thick crowd and whispered to Byron that Keisha could be standing next to them, and they probably wouldn't even know it.

¹⁵Byron told Jill something else that he remembered Keisha saying. She said she would be wearing a bright red blouse. Jill looked around and noticed a lot of people were wearing red—and none of them seemed to be looking for anyone.

¹⁶The speaker went on with the story of Juneteenth. He said that after the Emancipation Proclamation, no one had bothered to let the slaves in Texas know that they were now free. So **slavery** continued for two-and-a-half more years. The crowd grew quiet.

¹⁷"I think I see her," Byron whispered to Jill.

¹⁸But Jill was busy listening to the next part of the speech. The speaker described how General Granger came riding into Galveston and announced to the people of Texas that all slaves were now free. That declaration of freedom happened on June 19, 1865—now called "Juneteenth." Jill clapped and cheered loudly along with the crowd. She suddenly realized that Byron was tugging on her sleeve. "What is it?" she shouted over the noise.

¹⁹Byron pointed in the distance. Jill stood on tiptoe and looked over the crowd. Two girls were standing by a booth, looking around. One wore a silky red blouse.

A family gathers to celebrate Juneteenth.

²⁰Jill and Byron tried to move that way, but just then the speech ended. The crowd started to move too. By the time they reached the booth, the two girls were gone.

²¹"I'm sorry about all this with Keisha," Byron said. "Let's just have some lunch and celebrate Juneteenth without her."

²²They headed back toward the barbecue, mouths watering. Then with sandwiches and sodas in hand, they found a patch of lawn where they could sit and eat. Afterward Byron lay back on the cool green grass. Up on the stage, the winner of the pie eating contest was being announced.

²³"Oh, Byron," Jill exclaimed, "take a look!"

²⁴A tall young woman with a bright red blouse stood at the center of the stage. Just then the speaker held up a blue ribbon and said, "This year's winner of the pie eating contest was a big surprise to all of us. Congratulations Miss Keisha Jackson!"

Coming to America

¹**W**hat if you had to move to another country—to a place you've never seen before? All around you are the odd sounds of a strange language. You don't understand what people are saying, and they don't understand you. You can't even understand what's happening on TV. People's clothes and ways of doing things seem unusual. There are new laws you don't understand. At the grocery store, you may not find the foods you know and like. You also have to get used to paying with different money.

²Although things are strange, you need to deal with them. First, you need to look for a place to live. Next, you have to figure out how to get into a school or earn money and to shop for things you need. Then you have to learn your way around town.

³These are some problems that immigrants face when they first come to live in the United States. Moving to another country can certainly be difficult. But even though it's difficult, many people still come here.

Hakeem Olajuwon

10

[4]Most immigrants come to **achieve** their dream of a better life. Sometimes that dream is to gain more freedom. Compared with people in some other countries, people in the United States have a great deal of freedom. They can practice their own religion, read the books they want to read, say what they believe, and listen to the music they like.

[5]Often the dream of a better life is to work and make money. In the old days, immigrants came to the United States because they heard the old saying that "the streets are **paved** with gold." When they arrived, they didn't find gold, of course, but many did find **opportunity**. They found the chance to work and succeed.

[6]That is still true today. People in the United States can choose from a wide **array** of jobs. They can work in factories, on concert stages, at schools, or in stores. They can work for themselves at home or for large companies in tall skyscrapers. Here are four success stories of coming to America. They are the stories of an athlete, a business woman, a musician, and an actor.

Hakeem Olajuwon

[7]Hakeem Olajuwon once lived in Nigeria, a country in Africa. As a teenager, he liked playing basketball, and he was good. In the 1970s, Olajuwon had the opportunity to come to the United States to play college basketball for the University of Houston. Later, he played for the Houston Rockets in the NBA. Olajuwon led the Rockets to two championships. Now that's success!

Jenny Ming

[8]Have you ever shopped at an Old Navy clothing store? If so, you were in a store that Jenny Ming is in charge of. Ming was born in Macau, China. When she was young, she moved with her family to the United States. While in college here, Ming studied home economics and planned to teach middle school students. But she also studied business and later went to work for Gap, Inc. In the middle 1990s, she helped Gap start a new store called Old Navy. In 1999, Ming became president of all Old Navy stores. Now that's success!

Carlos Santana

[9]Carlos Santana was born in Mexico in 1947. When he was very young, Santana learned to play the violin and guitar. In the 1960s, he came to San Francisco, where his family had recently moved. He formed the band Santana, whose music is a mixture of rock and Latin, and played at the Woodstock music festival. Santana continues to play music today. One of his albums, *Supernatural*, won nine Grammy Awards. Now that's success!

Arnold Schwarzenegger

[10]Arnold Schwarzenegger was born in 1947 in the tiny town of Thal, Austria. When he was young, he became interested in bodybuilding. After much hard work lifting weights, he won bodybuilding championships in Europe. In 1968, he moved to the United States, even though he spoke very little English. After going to college and becoming a U.S. citizen, Schwarzenegger became a famous Hollywood actor in movies such as *The Terminator, Kindergarten Cop,* and *Jingle All the Way*. Schwarzenegger's more **recent** achievement was a big one. He became the governor of California. Now that's success!

The Rock 'n' Roll Band

[1] **R**.J. slipped a hand over the phone receiver and turned to the other band members in his basement. "It's a client on the phone. She wants to know if we'll play Tejano music at her daughter's wedding."

[2] "Tejano?" Alana asked. She set her microphone back in the stand.

[3] Antwan strummed his electric guitar and laughed. "We play rock 'n' roll!"

[4] "But that's the second person who's asked if we play Tejano," Sara said, shutting off her keyboard.

[5] R.J. told the person on the phone that he'd have to call her back.

[6] The band members discussed the phone

call. Sara said they really should learn to play various kinds of music. But Antwan said they should stick just with rock 'n' roll because that's what they played especially well.

[7]"I agree with Antwan," Alana said.

[8]"The business of music is getting more complicated now," R.J. said. "People want us to play different kinds of music from all these different cultures. But they're also willing to pay us for it." He told the group that the woman on the phone offered to pay them $500 for three hours of playing Tejano.

[9]The band members were quiet. That was the most money they'd ever been offered to play.

[10]Alana said they were worth $500 because they were good. But Antwan pointed out that they weren't good at playing Tejano.

[11]"If it's so popular, we could be good at it," Sara said.

[12]Antwan slowly stood up and put the strap of his guitar over his shoulder. He asked the group members if they knew what instruments they would need to play Tejano. "I know one instrument is an accordion," Alana said. Sara told them her keyboard could sound like an accordion.

[13]"Let's go for it," Antwan said. "Let's get some music and practice."

[14]Alana, Sara, and R.J. quickly agreed. Alana said that they should learn a variety of other music styles, too, like jazz and hip-hop.

[15]Just then R.J.'s phone rang. He joked that it was probably someone asking if they play classical music.

[16]Sara laughed. "If they want to pay us $500, they've got it!"

American Music

¹**H**it the scan button on a radio, and what kind of music do you hear?

²First, you might hear Tejano music. *Tejano* is the Spanish word for Texan. This style of music developed near the border of Mexico and Texas. Tejano musicians play lively Mexican-style music with accordions and guitars.

³A blues station is next on the radio. African Americans developed the style of music called the blues in the late 1800s. Early blues singers told of slavery and their hopes for better times. Today, singers of many different cultures, especially African Americans, sing and play the blues. Blues music has also influenced many other types of music.

⁴Now the radio scanner comes to jazz music. Early jazz was one type of music influenced by blues and African Americans. Since then, jazz artists from different cultures have

The Olympia Brass Band marches in a parade.

Tejano music group, La Mafia, winners at the 39th Grammy Awards ceremony

developed a variety of styles, and jazz is popular all over the world. Jazz musicians sometimes invent the music as they play. Some people think jazz is truly *the* American music.

[5]Next on the radio is rock 'n' roll, with its strong, repeating drum beat and electric guitars. Rock 'n' roll is a combination of different types of music. They include jazz, blues, and especially rhythm and blues, another style developed by African Americans.

[6]Finally, your radio scanner stops at hip-hop. The rapper on the air calls out his story in rhythm and rhyme. Hip-hop, like so many other kinds of music in the United States, began with African Americans.

[7]What type of music would you like to go back and select on the radio dial? What type of American music do you prefer?

FORENSICS
Digging into the Past

- *What can we learn from an old bone?*
- *How can forensic science unlock mysteries from the past?*
- *How does studying the past help us understand ourselves?*

The Case of the Rich Man's Will

Howard Hughes was a pilot who designed and tested his own aircrafts.

A Mysterious Man Dies

[1]In 1976, one of the richest people in the world died. This man had acted very strangely at the end of his life. He locked himself away from the world and saw very few people. He never appeared in public. His hair had not been cut in years, and he was extremely skinny.

[2]The man was Howard Hughes. Hughes was not only rich. He was also a **brilliant** inventor. He had worked closely with the U.S. government on many secret airplane and rocket projects. The FBI was called in when the

government learned of Hughes's death. They wanted to be sure the dead man really was Hughes. Perhaps someone had **kidnapped** Hughes to learn government secrets, leaving another body behind to throw off investigators. Forensic experts at the FBI compared the fingerprints taken from the body with those of Hughes they had on file. The fingerprints matched.

A Mysterious Will Appears

[3]Then the strange case of Howard Hughes got even stranger.

[4]Many people create a legal **document** that tells who should get their money and property when they die. This piece of paper is called a will. At the time Howard Hughes died, he left no known will. When there is no legal will, a court divides the money and property, called the estate, among the person's closest relatives.

[5]Shortly after Hughes died, a will was mysteriously delivered to a church. It appeared that it had been written and signed by Hughes. The will gave a **portion** of Hughes's huge estate to a man named Melvin Dummar. Dummar claimed that years before, he had found Hughes lying injured in the desert. He said that he gave Hughes a ride and lent him some money. Now a will was leaving Dummar a portion of Hughes's estate that was worth millions of dollars.

Was the Will Real?

[6]The court had to determine if the will was **authentic**. The judge needed to be sure it really was Hughes's will. Forensic experts were called in. A forensic expert uses science to test and present material for a court of law. One forensic **method** used to make sure a document is authentic is comparing handwriting. Different handwriting experts compared the writing on the will with samples of Hughes's writing, and they said the writing did not match. Then Dummar's own fingerprints were found on the envelope in which the will was delivered. The court threw out Dummar's claim.

A History Mystery:
The Athlete and the President

The Death of an Athlete

[1]In 1986 the U.S. women's volleyball team was one of the best teams in the world. The star and captain of the team was Flo Hyman. She was likable and very good. She was a 6-foot, 5-inch champion who was one of the greatest players ever in the game.

[2]On January 24, Hyman played in a match in Japan. She was at the top of her game. Her blocks were perfect, and her spikes were unstoppable. She was a world-class athlete at the height of her abilities.

[3]Then, while resting on the bench, Hyman collapsed and died. No one knows why she had suddenly fallen to the floor. Doctors later examined her body to try to explain the cause of her death. They learned that Hyman had a physical condition called Marfan syndrome, yet she never knew she had it.

The Condition That Killed Hyman

[4]Marfan syndrome is **inherited**. A person who has Marfan syndrome is born with it and gets it from his or her parents. About 1 in every 5,000 people has Marfan syndrome. It can weaken the material that holds the body's tissues together. In fact, it can **affect** the bones as well as the tissues that connect the bones. It can also cause weakness in the aorta, the main blood vessel from the heart. That, investigators learned, is what killed Flo Hyman.

[5]Her death brought new attention to Marfan syndrome. This attention reopened an old **debate** about President Abraham Lincoln. Since 1960, forensic researchers have argued that Lincoln may have had Marfan syndrome.

20

Flo Hyman

People with Marfan syndrome often have very long, narrow faces with sunken eyes.

Abraham Lincoln

Did Abraham Lincoln Have It?

[6]People with Marfan syndrome are usually very tall and thin. Their arms and legs are very long in **proportion** to their torsos. Their joints are often loose. Many people with Marfan syndrome can bend a finger back to touch their wrist.

[7]People with Marfan syndrome also usually have long, narrow faces. Their chests may seem caved in, or the chest may **protrude**, like a bird's chest. Their eyes may appear to be sunken. They are often nearsighted, and in half of the people with Marfan syndrome, the lens of the eye is out of place.

[8]Most of these things were true about Hyman, and many were also true of President Lincoln. All these things lead scientists to wonder if Lincoln had Marfan syndrome. There is no clear agreement, though. Some researchers are sure Lincoln had the condition, while others are equally sure he did not.

The Case For Lincoln Having Marfan Syndrome

[9]The **image** we have of Abraham Lincoln is that of a long and lanky man. His face looked almost like that of a skeleton. Even as a child of 7, he was described as a "tall spider" of a boy. By the time he was 17, Lincoln was 6 feet, 4 inches tall. At the time, the average male adult in America was only 5 feet, 6 inches tall. That's almost a foot shorter than Lincoln.

[10]President Lincoln's legs were unusually long. When he was sitting, he did not seem taller than anyone else. When he stood, though, he towered over others. He had very large feet and could wear only custom-made, size 14 shoes. His arms and fingers also seemed too long. They were out of proportion with the rest of his body. His eyes were sunk deep in their sockets.

The Case Against Lincoln Having Marfan Syndrome

[11]The signs of Marfan syndrome vary greatly from one person to another. Not everyone with the syndrome is tall. Lincoln's fingers were long, but they were also very powerful by many accounts. Most people with Marfan syndrome do not have such strength in their hands.

What's Important Today?

[12]Forensic scientists could end the debate by testing tissue taken from President Lincoln in his grave. Every few years, a researcher will suggest digging up the 16th president's remains to do that, but so far, no one has.

[13]Knowing Lincoln had Marfan syndrome won't benefit anyone very much. It will have very little meaning for people who have the condition today.

[14]Marfan syndrome is a serious condition, but it is treatable. In fact, today there are many successful treatments. Often it can be treated simply with drugs. For people who have a heart risk, like Flo Hyman had, surgery may be required. But people have to be tested for the syndrome before they can be treated for it.

[15]That is the true sadness about Hyman. She died from Marfan syndrome, but she could have lived with it.

How Can a City Disappear?

Cahokia Mounds

Tourists view a mound at the Cahokia Mounds State Historic Site.

¹**A**bout 1,100 years ago, a great city was built on the banks of the Mississippi River. We now call it Cahokia. It was located 8 miles east of what is today St. Louis, Missouri, and was a city unlike any other place north of Mexico.

²Cahokia was the largest city of a civilization that covered much of eastern North America. The people of this civilization were called the Mississippian Culture. They built cities and towns from Florida to Wisconsin and from Oklahoma to Pennsylvania. Within their communities, they used dirt and rock to build earth mounds of different shapes and sizes. Many of these earth mounds still exist today. Scientists have learned about these people by studying the mounds they built throughout the country.

³Some towns had many mounds, and others had only a few. The largest group—more than 120 mounds—was in Cahokia. Cahokia also had the

largest mound. In fact, it was the largest earth **structure** north of Mexico. This giant mound still rises three levels to a height of 100 feet. Its base covers 14 acres, or more than 10 football fields. The mound once stood in the center of the city and was surrounded by a stockade made of tree trunks. This wall was about 2 miles long.

Digging for artifacts at the Cahokia Mounds

[4]The people of Cahokia traded with other people all over North America. They used shells from the Gulf of Mexico, copper from the northern Great Lakes, and stones from the Appalachian Mountains.

[5]At one time more than 20,000 people lived in Cahokia. In the 1100s, it was a larger city than London. But by 1400, Cahokia was **deserted.** No one lived there anymore.

[6]What caused Cahokia to **decline** and its people to disappear? There is no **evidence** of a natural disaster. There is no sign that the city was invaded by enemies. How could a city of such wealth and power simply be abandoned?

[7]Forensic scientists may have found part of the answer. They have examined pottery and other items from the site. They have also examined human **skeletons**. These remains give us important clues about what actually happened.

[8]Scientists can learn a lot about a person's health and diet by studying bones and teeth. For example, the way teeth wear down shows what foods a person ate. It also shows how the foods were prepared. Foods with a hard **texture** wear out teeth faster than softer foods.

[9]Forensic scientists can learn a lot from skeletons as well. For example, they can tell:

- A person's gender—whether a person was male or female. Males and females have clear differences in the shape of the forehead, the base of the skull, the jaw, and the hip bones.
- A person's age. Bones, joints, and teeth show age differently. For example, an older person has a smoother skull than a younger person.
- A person's height and weight. Scientists figure this by measuring the length of certain bones in the body. For example, finger bones provide clues to a person's height.
- If a person was left-handed or right-handed. This is shown by the thickness of the bones and marks from muscles on the bones of either the left or right arm.
- What a person ate and did not eat. Scientists study different kinds of carbon in the bones to learn what kind of food was the most important part of a person's diet. For example, the disease anemia can come from a diet that is low in iron. Bones can show that a person had anemia. This may mean that the person's diet was low in meat, which contains a lot of iron.

[10]Forensic scientists who examined skeletons from Cahokia could tell that the city's people lived on corn. The people's success in raising corn was what made the huge city possible.

[11]But corn may also have been responsible for the city's decline. Analysis of the people's bones showed that they ate too much corn and not enough other kinds of foods. Not having a balanced diet can be very unhealthy. This put them at risk for developing diseases. Also, any kind of change in the climate that reduced the corn crop would have caused widespread starvation.

[12]It was probably a combination of these and other reasons that led to the end of Cahokia. We don't know for sure. What we do know is that the greatest early city in North America was empty by the time European explorers first saw it.

HOW DID THE BOG MAN DIE?

A peat bog in Cheshire County, England

¹**A** bog can be a quiet, mysterious place. It is a wetland with soft, muddy ground. Often the hum and buzz of insects are all that can be heard. In a bog you'll also find many rotting plants. In fact, bogs produce more plants than can rot completely. When plant material cannot **decay** completely, it builds up and becomes peat. Sometimes peat in a bog can be several yards thick.

²For thousands of years, people in Europe have used peat as fuel. Peat is cut into blocks, dried, and then burned for cooking and for heat. Long ago, people also used peat bogs to bury their dead.

A Body Found in a Bog

³These days, peat is cut from the surface of bogs with machines. In 1984, at Lindow Moss in England, workers were collecting peat at a bog. One of them uncovered what he thought was a piece of wood. It turned out to be a human foot.

⁴A local scientist heard about the discovery. When he searched the **site**, he found signs of a buried human body. The body was moved to a laboratory where scientists examined it to find the cause of death, and they made some interesting discoveries.

⁵For example, the body still had skin and hair, which was very unusual. The scientists **estimated** that the age of the body was about 2,000 years.

26

They used a method called carbon dating to help them form this opinion. The diagram explains how carbon dating works. The scientists also found that parts of the body were remarkably well **preserved**. The stomach and intestines were still in excellent condition.

[6]Why was the body in such good condition? It did not decay in the same way bodies buried in the ground do. Bacteria in the ground usually cause the breakdown of tissue in a dead body. Eventually, only bones and teeth are left. This does not happen in a peat bog.

[7]Bacteria cannot grow in the bog because there is no oxygen available below the surface. In addition, the bog is cold, and there is a lot of acid in the water. All of these things prevent **typical** decay.

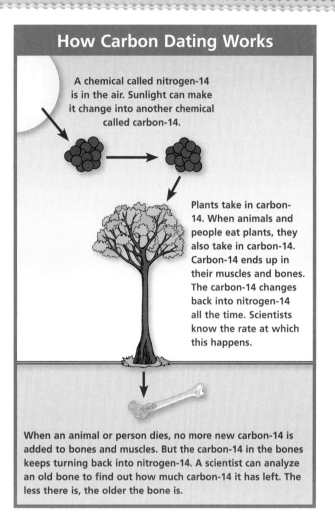

How Carbon Dating Works

A chemical called nitrogen-14 is in the air. Sunlight can make it change into another chemical called carbon-14.

Plants take in carbon-14. When animals and people eat plants, they also take in carbon-14. Carbon-14 ends up in their muscles and bones. The carbon-14 changes back into nitrogen-14 all the time. Scientists know the rate at which this happens.

When an animal or person dies, no more new carbon-14 is added to bones and muscles. But the carbon-14 in the bones keeps turning back into nitrogen-14. A scientist can analyze an old bone to find out how much carbon-14 it has left. The less there is, the older the bone is.

Signs of a Violent Death

[8]The big surprise was that the bog man seemed to have been murdered. His skull was fractured in two places, and his neck was broken. His throat may have been cut. A piece of leather around his neck dug into the skin, suggesting he had been choked.

[9]Because the body was 2,000 years old, scientists believed the man was a Celt. The Celts were people who lived in small villages all across England at that time. In addition, the man's appearance was unusual in several ways that made scientists think he was an important person in Celtic society:

- His hair had been cut with scissors two or three days before he died. This was unusual 2,000 years ago. Only powerful people had scissors at the time.

27

- His fingernails were in very good condition. This made scientists think the man did not have to work hard.
- He had a neatly trimmed beard. No other bodies of Celts they had found had beards.
- Scientists examined the contents of the man's stomach and found the pollen of mistletoe and burnt bread. Both had a special, sacred meaning to the Celts.

Was It Murder?

[10]Scientists had the well-preserved body of a 2,000-year-old man who apparently had died violently. He wore nothing but a fur armband. He had been healthy and well groomed. He had eaten mistletoe pollen and burnt bread before he died.

[11]Scientists can only guess what all this means. Using their knowledge of the Celts, some scientists believe the man was murdered as part of a sacred ceremony. Others disagree, saying there is not enough evidence. They point out that his **windpipe** shows no sign of being choked. If he had been choked, this tube in the throat that brings air to the lungs would have been damaged. Also, they say that the leather around his neck could have been a necklace that shrank over the years. His other injuries could have been caused by the peat-cutting equipment.

[12]The real story of the bog man may never be known. Now called the Lindow Man, he is the best preserved Celtic body in England. You can see him on display at the British Museum in London.

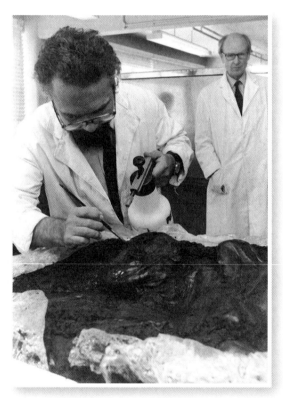

A scientist carefully examines the body of the bog man, using special tools.

What *Really* Happened at JAMESTOWN?

This drawing of Jamestown shows the three-cornered fort built as protection against American Indians.

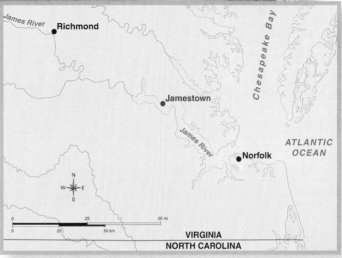

[1]There's a 400-year-old mystery in our country. If you want to learn the facts about it, you have to study the Age of Exploration. That's when Europeans first came to the Americas.

The Facts

[2]The basic facts are well known. In the spring of 1607, 104 men and boys from England arrived in what is now Virginia.

[3]The men came for several reasons. They wanted to start a settlement, and they were searching for gold. They also were looking for a waterway between England and East Asia, where spices and other fine goods could be bought and sold. To do all this, they needed to find a good site for a town. They chose a small island, and on May 14, 1607, they founded the settlement of Jamestown.

[4]However, life in Jamestown was a struggle. By the end of the year, just 38 of the 104 settlers were still alive. Supply ships and new settlers arrived in January 1608. More came nine months later. Without them, the Jamestown settlement probably would have disappeared for good.

[5]What went wrong?

People Called Jamestown a Failure

[6]For many years, people blamed the Jamestown settlers for their failure. Some people said the settlers chose the wrong site for their town. The settlers built in a swampy bog filled with insects, whose bites could spread disease. No settlement could succeed in such an unhealthy wetland.

[7]Other people accused the settlers of being unwilling to work and unable even to feed themselves. The settlers' servants had done all the real work in England. This dependence on servants doomed the settlement from the start.

[8]Still other people believed that greed for gold was the problem. They thought the settlers had not come prepared to survive in the wilderness. The settlers were too busy looking for gold to grow food.

New Evidence Changes These Ideas

[9]Then, in 1996, scientists began to find evidence that had been hidden for almost 400 years. It suggested another story entirely.

[10]The first thing found was a buried portion of the fort that had been built in 1607. Next, scientists discovered the entire outline of the structure. This was important because it showed where the original settlement was.

Artifacts found in Jamestown

It had been built on a riverbank, not in a bog. Scientists now knew where to look for more ruins. Finally, they uncovered the remains of buildings and thousands of items that the settlers had used.

[11]In fact, half of a million items have been found. Some were well preserved and are in excellent condition. The settlers had all kinds of useful tools. This shows that they were well prepared to survive in the wilderness.

[12]Trash pits also have been recently uncovered. They contain the bones of horses, dogs, and rats. Forensic scientists have examined these items, and they believe the animals were butchered for food. The skeletons of people have also been found in mass graves.

[13]These clues are from 1609 to 1610, a period called "the starving time" in Jamestown. The settlers and the Powhatan Indians were at war. Without food, the people inside the fort became ill, and many died. But it was probably not laziness or neglecting farm fields to search for gold that caused the lack of food. Instead, a 1998 climate study may have found the explanation. Tree rings from that part of Virginia show that there was a

31

This water well, built in the 1600s, was discovered at the Jamestown settlement.

drought from 1606 until 1612. So Jamestown was built in the middle of a terrible dry spell. The drought may have dried up fresh water and killed the corn crops that the settlers and Native Americans needed. This in turn might have led to deadly conflicts between the settlers and Native Americans.

Was Bad Luck the Reason?

[14]Instead of being failures, the Jamestown settlers may simply have been unlucky. By the middle of 1610, about 500 settlers had come to live in Jamestown. Only 60 of them survived. These 60 settlers were going to abandon the town. They decided to bury their cannon and armor and go back home to England. But the lucky arrival of more ships and supplies stopped them. The settlement began to recover, and it became the first permanent English settlement in America.

SPACE
Traveling into the Unknown

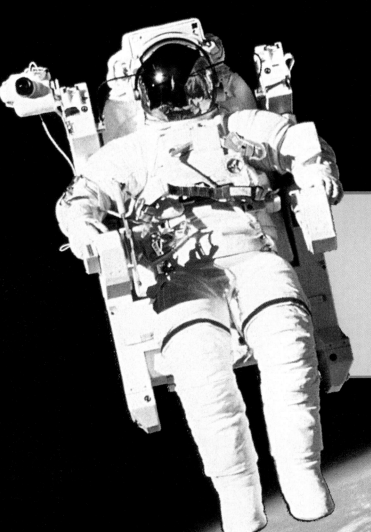

- *Why do we travel into space?*
- *What can we gain from space travel?*
- *Who should be able to travel into space and why?*

Buzz Aldrin saluting
the American flag
on the moon

The Space Race

¹On October 4, 1957, Americans were shocked. For the first time, an object other than the moon was in **orbit**, circling the Earth. This new satellite was about the size of a basketball and was made by humans. Furthermore, the satellite was made by the Soviet Union, a nation many people considered our enemy. How could this have happened? What could we do about it? The United States decided to race the Soviet Union into space. The space race was on.

The Race Begins

²In 1954, an **international** group of scientists said satellites could help map Earth's surface. Both the United States and the Soviet Union announced plans to send up satellites. The two countries were rivals. Each believed it was better and stronger than the other. So when the Soviets launched that first satellite, *Sputnik I*, Americans were upset and embarrassed. But many Americans were also afraid. Was *Sputnik* spying on us? Would it be used to fire a weapon? The United States wanted to catch up in the space race.

34

The United States in Space

³A major push to develop a space **program** began. In December 1957, the United States launched its first satellite. The rocket rose 4 feet into the air, then fell back and exploded. A London newspaper reported, "Oh, what a Flopnik!" But on January 31, 1958, the first successful U.S. satellite, called *Explorer I*, was launched.

⁴However, Americans still felt they were trying to catch up. In May 1961, Alan Shepard became the first U.S. **astronaut** in space. But 23 days earlier, a Soviet pilot had become the first human in space. The Soviet Union seemed to be winning all the "firsts." Then President John F. Kennedy gave Americans a **goal**. He said the nation should commit itself to "landing a man on the moon and returning him safely to the Earth."

Race to the Moon

⁵Americans became determined to land the first man on the moon. Mission after mission helped get the space program closer to this goal. First, astronauts orbited Earth. Later, Edward White became the first U.S. astronaut to walk in space. Eventually, a crew of American astronauts orbited the moon before returning to Earth.

⁶Sadly, three American astronauts lost their lives in the space race when a fire started in the spacecraft during a test on the ground. Some Soviets died in tragic accidents too.

⁷In July 1969, American Neil Armstrong became the first person to walk on the moon. Around the world, people could not take their eyes off their TV sets as Armstrong stepped down from his spacecraft and said, "That's one small step for a man, one giant leap for mankind." When the astronauts planted a U.S. flag on the moon, it was not to **claim** the moon as a U.S. territory. It was just to show we got there first. The space race was over, and the United States had won.

A footprint
on the moon

35

THE INTERNATIONAL SPACE STATION

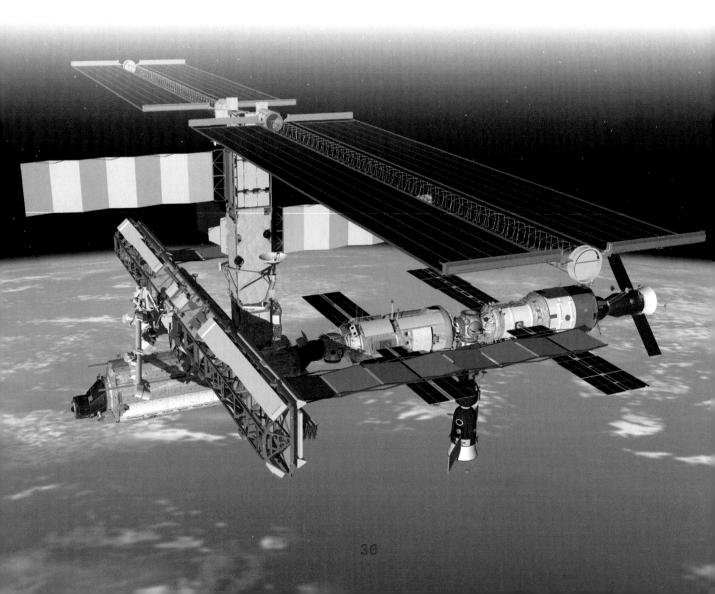

[1]More than 30 years have passed since an American first walked on the moon. Following that event, the excitement about space exploration cooled. Today there is a **renewed** interest in space travel. But there are questions to answer first. What will people need in order to survive in space for long periods? How can we be sure they will have everything they will need? To find out, the United States is working with other countries to build an International Space Station (ISS). The ISS, a giant spacecraft, will orbit Earth. People will live on the station for several months at a time.

[2]Completing the space station and living there for long periods will be a **challenge**. But scientists have already figured out how to solve some of the problems. They already know how to:

- build the station.
- provide air and water.
- feed the astronauts.
- handle waste.
- provide for communication between people on the space station and on Earth.
- offer opportunities for leisure.

The Expedition 10 patch forms the letter "X" with the American and Russian flags.

Building the Space Station

[3]A completed space station would be much too large to launch from Earth. Astronauts are building most of the station in space—one section, or module, at a time. Some of the station's modules are already in orbit. Several crews have already spent months living on the station. Space shuttles bring new modules, supplies such as food, and relief crews to the station.

[4]Astronauts on the ISS have many jobs. They **expand** the station by adding modules. They repair **equipment** and perform experiments. They catch satellites that are already in orbit in order to repair them.

Air and Water on the ISS

[5]The ISS must provide everything astronauts will need during their stay, including air and water. Air inside the station must be like the air we breathe

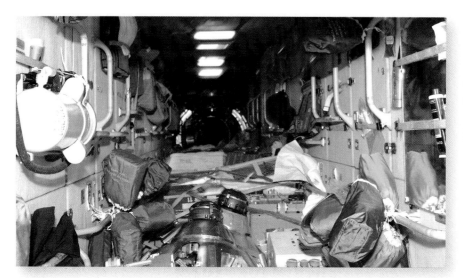

Items and spare parts stored onboard the ISS during the Eneide Mission in April 2005

on Earth. It contains two gases. Supply spacecraft bring tanks of one of the gases to the station. The space station gets most of the other gas by taking it out of water.

[6]ISS astronauts need water for drinking and preparing food. They also need water for washing. In fact, each astronaut uses about a ton of water each month. It's too expensive to ship water to the space station. Instead, the ISS **recycles** water from every possible **source**. The station even cleans, treats, and reuses water from astronauts' tooth brushing, hand washing, and urine!

[7]To save as much water as possible, astronauts use wet washcloths to wash their hands. Their shower uses 12 times less water than a shower on Earth. Astronauts wipe dirty dishes with a wet cloth. They're lucky. They don't have to do laundry. Instead, they send some dirty clothes back to Earth. Other dirty clothes become part of the station's trash. Trash is loaded into a spacecraft and set free from the ISS. Eventually, the spacecraft burns up as it moves through Earth's air.

Food

[8]Space station astronauts eat three meals and one snack each day. Much of the food is canned or in pouches. There is no frozen food because the station does not have a way to keep food frozen. Crews enjoy fresh fruits and vegetables only when the supply spacecraft arrives.

[9]Astronauts make their own meals. Some choices include spaghetti, beef stew, and macaroni and cheese. To make these meals, astronauts add water to

pouches of dried food and then heat the food in the space station oven. They eat snacks such as dried fruit and nuts straight from small packages.

[10]Astronauts can add several different toppings to their food, including ketchup, mustard, and hot sauce. They can add salt and pepper, too, but in an unusual way. Salt is in water. Pepper is in oil. That's because astronauts can't shake salt or pepper onto their food. The grains would float away because there is little gravity in space.

Waste

[11]Many people wonder how astronauts go to the bathroom. They use something that looks like a toilet seat. Under the seat, a force draws the waste into tubing. Solid waste is placed in bags, which are then sealed. These bags are stored in a tightly closed container. Urine is saved, cleaned, and treated to recycle the water in it.

Communication and Leisure

[12]The astronauts must be able to communicate with Earth. A ground crew is responsible for keeping the astronauts safe. Astronauts talk to the ground crew by radio. The ISS computers let the ground crew know if any equipment is leaking or broken. Astronauts also talk with their families and friends by e-mail. On weekends, they can visit with their families using equipment that acts like a two-way TV. Sometimes they answer questions from schoolchildren.

[13]For an astronaut, a work day usually begins at about 7:00 a.m. Each crew member has a list of things to do throughout the day. Usually, work is finished by 7 p.m. Astronauts get weekends and some holidays off.

[14]Astronauts enjoy their free time. Often they choose from the station's small library of books, tapes, and computer games. At other times, they exercise. One popular activity is running from one end of the space station to the other. However, nearly all astronauts say that looking out the station's windows is their favorite activity. They wonder at seeing constant lightning sparks over the surface of Earth. They are treated to several amazing sunrises and sunsets each day. But most of all, astronauts enjoy gazing at their distant home—the planet Earth.

What's Next In

¹**A**stronauts have been traveling into space for more than 40 years. They have orbited Earth, walked in space, and landed on the moon. What's next for humans in space?

²Many people other than astronauts want to visit space. American Dennis Tito became the world's first person to fly into space who was not a trained astronaut. He flew on a Russian rocket to the International Space Station in 2001. In the future, some people may travel to space for their vacations.

Space Tourism

³As space tourism develops, several choices will be **available**. Some people may want to orbit Earth in the ISS, like Dennis Tito did. A spacewalk adventure will attract other tourists.

⁴Space tourists will need some astronaut training. For this reason, a few schools now offer courses in space tourism. Courses help prepare students to meet the needs of space tourists. For example, tourists will need to understand the risks of flying in a spacecraft. Tour operators will offer special zero-gravity flights to prepare for space travel. These give passengers the feeling of weightlessness that happens in space.

⁵A vacation in orbit around Earth will be expensive. A stay in a space hotel will cost a lot of money too. That's because it costs so much to send people and supplies on the spacecraft we have now.

Lowering the High Cost of Space Travel

⁶One way to make space travel less expensive is to design better spacecraft. To encourage the design of better spacecraft, a contest was held. The Ansari X Prize offered the winner $10 million. The winner had to design a **vehicle** that could carry people into space. Twenty-six teams from seven countries competed in the contest. In 2004, a California company claimed the

Space7

SpaceShipOne flies attached to its launchship.

$10 million prize with its vehicle called SpaceShipOne.

[7]The Ansari X Prize will lead to other benefits besides cheaper space vacations. Launching satellites will cost less money as well. This will make services such as satellite TV and satellite radio less expensive.

A New Reason to Go to the Moon

[8]In 2004, President Bush announced a big change in the space program. He suggested that the nation should send astronauts to explore the solar system. First, the United States would have to return to the moon. From the moon, we would launch spacecraft headed for **destinations** farther out in space.

[9]Moon launches would be less expensive than those on Earth. Objects, including spacecraft, weigh less on the moon than they weigh on Earth. As a result, they can be launched using less fuel. This would lower costs.

[10]To meet this goal, people would have to live on the moon. Of course, people would need food, water, and shelter there. One of the biggest challenges to a long stay on the moon is the need for building supplies. It would be **extremely** expensive to bring all the building supplies from Earth. But there is another possible source for the materials we would need.

Space Mining

[11]An asteroid is a small **rocky** object that orbits the sun. The smallest asteroids are about a mile across. The largest are as much as several hundred miles wide. Asteroids are probably a much better place than Earth to get materials to make supplies for people living on the moon.

[12]Research shows that asteroids are **valuable**. They have materials worth trillions of dollars. A single asteroid may contain a huge amount of metal. About half of the asteroids contain water. Asteroids have some materials that could be used for fuel. They also have materials for manufacturing computers and building solar energy cells. Asteroids even have materials useful for making medicines.

Who Owns the Moon?

[13]Several organizations are already making plans for taking materials from space. That brings up some interesting questions: Who owns space? Who owns the moon? And who has the right to remove valuable materials from the moon or from other objects in space?

[14]While exploring space, the United States has not claimed any land as its own. The nation is following the Outer Space Treaty of 1967. This agreement forbids a nation to own land in space. For now, everyone on Earth may be able to share the moon, the asteroids, and other objects discovered in space.

Spinoffs
FROM SPACE

[1]Imagine all of the products that are made especially for space travel. Are these a waste of time and money? Not if you think about the many "spinoffs" of these products. A spinoff is something that was meant to be used in one way but is useful in many other ways also. Some things used in space have been found to be very useful right here on Earth.

Cordless Tools

[2]Astronauts landing on the moon planned to collect some moon rocks. They needed a tool to break apart large rocks. The tool needed to have its own source of electricity. It had to be easy to carry and use. Scientists developed a battery-operated drill for use on the moon. Later, a company used the same **technology** to make cordless tools for home use. Today you can buy cordless drills, cordless screwdrivers, and a variety of other cordless tools.

Smoke Alarms

[3]Astronauts need to know when dangerous gases leak into the spacecraft. Scientists developed a **sensor** to warn them when dangerous gases were present. The sensor had a tiny electric current. If a dangerous gas entered the sensor, it stopped the current. When the current stopped, an alarm sounded.

[4]Other people saw that the same idea could apply to **detecting** smoke from fires. The alarm could warn people if smoke was present. Today smoke alarms save lives. Experts say that every house or apartment should have a working smoke alarm near every bedroom.

Identifying Bar Codes

[5]Look at a carton of milk or a box of cereal. You'll find a bar code on one side of each package. The bar code is made up of bars and numbers. The bars are a series of thick and thin lines and spaces. The numbers written underneath the bars identify the maker and the product.

[6]Bar codes were developed by scientists to keep track of the millions of parts in a spacecraft. Today they are on nearly every product you buy. At the store checkout counter, a scanner "reads" the lines and spaces of the bar code. It matches them to the numbers from 0 to 9. The numbers give the product's price.

[7]Bar codes are **accurate** and save time. Before bar codes existed, people had to mark the price on everything in the grocery store. They had to mark every can, bottle, jar, package, and box. At the checkout, another person had to enter each price, one at a time. By the time you paid for your groceries, you could be truly hungry!

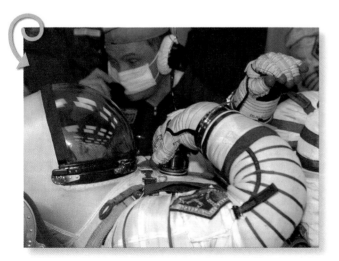

Sports Wraps

[8]On the moon, astronauts wore special cooling suits. The suits protected them from the moon's high temperatures. One kind of moon suit had a lining of small tubes. A tiny battery-operated pump moved cool water through the tubes. The water kept the astronauts comfortable. This idea has been applied to suits

worn by some racecar drivers. They wear them because some parts inside the racecar get hot enough to boil water.

[9]The "cool suit" idea was also applied to sports wraps. Athletes can put wraps on their injuries instead of ice packs. Wraps are easier to apply than ice packs. They are smaller and less **bulky**. They are less messy too. Different wraps fit ankles, knees, and the back. Others fit shoulders, elbows, and wrists. Trainers claim that athletes heal more quickly with cooling wraps than with ice packs. In fact, some athletes heal twice as fast.

Thermal Packs

[10]On a spacecraft, some parts need to be sealed using heat. A scientist took the special heat-sealing material and developed a new material from it. If the material is heated in a microwave oven, it stays warm for hours. If the material is cooled in a freezer, it stays cool for hours.

[11]This new material, covered with a cloth, is called a thermal pack. You can buy thermal packs at your local drugstore. A warm thermal pack can lessen muscle pain. A cool thermal pack can **ease** swelling and the pain of sunburn.

[12]There are thousands of spinoffs like these. Some are used in simple everyday living. Some have very special uses. Each spinoff came from an idea that originally was developed for space exploration. Each offers an answer to the question, "What does the space program do for me?"

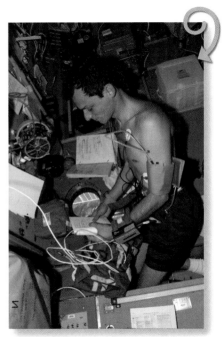

Thermal packs are similar to ones this astronaut is using to conduct stress and heart experiments in space.

Working on the Space Station

[1]What weighs 200 tons, has 8 miles of wires, and needs 20,000 pounds of food? The answer is the International Space Station, or ISS.

[2]Although most of the ISS is being assembled by astronauts in space, much work has to be done on Earth as well. Around the world, about 500 different companies work on the ISS. They employ about 100,000 people. Not all of them are astronauts or scientists.

[3]Some ISS workers have unusual jobs. For example, professional sniffers test the air to be delivered to the ISS. Their job is to keep it free from bad odors. And you might not expect to find diving instructors working on a space station; yet you will find them working at the Johnson Space Center. The center has an underwater model of the ISS. The instructors help astronauts train underwater. The training prepares them for the challenge of working in weightlessness.

Metalworkers and Machinists Build the Parts

[4]Astronauts are expanding the ISS in several stages by adding sections to it. One section of the ISS is the U.S. research laboratory. This section is made of two layers of aluminum. One layer has a "waffle" surface, which adds strength. The other is smooth and shiny to reflect sunlight. These different forms of aluminum are just two of the many metals used in building the ISS. Metalworkers in different states on Earth help make these large metal parts.

[5]Machinists produce the small metal parts for the ISS. They use tools such as lathes, drill presses, and milling machines. As they work, they follow blueprints, or written instructions. After the parts are made, machinists must check their work to make sure it is accurate. If even one small part is not built correctly, disaster could result.

Astronaut Susan J. Helms, Expedition Two flight engineer, works at a laptop computer on the International Space Station (ISS).

Electrical Workers Bring the Power

[6]The ISS relies heavily on electronic equipment. Some of the equipment checks things like temperature and air quality. It also checks and controls the orbit of the ISS. Other electronic equipment collects, records, and sends research information back to Earth.

[7]All this equipment must be installed. Electronic installers do this work. They install all the wiring in the sections of the ISS before the sections are carried into space. They also perform regular checks on the equipment. They use special tests to help them find problems before they become serious. Think of what happens in your home when the power goes out. In the darkness of space, an astronaut certainly doesn't want the power to go out on the space station.

European Space Agency astronaut Kuipers and his NASA colleague Foale eat Dutch cheese for breakfast aboard the International Space Station.

Food Service Feeds the Astronauts

[8]Astronauts need to eat, of course. Food service workers at the Johnson Space Center on Earth make that possible. They prepare the meals astronauts will eat in space. First, astronauts choose their favorite foods from a menu. Food service workers study their food choices and then develop and test food preparations. They make sure the foods are suitable for use in space.

[9]It takes quite a few workers to feed hungry space station crews. Diet experts make sure the crews' diets are balanced and healthy. Food scientists study how well food keeps. Some workers test foods for taste and texture. The ISS chef oversees food preparation. Cooks create the recipes. Food preparation workers get the ingredients ready and keep work areas clean.

[10]Packaging space food for astronauts is important too. Some workers study and develop ways to package and serve individual portions. Many space foods are the same foods that are available in your neighborhood grocery store. However, Earth-food packages are not easy to use in weightless surroundings. Food preparation workers must repackage these foods for special space use.

[11]One popular ISS menu choice is called Space Wraps. It has only three ingredients. If you have these ingredients at home, you can taste-test Space Wraps for yourself. Just follow this recipe: Spread a thin layer of peanut butter on a tortilla. Add a thin layer of jelly. Fold and enjoy!

[12]Not everyone can be an astronaut. But many different kinds of workers help astronauts live and work in space. They are all needed to make space exploration a success.

YOUR HEALTH
Fit Minds, Fit Bodies

- What choices do you make each day about your health?
- How do you have the power to change the way you look and feel?
- How do food and exercise affect your body?

FUELING THE FIRE:
Energy, food, and Nutrition

Carl Lewis

¹If you blinked, you might have missed him. Track star Carl Lewis could cover many yards in only a few seconds. What gave him the energy to run so fast? Part of the answer is nutrition.

²Nutrition is about the way you feed, or nourish, your body. Your body uses food to give you energy to live and move. If energy is like a fire, food is the fuel that keeps it burning.

³The energy you get from food is measured in **calories**. When Carl Lewis was in college, he skipped meals during the day. Then he would run out of energy. This **prompted** Carl to think about nutrition. He began to eat more during the day to give his body the calories he needed to keep his energy up.

The Nutrients You Need

[4]Carl also started to think about the types of food he was eating. All foods have calories, but they contain different nutrients. Nutrients help your body in many ways. Carl began to eat more fruits and vegetables. They are loaded with nutrients. They have minerals and **vitamins**, which help your body perform at its best.

[5]In addition to nutrients, fruits and vegetables contain fiber. Fiber helps you **digest**, or break down, foods. Through digestion, your body gets the nutrients it needs and rids itself of wastes. Carl is sure that the nutrients he received by eating fruits and vegetables helped him become a great athlete. "Your body is your temple," he says. "If you nourish it properly, it will be good to you."

[6]Many other athletes are also interested in nutrition. Olympic track star Jackie Joyner-Kersee **encourages** people to eat a **minimum** of five servings of fruits and vegetables a day. Her program is called "Get Fit with Five." Many people eat too much fat. Fruits and vegetables have less fat than other foods. Fat is a nutrient that gives us extra energy, but too much fat can cause obesity and other health problems.

[7]Another athlete who wants to help children and teens with nutrition is NFL player Tim Brown. Tim didn't realize the importance of nutrition until late in his career. When he started to pay attention to what he ate, his performance as a football player improved. Tim developed a nutrition program to help children and teens eat better too.

Jackie
Joyner-Kersee

51

Tim Brown

[8]Tim worked with scientists to develop his nutrition program. They made products with the nutrients people need. Some of the most important nutrients are carbohydrates. Carbohydrates are sugars and starches that give you energy. Whole-grain foods such as brown rice and oatmeal are full of starches. Vegetables such as potatoes are too. Fruits like apples have sugars that give you energy.

[9]Protein is another nutrient our bodies need. Foods like nuts, eggs, meats, and fish have a lot of protein. Your body uses protein to grow and to strengthen your muscles and bones.

Especially for Teens

[10]It is especially important for growing teens to think about nutrition. During your teen years, your bones are growing fast. You need a lot of calcium, a mineral that helps your bones grow. You can find calcium in milk, cheese, orange juice, and broccoli. Teens also need a lot of iron. Iron is a mineral that helps make healthy blood and strong muscles. Eat foods such as meat, peanut butter, nuts, spinach, peas, and strawberries to get iron.

[11]Carl Lewis, Jackie Joyner-Kersee, and Tim Brown found out the importance of nutrition in their sports careers and in their lives. They work to help others learn that importance too. If you now know how to give your body the fuel it needs to grow healthy and strong, they have succeeded.

Y Workout

¹**E**ric slumped his shoulders and hung his head as he walked down the street after school. Maybe the bully wouldn't notice him this way. Maybe the bully wouldn't see his face, and he would think Eric was someone else. Maybe—

²"Hey, wait a minute, kid." The voice made Eric's stomach feel sick. Stepping out from the narrow walkway between two buildings was the bully. He demanded that Eric give him his money, and Eric did. The bully was almost twice Eric's size, and though he had never actually hit Eric, he made

it obvious that one day he might. Eric had tried walking a different way home from school. He had tried walking near groups of other kids. But the bully managed to find him alone at least once a week.

[3]When Eric reached home, he did what he always did after school. He turned on the TV and lay back on the couch.

[4]The next day Eric noticed a poster outside the school counselor's office. It was from the YMCA, and it was about the Y's mentoring program. YMCA **mentors** were available to help young people with activities such as working out and doing homework. If an individual couldn't afford to be a member of the Y, aid was available. "Ask at your local YMCA," the poster said.

[5]Eric was **doubtful**. But that afternoon, the bully stopped him again. When Eric got home, he thought about the poster. If he could join the mentoring program, he'd go to the Y after school. That way, he could avoid meeting the bully. He didn't care much for exercise, but he was tired of just plopping down in front of the TV every day. Maybe he would ask the school counselor about the Y. It wouldn't hurt to try.

[6]It didn't. Mr. Gregory, the school counselor, thought Eric had an excellent idea, and Eric hadn't even mentioned the bully. Mr. Gregory said he'd contact Eric's mother and then the YMCA to make arrangements.

[7]Two weeks later, Eric found himself at the front desk of the YMCA. The woman there led him up some wide stairs. He was panting a little by the time he reached the exercise room at the top of the steps. It was big and open, with strange-looking machines placed in rows.

[8]A group of teens relaxed on some mats. Eric thought he recognized a couple of them from school, but he didn't know their names. Then a young man in his twenties came over and shook Eric's hand.

[9]"Hi, I'm Josh," he said. He glanced at the papers on his clipboard and smiled. "You must be Eric. Welcome to the mentoring program." Josh gathered the teens and explained that they would meet three days per week after school to work out.

[10]Josh asked the teens in the group to introduce themselves to one another. Then, he spent some time introducing them to the weight room. He showed them how to use the weight machines and had everyone try a few **repetitions**. "You'll see your strength improve so that you'll be able to lift more and more weight," he told them. He gave them charts to record how much weight they lifted each day.

[11]After Josh **demonstrated** how to use the treadmills and exercise bikes, he handed each of the teens another chart. "You can record how many minutes you go so you can see how much your endurance increases. You'll be amazed. Soon you'll all be able to go twice as long and twice as fast."

[12]Over the next few weeks, the group met three days per week. Eric didn't like the sweating, and his muscles felt sore for a while. But Josh let them listen to music while they worked out, and the time went by fast. The teens started to joke around with one another too.

[13]"This beats sitting at home by myself after school every day," Eric told Tamara, one of the girls. He wasn't sure why Tamara was a member of the mentoring group, but the reason wasn't important to him anyway.

[14]"It sure does," Tamara agreed. "I like hanging out here, now that I'm used to it. I noticed some other good things too, like how I sleep better at night. I used to wake up a lot and think about the things that were bothering me. Now I don't get as upset when things go wrong."

[15]Eric nodded. He was sleeping better too. These days, he walked home right after school only twice a week, and he hadn't run into the bully in that time. Eric had begun to feel like another person. He was stronger, with a little more **confidence**. He still did not want to meet the bully, but he knew that if he did, somehow it wouldn't be so bad.

Getting Stronger, Getting Fit

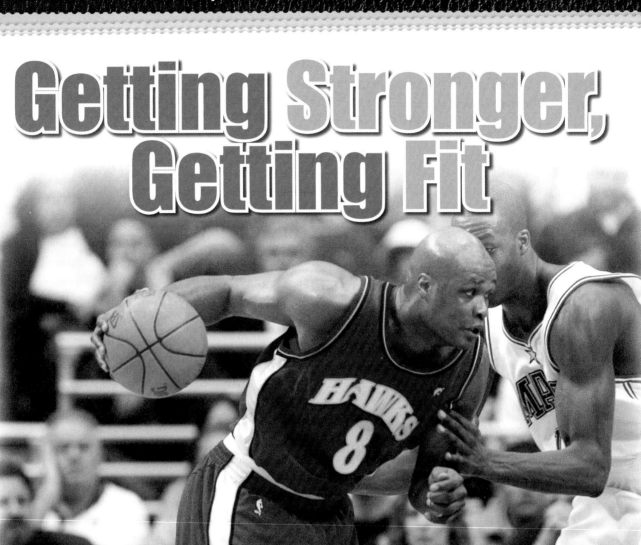

Antoine
Walker

[1]Professional basketball player Antoine Walker was in a slump. He wanted to become lighter and quicker on the court to improve his game. Antoine achieved success by changing the way he worked out. Basketball star Kobe Bryant also wanted to improve his game. He needed to get bigger and stronger, so he changed his workouts too. Both athletes understood that working out is more than just staying fit. A workout can change a body so that it performs at its best.

Getting Lighter and Quicker

[2]A few bad games on the basketball court left Antoine Walker feeling slow. Antoine weighed 245 pounds. He decided to increase his quickness to improve his game. One summer, Antoine worked out 4 hours a day. He used the help of a trainer who had worked with former basketball star Michael Jordan. Antoine spent a large amount of time running on the treadmill.

[3]Running changed Antoine's body. First of all, it increased his endurance. Running is an aerobic exercise. It makes you breathe more deeply, which means you take in more air. That air contains oxygen, which energizes your muscles. Because of his running, Antoine's lung **capacity** increased. His lungs could hold more oxygen. In addition, his heart muscle grew stronger. It could pump more blood, which carries oxygen to all parts of the body. So Antoine's lungs and heart started working together to bring more oxygen to his muscles. His energy level went up.

[4]Antoine's running also burned calories. It used up the extra fat his body was storing. The long workouts probably burned some protein from his muscles too. This helped him slim down even more. Antoine's weight decreased by 15 pounds.

[5]Antoine reached his goal through aerobic workouts. His endurance and his conditioning got better. As a result, his game improved.

Getting Bigger and Stronger

[6]Kobe Bryant's coach on the Los Angeles Lakers wanted him to play more **aggressively**. He wanted Kobe to go to the hoop, get more rebounds, and improve his 3-point shot. Kobe was fairly thin. He knew these skills

required more muscle. Going to the hoop and getting rebounds meant pushing past opponents. Improving the **range** on his shot would take strength too.

[7]Kobe turned to his **fitness** trainers to change his workouts. Kobe had always been a workout maniac. In high school, he would wake up at 5 a.m. to work out before school. During his professional basketball career, he had trained for 8 hours at a time. Now, he wanted to build extra muscle mass. This would help him play a more forceful game of basketball.

[8]Kobe's new workout involved lifting heavy weights. When he lifted weights, he pushed his muscles to their limit. Muscles grow when they are pushed to their limit. Kobe continued to increase the amount of weight he was lifting. His muscles continued to grow in size and strength. His bones also got stronger. They became more **dense**, with more bone matter in them, to help support the weight he was lifting.

[9]When a muscle works, it shortens, or contracts. It then pulls on the bone it is attached to, moving the bone. For example, put a hand on one of your biceps muscles on your upper arm, and then bend your arm up at the elbow. You can feel your biceps muscle squeeze tighter and get shorter. When you relax your arm, you can feel it **decompress**. By contracting and relaxing like this, the muscle is pulling on one of the bones of your lower arm. During Kobe's workouts, his muscles were contracting over and over again as he lifted the heavy weights.

[10]An important part of weight training is stretching your muscles. Stretching makes muscles longer and more flexible. Being flexible helps a

person prevent injuries, avoid muscle cramps, and keep a good range of motion.

[11]Kobe achieved his goal through weight training. He put on extra muscle weight. As a result, his game improved.

Strengthening the Core

[12]In addition to aerobic exercise and weight training, core workouts can improve conditioning. Your "core" muscles are the muscles of your abdomen, lower back, and hips. Special exercises strengthen these muscles. Sometimes people use big balls and weights to develop their core muscles. The more muscle mass you have, the more calories you burn. So you'll burn more calories every day just by building your core and other muscles.

Your Personal Workout

[13]Athletes are not the only ones who can work out to change their bodies. Everybody can. If you don't like to run, you can get aerobic exercise in other ways. For example, you can go for a brisk walk, a bike ride, or a swim. Basketball is aerobic exercise if you're playing defense as well as offense and running up and down the court, but just shooting hoops is not aerobic. Weight training to strengthen your muscles includes using special workout machines as well as free weights. The trick to workout success is to find out the kinds of exercises you like to do, and then to do them.

Pushing Past Normal:
Forcing Body Changes

[1]Take a look at people on TV, in movies, and in magazines. What do you see? You often see people with "perfect" bodies. You see slim women and men with muscles. Nobody has a pimple or a freckle on his or her face. Everybody's hair is just right.

[2]Now take a look at the real world, at the people around you. Look at yourself too. You see people of all shapes and sizes. People have different body types. There are many "normal" ways to look.

[3]However, our American culture puts a great deal of pressure on people to all look the same. Because of such pressure, many people become unhappy with the way their bodies look. They develop a negative body image. Many try to change their looks. Exercising and eating healthy foods are positive ways to change your body. Some people, however, believe that those changes are not quick enough or good enough. They may turn to **artificial** means, such as taking pills. Or, they may turn to **extreme** means, taking their bodies past their limits.

Becoming Too Thin

[4]Girls in our culture often believe they should be slimmer. They see actresses and singers with **miniature** waists and no fat on their bodies. Such **thinness** is seen as normal. If a girl actually weighs too much, she can lose weight with a good diet and workouts. Studies, however, show that 30 percent of teen girls take diet pills. Some diet pills keep the user from feeling hungry. Others increase the rate at which the body burns calories from food. Diet pills, however, can be dangerous. They can lead to poor nutrition, a loss of muscle tissue, less dense bones, and injury.

[5]A "too fat" body image can also lead to an eating **disorder**. An eating disorder is an extreme, dangerous way to lose weight. With one type of eating disorder, people actually starve themselves. They see themselves as fat, no matter how thin they really are. Sometimes they eat as little as one apple a day. With another type of eating disorder, people eat big meals. But they make themselves throw up afterward.

[6]Girls aren't the only ones who suffer from eating disorders. Women, men, and boys may too. But most people with eating disorders are girls. Some of the actresses and singers that young girls admire are thin because they have eating disorders. Even some athletes have eating disorders. Christy Henrich was a world-class 1980s gymnast. She died at age 22 from an eating disorder. She had become so thin that her body was too weak to survive.

Building Muscles the Wrong Way

[7]Some boys in our culture want more muscles. They see athletes who are "beefed up" smacking home runs and sacking quarterbacks. If a boy wants to build muscles, he can lift weights in a safe workout. Girls can

too. Studies, however, show a big increase in the number of teen boys who use artificial means to build muscles. They take anabolic steroids.

[8]Anabolic steroids are artificial hormones. They are similar to a chemical that your body naturally produces, but they are created in laboratories. Steroids help muscles grow. However, these drugs also have many dangerous side effects. They can affect the user's mood. He might become easily angered and **prone** to fits of rage. Steroids also hurt the body. They can cause liver disease and high blood pressure. In teens, steroids can cause bones to stop growing. Once a user stops taking steroids, injury becomes more likely.

[9]The use of anabolic steroids is a big problem with professional athletes. Many athletes take steroids to help them perform better. In the past, taking these drugs was not against the law. Arnold Schwarzenegger, the governor of California, used to be a professional bodybuilder. Schwarzenegger admits that during that time, he took steroids. He took them legally, with his doctor's help. The steroids helped him build his muscles and win contests. However, after the dangerous side effects of anabolic steroids became known, the steroids became illegal. Now, as the governor of California, Schwarzenegger warns teens and athletes not to use steroids.

[10]One well-known baseball player, Jose Canseco, admitted to steroid use. Because of back problems, Canseco's doctors gave him steroids as medicine. "I needed steroids and growth hormones just to live," he wrote in his book, *Juiced*. However, Canseco used steroids to help improve his performance in baseball too. That gave him an unfair advantage over players who didn't use them. Most professional sports now test athletes for steroid use.

Safe and Healthy Paths to Change

[11]Clearly, there are serious risks in trying to push past normal. The risks can include loss of health, social problems, and even loss of life.

[12]Body change through diet and exercise takes time—but it's time well spent. The benefits include fitness, good health, and a positive attitude. The changes you earn in safe and healthy ways can stay with you for life.

What's in a Good Night's Sleep?

[1]You're falling, falling, falling. Or maybe you're all alone, then suddenly you're in a large crowd. Or you're with a couple of really good friends, but they don't really look like your friends. These are all common dreams.

[2]We spend a lot of time each night dreaming. We spend even more time sleeping. In fact, we sleep about a third of our lives away. There are good reasons we sleep so much. Scientists now think that teens should sleep even more than they do.

The Stages of Sleep

[3]When you go to bed at night, you should be ready for a roller coaster ride. That's what your brain takes every night. You sleep in stages. You move from light sleep through medium sleep to deep sleep. Then you go back up from deep sleep through medium sleep to light sleep. Then you go back down again, then back up again. The roller coaster ride of sleep has four or five up-and-downs each night.

[4]At each stage your brain waves—which are a sign of brain activity—change. During light sleep, brain waves are low and fast. They are almost like they are when you're awake. During deep sleep, however, brain waves are high and slow.

Sweet Dreams

[5]At each peak of the sleep ride, before you go back down into deep sleep, you enter a special stage of sleep. This is the stage where dreams happen.

[6]The dream stage is called REM sleep. REM stands for Rapid Eye Movement. During REM sleep, your eyes move back and forth very quickly. Your brain waves at this time are similar to how they are when you're awake. However, your muscle activity is very quiet. Scientists think the body "shuts down" most muscles during REM sleep so that people can't act out their dreams. That could be dangerous.

[7]Everybody dreams, even though some people say they do not. They just don't remember their dreams. If you have a problem remembering yours, try this: Have someone watch you sleep. When your eyes seem to be moving back and forth, that person should wake you up. Your dream should be fresh in your mind.

The Reasons for Sleep

[8]Why do we sleep about a third of our lives away? Isn't that an extreme amount of time? Research suggests it is not.

[9]Many scientists think that sleep—especially deep sleep—helps your body recover from the day's work. Studies show that exercise increases deep sleep. The more exercise you do during the day, the more time you spend in

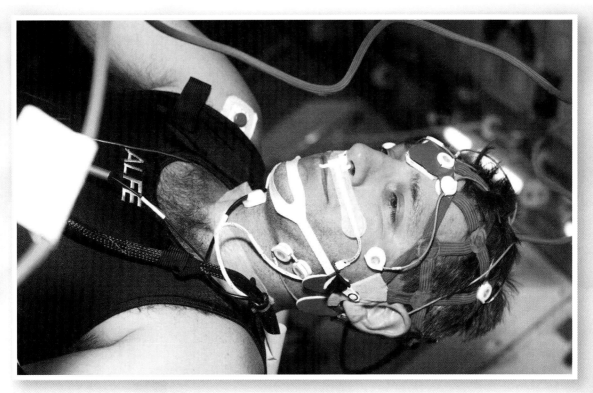

Astronaut Richard Linnehan participates in a sleep experiment on the space shuttle. Astronauts can have difficulty sleeping in space.

deep sleep at night. Also, if someone is awakened each time he or she gets to deep sleep, that person will be tired the entire next day.

[10]If people are awakened each time they enter REM sleep, they may be anxious and irritable the next day. What happens if someone has lost a lot of "dream sleep"? When he or she goes to bed, REM sleep tends to start very quickly and continue for a while. The body is trying to make up for the lost REM sleep. Scientists think sleep—especially REM sleep—is important for memory and learning. Dreams may help us form memories.

Sleepy Teens

[11]How much sleep does a person need? That depends on age. Of course, babies need more sleep than others. But many people are surprised to learn that teens need a lot of sleep too. In fact, studies suggest a teen should sleep more than 9 hours each night.

[12]Research also suggests that waking and sleeping patterns change during the teen years. Teens seem naturally to get sleepy later—at about 11 o'clock at night. Their bodies also tend to wake up later in the morning.

[13]Yet teens' need for sleep and their late-night sleep pattern leads to problems. Middle and high schools often start very early in the day. Some start as early as 7:30 a.m., which means teens have to get up earlier still. Because many teens do not go to bed until about 11 p.m., they do not get enough sleep. That makes it difficult for them to perform well in school. In fact, just staying awake is difficult. To solve the problem, some people are encouraging schools to start no earlier than 8:30 a.m. Sleep is just too important to health—as well as to learning.

SHOCKWAVES

Earthquakes, Volcanoes, Tsunamis

- *How has Earth changed over time?*
- *How are Earth's changes and natural disasters connected?*
- *How can science help protect us from natural disasters?*

LESSONS FROM EARTHQUAKES

San Andreas Fault, California

San Francisco, 1906

[1]In 1906, a strong earthquake shook San Francisco. The earthquake had a **magnitude**, or strength, of 7.7 to 7.9. So far, the most powerful earthquake known has been 9.5 on the magnitude scale. Any earthquake with a magnitude over 7.0 is very strong.

[2]People throughout California and Nevada felt the 1906 earthquake. It toppled thousands of buildings and caused countless fires. More than 3,000 people died, and 225,000 were injured.

[3]The 1906 earthquake was deadly, yet it taught scientists something. It helped them understand what causes quakes. They

studied the damaged buildings and marked where each was on a map. Together, the marks showed that the earthquake had taken place along a line. The damage was greatest near this line. Scientists also found out that the amount of damage to the buildings depended on the kind of soil under them. Scientists learned a lot from the 1906 quake. In fact, this quake marked the beginning of earthquake science.

Investigators examine damage by earthquake.

What Causes an Earthquake?

[4]By 1960, scientists had discovered that just below Earth's surface are about 12 huge, jagged pieces of rock. These pieces are called plates. The plates fit together like the pieces of a puzzle. But unlike puzzle pieces, they don't stand still. Each plate is moving very slowly. The cracks between the plates are called faults. At a fault, two plates bump and rub up against each other.

[5]As plates rub, energy builds up. When the **pressure** becomes too great, the plates suddenly slip and move. Then energy that had been building for years is released in seconds. It travels through the ground in waves. We call these waves of energy an earthquake.

[6]Scientists figured out the location of faults in California and in other places. For example, they learned that the San Andreas Fault runs from southern to northern California and lies under San Francisco. Scientists also began to track and measure the movement of Earth's plates. They were able to tell where pressure was building up along a fault. People then knew where earthquakes were likely to happen. As a result, they rewrote building codes. These laws told how new structures, such as homes and office buildings,

must be built. A structure built anywhere near a fault had to be designed to **resist** the effects of an earthquake. It had to be able to stand firm even when the ground shakes.

Northridge, 1994

[7]Since 1906, many more earthquakes have shaken the ground. Each has added to our knowledge. For example, a quake on January 17, 1994, had a magnitude of 6.7. It was centered in Northridge, California, but it jolted an area for miles around. This quake was followed by 15,000 aftershocks, or smaller quakes.

[8]Far fewer people died or were injured in this quake, as compared with the 1906 quake. By 1994, many structures had been built to resist earthquakes. For example, one hospital was built on a special base that could absorb some of an earthquake's energy. The base helped keep the building from swaying from side to side when the quake hit. As a result, the hospital had little damage.

[9]Other building methods did not work as well. The Northridge earthquake damaged the steel frames of more than 100 buildings. After the quake, the building codes were changed again to try to prevent such damage.

[10]In the future, more quakes are likely to **occur** in Northridge and along other faults in California. Equipment now measures ground movement in 1,000 places throughout the state. Maps show which areas will probably be shaken the most during a quake.

Learning from Earthquakes

[11]Of course, quakes will also happen along faults in other places in the United States and the world. New research now shows us why earthquakes occur and how their energy moves through the ground. These models are helping scientists figure out when quakes might happen and how strong they might be. Scientists also continue to study how earthquakes affect different kinds of buildings. This information helps improve construction methods.

[12]When and where will the next earthquake happen? No one really knows, but past quakes have helped us get ready.

Volcano Camp

This huge cave is a tube of hardened lava.

[1]**W**hen the family finally got to the campground, James was puzzled. "Where's the volcano?" he asked. All he could see were the trees towering over their van. They had spotted the flat, snow-covered top of Mount St. Helens a while back, but where was it now?

[2]"You know we can't camp on the mountain, James," Dad reminded him. "The volcano is so active now that we'll be lucky to get near it."

[3]James had learned that a dome, or huge bulge, was growing on one side of the volcano. The same thing had happened before its destructive 1980 eruption. The new dome was about half as big as the old one. "I really hope the volcano will erupt while we're here. I want to tell all my friends about it!"

[4]"I'll have to disagree with you there, James," Dad said, with a glance at Mom.

[5]James sighed. He thought they'd at least be able to see the volcano from their campsite. "Can we go see it up close now?" he asked.

⁶"Don't be so **impatient**!" his mom told him. "As soon as we set up our tent, we'll head over to the visitor center. It has a great view of the volcano and plenty of exhibits. And we've arranged for a guide. He said he would meet us there at 2 p.m."

⁷An hour later, James and his parents were standing on a platform with an awesome view of Mount St. Helens. His mother was taking photos when the platform began to jiggle. It jiggled for a few seconds. Everyone grabbed for the handrails. It was an earthquake!

⁸Grinning, the guide said, "That was just a hint of what can happen here. The earthquakes before the 1980 eruption came in swarms. Once in a while we'd feel a bigger one, and we'd think that Helen was finally going to explode, but she was just waiting until she had everyone's attention, I guess."

⁹James had learned from the exhibits about the big earthquake on May 18, 1980. It had caused the top of the mountain to cave in. In the weeks before the eruption, rising magma had created a bulge on one side of the volcano. That bulge had grown 5 feet taller—the height of a 12-year-old like James—every day. By May 18, it was huge.

¹⁰Then came the eruption. The bulge burst open. The magma, now called lava, flowed down the volcano. Tons of rock rushed down the mountainside at 180 miles an hour. That's faster than many racecars. A blast of hot gases also exploded out of the volcano into the air. Gases are usually **invisible**, but these gases carried dust, ash, and even stones with them. The blast could be seen for miles. James could see still hundreds of **scorched** tree trunks that it had knocked down. The smaller plants had been buried under the hot lava or beneath a thick layer of ash.

¹¹Yet now the mountainsides were not **barren**, but green and filled with life. The guide explained that some plants had survived beneath the ash until the rain washed it away. Other plants grew from seeds blown onto the ash by the wind or dropped there by birds. Before long, many types of plants were growing on the mountainsides.

¹²"Of course, these aren't the same kinds of trees that grew here before," the guide pointed out. "Before that eruption, fir and hemlock were the most common trees. Now what you see are red alder, black cottonwood, and willows. These fast-growing trees will be replaced someday by more fir and hemlock. Scientists predict that by about 2200, this forest will look much like it did before—unless Helen erupts again."

[13]That night, James lay awake in his sleeping bag for a long time. For a moment, he thought he felt an earthquake. Then he decided that maybe it was just his imagination.

[14]The next day, the family visited Ape Cave. There were no apes there. The cave had been named long ago by a scout troop. It was a lava tube that stretched for a mile and a half. A guide explained that lava tubes form when really thick lava flows down a mountain. The lava on top cools and hardens into a crust. The lava **underneath** keeps flowing until the eruption is over. What's left is a hollow tube of hardened lava. This tube can be as small as a finger or as huge as this cave. The guide told them that Ape Cave had formed after a powerful eruption about 2,000 years ago.

[15]The cave was cold and very dark. The family used flashlights to find their way. James hoped that Mount St. Helens would not erupt right then. This would be an awful place to get trapped. The "lava-sicles" hanging from the ceiling and the slime on the walls did not help. The cave made James realize how much power is **unleashed** when a volcano explodes. A flow of lava twice as tall as he was had formed this cave.

[16]A long hour later, James and his parents stumbled to the cave exit. At least they had not taken the longer upper route. That one took 2 1/2 hours to walk! Blinking in the sunshine, James noticed some smoke rising from the volcano. It came from near the new dome!

[17]Suddenly James hoped the mountain would not erupt while they were there. He didn't want to be anywhere nearby. In fact, he was glad they were going home the next day.

Krakatoa!

[1]One of the worst natural disasters in history was the 1883 eruption of the island volcano called Krakatoa. The good news is that in 1883 the island of Krakatoa was not **inhabited**. No one lived there. However, when Krakatoa erupted, it created huge tsunamis, or destructive waves, in the ocean. These waves drowned thousands of people living on nearby islands. In fact, Krakatoa affected the **entire** world for years afterward.

1887 woodblock print of Krakatoa eruption

The Eruption

[2]Long ago, Krakatoa was a large volcanic island that was part of the country of Indonesia. The map shown on page 77 shows an outline of the island before 1883. You can see that Krakatoa was in the Indian Ocean. That's also where the killer tsunami in 2004 began. You may have heard about that disaster.

[3]Krakatoa had been quiet for nearly 200 years, but in 1883 it became active once more. First, the earthquakes began. Then they became stronger and closer together. On May 20, people 100 miles away heard the first eruptions. Steam and ash rose nearly 7 miles above the volcano. By mid-August, more than a dozen vents on the volcano had opened. They were erupting in lava or releasing steam and ash. Yet Krakatoa's main vent remained plugged with lava.

[4]Then, on August 26 and 27, four **tremendous** explosions occurred. The first eruptions were so strong that they cracked the walls of the volcano, letting ocean water flow inside. As the water hit the **fiery** lava, the water turned into hissing steam. The steam built up more pressure inside the volcano, leading to the last explosion. This one blew away two-thirds of the island. The remaining one-third broke into four parts.

[5]The last eruption of Krakatoa was the most powerful explosion ever recorded. The volcano's blast was heard by people living as far away as Australia, about 2,200 miles from Krakatoa. It cracked walls and broke windows miles away. Shock waves circled Earth seven times. The blast also collapsed the walls of the volcano itself. As the gigantic walls of rock collapsed into the ocean, they caused the first great tsunami.

Water and Fire

[6]The first tsunami rose 120 feet into the air as it roared away from the remains of Krakatoa. More explosions followed, causing smaller tsunamis. About an hour later, these waves wiped out the closest islands. The islands vanished under the water. On other islands, the tsunamis stripped everything away. About 3,000 people were washed out to sea. Some people were able to climb trees and avoid drowning. Altogether, the tsunamis destroyed 295 towns and villages, and about 36,000 people drowned.

[7]The eruption also sent out flows of very hot ash, pumice, rock, and gases. The flows traveled long distances, even over water. For example, in Sumatra, an island 25 miles from Krakatoa, 2,000 people were severely burned. Entire villages were set on fire.

Disaster in the Air

[8]The eruptions shot miles of dust, ash, and vocanic rock high and wide into the air. Ash and rock rained down around Krakatoa. It buried most plants on nearby islands. The ash left a thick layer on the decks of ships as far as 160 miles from the blast. In the seas, the ash formed floating rafts 3 yards thick. These rafts of ash **clogged** the waters. They kept ships from bringing help to some of the islands. Some of these rafts floated for 2 years. One huge ash raft floated to South Africa, more than 5,000 miles away.

[9]The cloud from the volcano was so thick and wide that it blocked the sun. The area around Krakatoa was completely dark for 3 days straight. Places more than 130 miles away were dark for 24 hours. Thirteen days later, this cloud was circling Earth. It had formed a "belt" above the equator. The cloud reduced the amount of sunlight that reached Earth's surface. Because of that, it lowered temperatures worldwide. It also changed weather patterns. In fact, it was 5 years before the world's weather returned to normal.

[10]The fine dust rose so high that it affected sunsets around the world. The dust particles caught and reflected different colors of the sunlight. For almost 3 years, even people in the United States and Europe saw beautiful, unusually red sunsets. Sometimes the sun was blue, and sometimes it was green!

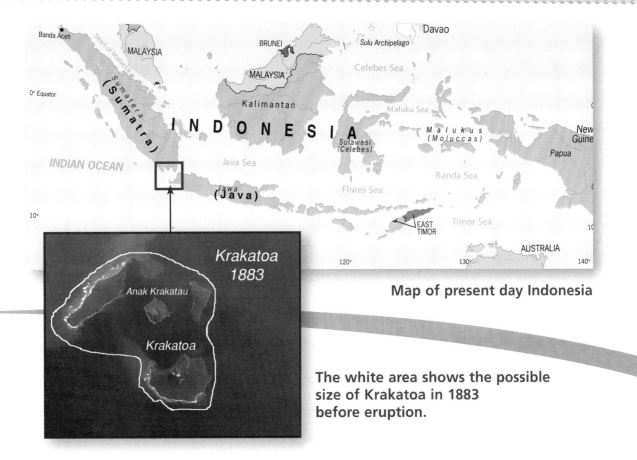

Map of present day Indonesia

Krakatoa 1883

Anak Krakatau

Krakatoa

The white area shows the possible size of Krakatoa in 1883 before eruption.

Krakatoa Today

[11]After Krakatoa exploded into four parts, one of those parts also became a volcano. Today it's called Anak Krakatau, which means "child of Krakatoa." In 1927, this volcano had a few weak eruptions. But from 1959 to 1963, it was very active, sending clouds of ash thousands of feet into the air. Small eruptions began again in 1994. Who knows what horror this "child" might bring upon the people living nearby?

[12]Back in 1883, the first announcement of the approaching tsunamis was the boom of the erupting volcano. Now this part of the world is only slightly better off. People can use **portable** telephones and e-mail to warn each other of an approaching tsunami, yet there is still no tsunami warning system for the countries around the Indian Ocean.

[13]People are working together to put a warning system in place. They hope that Anak Krakatau and the other volcanoes in this region will stay quiet until then.

Earth's Moving Continents

[1]Fifty million years from now, Africa may smash into Europe. This force may cause a great mountain range to rise. These mountains will be much like the Himalayas, which rose when India crashed into Asia.

[2]Are Africa and Europe and Earth's other continents really moving around? Yes, they certainly are! You have read that huge, rocky plates lie below Earth's surface. These plates are part of Earth's crust, or its outer layer. The continents and the oceans rest on these plates. The continents and oceans move as the plates under them move.

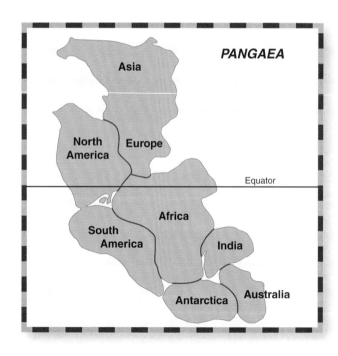

250 Million Years Ago

[3]What did Earth look like before all this traveling began? The diagram to the left might give you an idea. All of the land on Earth was one super continent that we now call Pangaea. *Pangaea* means "all lands" in Greek. One vast ocean surrounded Pangaea. The lines on the diagram show the borders of the future continents, but back then there was just one big piece of land.

78

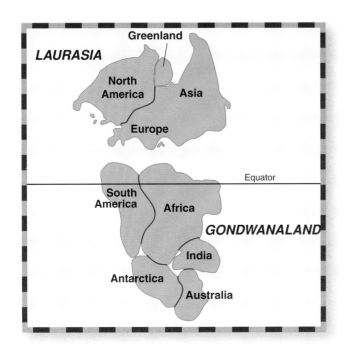

200 Million Years Ago

[4]In time, the movement of the plates caused Pangaea to break up. It split into two smaller landmasses:

- Laurasia, which included North America, Greenland, Europe, and Asia, and
- Gondwanaland, which included South America, Antarctica, Australia, Africa, and India.

These two areas of land were still huge in comparison to today's continents.

135 Million Years Ago

[5]As Earth's plates kept moving, Laurasia was pulled apart into three **distinct** continents, and Gondwanaland was torn into four. At this point, India was part of Africa. But it eventually broke away. It drifted north and slowly crashed into Asia. The force of that crash pushed up tons and tons of rock, forming the world's tallest mountains, the Himalayas.

[6]At the beginning of this period, dinosaurs and other animals could roam from one continent to another. After the continents pulled apart, animals could not roam as freely. Bodies of water stood in their way.

[7]You might wonder how scientists know which continents were once part of Laurasia and which were part of Gondwanaland. After all, no humans were alive back then. Scientists have found several clues.

Some Moving Clues

[8]Long ago, people did not know why mountains form. To explain such events, they made up myths and stories.

[9]Scientists, however, don't rely on myths and stories. They gather facts and look for evidence. Then they use this information to come up with a **theory** that explains how something happens. Back in 1912, a scientist named Alfred Wegener studied Earth closely. He was the first to suggest that all the continents had once been joined. He based this theory on three main types of evidence:

- The shapes of the continents. Wegener compared the west coast of Africa with the east coasts of North and South America. They fit together like puzzle pieces.
- Types of rocks. Wegener knew that very similar rocks could be found in Africa and South America. Scientists had studied the rocks from these two separate continents. They learned that some of the rocks had been formed at the same time and in the same place.
- Plant and animal remains. Millions of plants and animals once lived on Laurasia and Gondwanaland. As they died, some left behind **fossils**. These fossils show the shape of their remains. Wegener noted that the same kinds of fossils, formed millions of years ago, were found in Africa and South America. These plants and animals could not have crossed the ocean. Instead, those two continents must have been joined back then.

[10]In fact, fossils of a certain ancient plant have been found in Antarctica, Australia, South America, Africa, and India. These fossils suggest that all these continents were once joined as Gondwanaland. However, the same plant has not been found in any continent that was once part of Laurasia. That is how scientists know which continents were once part of Laurasia and which were once part of Gondwanaland.

[11]Wegener was also sure that Antarctica had moved because he knew that coal had been found under the ice there. Coal formed millions of years ago from decaying plants in swamps. Antarctica must have been warmer back then. But for it to be warmer, it had to be closer to the equator. Since then, Antarctica has moved toward the South Pole. This icy, frozen continent certainly has no swampland now.

[12]You know about the rocky plates that are part of Earth's crust, and you know that when these plates move, the land or ocean above them moves too. But Wegener didn't know these things. Instead, Wegener thought that the

continents pushed their way across the ocean floor. Few people believed this.

[13]"**Impossible!**" many said. Back then, people thought that the continents were permanently **attached** to a certain spot on Earth's surface.

[14]Wegener froze to death in 1930 while exploring Greenland. Scientists were still arguing about whether the continents could move. They did not agree that this was possible until 1960. Then, scientists finally proved that Earth's crust is made of 12 large plates.

Earth Today

[15]The continents are still moving. Can you feel it? No, you can't, because the movement is too slow. North America and South America are inching toward the Pacific Ocean. Australia is slowly traveling northward. Some day, millions of years from now, the western part of Africa may turn and hit Europe. It will be a slow-motion crash. People will have plenty of time to get out of the way as the new mountains form.

[16]The movement of plates continues to cause mountains to form, volcanoes to erupt, and earthquakes to bring down buildings. As always, living on Earth is a moving experience.

To the Rescue!

This rescue worker makes sure no one is trapped.

[1]At 4:31 a.m. on January 17, 1994, a tremendous earthquake shook millions of people out of their beds. The quake had a magnitude of 6.7. It rattled California's San Fernando Valley. The governor knew his state needed help. He quickly called FEMA, the Federal Emergency Management Agency. FEMA is the government agency in charge of helping people in disasters. Its Urban Search and Rescue Teams rush to cities and towns where disasters have happened. Their job is to find and rescue trapped people.

About the Rescue Teams

[2]An Urban Search and Rescue Team is a partnership. The partners are fire departments, police departments, government agencies, and private companies who have agreed to work together. The team includes many

specialists, such as firefighters and search dogs and their handlers. The team's engineers check the safety of damaged structures. Other experts look for dangerous materials. Heavy-equipment operators use cranes and other machinery to help uncover trapped people. Paramedics handle medical problems. Communication specialists keep team members in touch.

[3]These teams help during and after hurricanes, tornadoes, mudslides, and floods. They also rush to airplane accidents and dangerous spills, and they are always needed after a major earthquake. Immediately after the 1994 California earthquake, the three closest Urban Search and Rescue Teams reported for duty.

Checking the Earthquake Damage

[4]First, local firefighters drove through their districts. Their main goal was to rescue people from burning buildings. Often, they had to let the buildings burn. Because the earthquake had broken water pipes, firefighters were left without water to put out the fires.

[5]At the same time, helicopter teams took to the air. They saw toppled buildings and entire blocks on fire. Flames shot out of gas pipes. It was soon clear that the Northridge area had the most damage. A science lab at Northridge College was on fire. This was serious because burning chemicals can release poisons into the air. In addition, people were trapped in a parking garage and an apartment building that had collapsed there.

The Work of Rescuing

[6]At the college, rescuers made a quick search and found no one trapped in the lab building. Then college teachers told the team which chemicals were in the buildings and where they were stored. Firefighters in protective suits rushed into the fiery building. They managed to keep the flames from reaching the chemicals.

[7]In the three-story parking garage, a man was trapped underneath concrete on the first floor. He had been driving a street sweeper. Gasoline from his crushed truck had leaked onto the floor.

[8]At the garage, rescuers from three agencies agreed on a plan. Some team members sprayed foam to reduce the chance of fire. Others worked to lift the

concrete off the driver. They put air bags under the chunks of concrete and slowly filled the bags with air. As the bags lifted the concrete a few inches at a time, the team wedged wooden beams under the concrete to give it support. Paramedics stayed with the injured driver the entire time. As the team worked, aftershocks threatened to collapse more of the garage.

[9]After 9 hours, the team had lifted the concrete about 12 inches off the driver. They had also cut away parts of the truck that had been trapping him. Finally, the driver was gently pulled out. A helicopter rushed him to a hospital. His legs were crushed, but he was still alive.

[10]Another team had rushed to the Northridge Meadows Apartments. This three-story structure now had only two floors. The first floor had completely collapsed. The team worked to reach the people trapped there. They lifted off chunks of concrete and cut through the floor of the second story. All the while, aftershocks kept everyone nervous and tense.

[11]Among other tools, this team used a SearchCam. This special camera could look through a small hole into the collapsed rooms. That way, rescuers did not need to create a large opening unless the camera showed that someone was trapped under layers of rubble. Rescue dogs also helped locate trapped victims. Nearly 24 hours after the earthquake, the rescuers had searched all 163 apartment units. Sixteen people had died, and more were injured. Still, the team had saved many lives.

A Team that's Always Ready

[12]Each FEMA Search and Rescue Team is made up of two 31-person teams and four dogs. Two people are always available to fill each position on the team. Both have completed hundreds of hours of special training. A team also has thousands of pieces of portable equipment, as well as food, cots, and tents. If necessary, team members can live on these supplies for 4 days.

[13]Today, 28 Urban Search and Rescue Teams are prepared to rush to disasters. After each rescue, team members go back to their everyday jobs. Many are the same firefighters and paramedics who answer 911 calls. They are well prepared for the next disaster, whatever and wherever it might be.

THE INTERNET

A Wired World

- *How is the Internet used differently today from when it first started?*
- *How have criminals misused the Internet?*
- *What role does the Internet play in your life?*

Online and In Touch

The Internet provides worldwide communication.

[1]Millions of people go online every day to "surf" the Internet and to communicate by e-mail. The Internet is an ever-growing worldwide **network** of computers. E-mail has become an important way to send and receive messages cheaply and quickly across long distances. Both the Internet and e-mail have made a huge **impact** on our lives.

How Did the Internet and E-mail Begin?

[2]In the late 1950s, the first satellites were sent into space. Satellite technology now allows us to communicate by telephone and to go online. In the early 1960s, scientists worked to **devise** ways to transfer information among computer users. By 1969, computers at several key places in the United States were joined in a network called ARPANET. The letters stood

for "Advanced Research Projects Agency Network."

[3]Ray Tomlinson is an engineer who worked on ARPANET. At the same time, he had an idea for a new communication tool. In 1971, he created the program for e-mail. It was "a neat thing to try out," he says of the program. Tomlinson created e-mail in just a few hours during his spare time.

[4]The invention of the telephone changed society. In the same way, e-mail **transformed** our daily lives. At first, e-mail was available only to a few people connected on ARPANET. Later, during the 1980s, improved computer and telephone technology allowed ARPANET and e-mail to grow. Connecting to other computers became faster. Then, in 1990, ARPANET became the Internet that we know today. The World Wide Web soon became the pathway to the vast resources on the Internet.

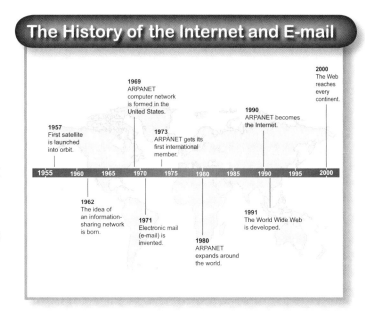

Can I Trust the Information?

[5]You can find information on any subject on the Internet. New knowledge is at your fingertips. This presents challenges and problems, though. The Internet is a tremendous jumble of information. You have to sort through the information and judge its quality. Here's where your critical reading skills come in handy.

[6]Can you trust what you read on a Web site? A site can be created by anyone. Opinions can be presented as facts. Knowing the purpose and creator of a site can help you decide if the information is of value. The first step in judging online information is to ask, who is providing the information? Is this source **reliable**? Next, ask, could someone gain money by offering this information? Many Web sites sell products and services. They want to entice you to buy something.

87

[7]Political groups and politicians have Web sites. Their goal may be to persuade you to accept their point of view. You may also come across blogs, or Web logs. These are written in several forms. Some are like personal journals. Others are like magazine articles. They present a wide range of views and opinions. But they don't necessarily present facts.

How Can I Judge a Web Site?

[8]Look for details that are clues to whether the information on a Web site can be trusted. Is the site well organized? Is the information easy to understand? Is the information up to date? Are facts well supported? Often, the last three letters of a Web site's URL, or address, can be helpful clues.

- Sites ending in *.com* are commercial. These sites are usually designed to sell products or services.
- Sites ending in *.org* are published by organizations and agencies. These sites are not usually set up to sell you something. Keep in mind, though, that some of these groups may have points of view to promote.
- Sites ending in *.edu* are maintained by academic, or educational, **institutions**. These are good sites to use when researching information for school reports or projects. You can't trust all the information on these sites, though. In some cases, students create personal Web sites using addresses ending in *.edu*.
- Sites ending in *.gov* signal a government agency. Federal, state, and local governments provide information on these sites.

[9]The Internet is an amazing invention. Keep in mind, though, that no person or agency supervises or controls the huge amount of information on it. Anyone can set up a Web site. Judge the quality of what you find online in the same way you judge information from sources such as newspapers and television programs. Be curious and open-minded. But be cautious too.

COMPUTER CRIME:
Identity Theft

[1]You've locked your valuables in a safe. Your money is in a bank. Your house is locked. You have a home alarm system. Are you safe from thieves? Not exactly. There's a new kind of thief out there. This thief doesn't break into your house or rob you at gunpoint. This thief works behind the scenes to steal your **identity**, along with your money.

[2]Early in 2005, a man found his life turned upside down by an identity thief. He owned a house in California but had been living outside the United States for four years. When the man decided to sell his California house, he learned that it was being inhabited by strangers. People were living there without his knowledge! Another person was **illegally** charging them rent. This person had pretended to be the owner. The man still doesn't know who the thief is or how the theft occurred.

[3]Unfortunately, this is happening to more people all the time. Identity thieves are devising smarter and more devious ways to get the information they need. Sometimes, they get people to practically hand the information to them. This type of theft has a great impact on a person's life, and the crime can take years to solve.

Personal Information

[4]According to some government estimates, more than 10 million people in the United States are victims of identity theft every year. Most often, a criminal steals someone's identity in order to cheat a credit card company. The criminals are able to do this by stealing important personal information.

[5]We all give out personal information at times. We do it in person, by mail, by telephone, and on the Internet. Millions of us have bought things online. Many of us pay bills online. We bank online and even apply for loans online. All of these things require giving someone information such as our Social Security number, credit card numbers, and bank account numbers.

[6]A thief who has **access** to a credit card number can use the number to buy things. The person whose name is on the credit card will get the bill. With someone's Social Security number, a thief is able to get credit card accounts in that person's name. Again, the victim will get the bills. In most cases, the person whose account was used will not have to pay for the purchases. But it will take a long time to straighten out the matter.

The Best Protection: Prevention

[7]The best way to protect yourself from identify theft is to follow a few simple tips.

1. Don't throw away papers or anything else that contains personal information. Thieves don't mind going through garbage to get this information. Instead, use a shredder, which strips paper into tiny pieces.
2. Do not carry your Social Security card or number in your wallet. If the wallet is lost or stolen, thieves will be able to use the number.
3. When you use a credit card, make sure to get the card back from the merchant. And make sure that you keep the receipt or shred it. The receipt may have your entire credit card number printed on it.
4. Don't give out personal information unless it is necessary and the person to whom you are giving the information is trustworthy.

Theft on the Internet

[8]The biggest risk of identity theft is on the Internet. Follow these steps when making purchases online.

[9]First, keep your passwords secret. A password is needed on many Internet sites where you can buy things. Use nonsense words as passwords, rather than your birthday or a pet's name. This will reduce the chance that a thief will guess the word. It's best to use letters, numbers, *and* symbols in a password.

[10]Second, use a credit card only at secure sites. Secure Web pages have *https* (not *http*) in the address bar. This appears just before the *www*. The *s* means "secure." The address bar should have a yellow background. Also, a little symbol should appear at the bottom of the window. The symbol looks like a closed padlock. On these sites, personal information is scrambled. It's impossible to read as it travels over the Internet.

[11]People who shop online often can use services that reduce the risk of theft. The services are called "third-party payers." People **authorize** these services to pay for their online purchases. A third-party payer will have that person's credit card information on file. The service will then bill the credit card company for purchases it makes online.

[12]Third, be careful about the information you share online. Make sure that a Web site will keep your personal information **confidential**. Read the site's privacy statement. Do not shop at a Web site that **permits** others to use your information.

[13]When you're online, be on the lookout for e-mails that try to trick you into sending personal information. These e-mails may seem to come from a company you already know, such as your Internet provider. The e-mail may ask for personal information. It may even ask for your Social Security number. Before giving out this information, call the company on the telephone to ask if they requested the information.

[14]You can also take care to keep personal information out of e-mails. Others may be able to read your e-mail and use the information for their own gain.

[15]Last of all, find out how to protect your computer. One kind of protection you can install is called a "firewall." A firewall is a program designed to obstruct outsiders. It keeps the files on a computer safe when the computer is connected to the Internet.

LOOKING FOR A JOB ONLINE

[1]**S**ooner or later, you'll begin the search for your first job. You may want to earn money to buy your own clothes. Perhaps you want to start saving money for college. Or you may want a job just to feel more independent. Whatever your reason, this will be an exciting step for you. In addition to making money, you'll gain valuable experience that will make you **eligible** for jobs in the future.

[2]Does the thought of searching for a job make you feel a little nervous? Most people feel this way at first. Here are some tips that may give you more confidence as you prepare to enter the world of work.

[3]For most jobs, you will fill out an **application**. The application is a form on which you provide information about yourself. You will describe your education and list any previous work experience. After a company reviews your application, you may be invited to an **interview** for the job.

Online Job Application
Fill in each box. Point and click to type your information.

①

PERSONAL INFORMATION
②

Last Name: [ ]
First Name: [ ]
Middle Name: [ ]
Social Security Number: [ ]
Street Address: [ ]
City: [ ]
State: [Please Choose ▼]
Zip Code: [ ]
Daytime Telephone: [ ]
Evening Telephone: [ ]

If you are under age 18, do you have a certificate of age or employment? ◯ Yes ◯ No

AVAILABILITY
③

What position are you applying for? [ ]
Are you currently employed? ◯ Yes ◯ No
Have you ever worked here before? ◯ Yes ◯ No
If yes, when? [ ]
Are you applying for full-time or part-time work? ◯ Full-time ◯ Part-time
What days and hours are you available? [ ]
What date are you available to begin work? [ ]

EDUCATION
④

Name and address of school [ ]
Dates attended [ ]
Did you graduate? ◯ Yes ◯ No

EDUCATION (cont.)

Name and address of school [ ]
Dates attended [ ]
Did you graduate? ◯ Yes ◯ No

EMPLOYMENT HISTORY
List your most recent employer first.
⑤

Company Name [ ]
Address [ ]
Telephone [ ]
Your Title [ ]
Dates Employed [ ]
Responsibilities [ ]
Reason for Leaving [ ]

Company Name [ ]
Address [ ]
Telephone [ ]
Your Title [ ]
Dates Employed [ ]
Responsibilities [ ]
Reason for Leaving [ ]

I agree that the statements in this application are true and complete. I understand that false statements on this application may be grounds for rejection or immediate termination of employment. I grant permission to verify any information I have given on this application.

◯ Agree ◯ Disagree **⑥**

[SUBMIT]

In an interview, a representative of a company will ask you questions about yourself and about your skills. The interviewer will decide if you are right for the job. You may also be asked to submit a résumé. This is a document on which you list your personal information and work experience. What if you haven't had a "real" job before? You can still prepare a résumé by listing any volunteer work or other activities that show you can handle responsibility.

[4]One way to begin your search is to use the Internet to visit Web sites that show job opportunities. Using a search engine such as Google™ or Yahoo®!, type in "job search." Then click on one of the listed sites.

[5]Similar to the want ads in a newspaper, Internet job sites **classify** openings by type of job. Suppose you want to find a job as a warehouse worker. You would type "warehouse worker" or "warehouse" in the search box of a job site, which will give you access to a listing of **potential** jobs. Look through the listing, and when you find a job that sounds interesting, you can contact the company through the site.

[6]The first step in applying is to fill out a job application. Nowadays, you can do this online for many jobs. Make sure to print out and save a copy of the completed application. You can use the information on it when you fill out other job applications.

Completing an Online Job Application

[7]Online job applications are much like the paper forms. Look at the model of an online application form. Follow the model as you read these guidelines.

1. First, read the instructions carefully. You will type in information or choose between two answers. Point and click to place your cursor in each box. Then type in the information or click the button as directed.

2. Type your last name, first name, and middle name into each box. Note that on this form, you must fill in your last name first. Some applications ask for a *first* name first. Fill in your Social Security number. Having a Social Security number is a requirement for a paying job. Then fill in your street address, city, state, zip code, and telephone numbers. Applicants under age 18 will need a certificate of age for employment. A teacher or school counselor can help you get this certificate.

3. The questions in this section are a sample of what an employer might ask. *What position are you applying for?* Type *warehouse worker* in the box. *Are you currently employed?* Click "yes" or "no." *Have you ever worked here before? If yes, when?* If your answer is "yes," the company will likely have a record of your employment, which can help in making a decision about whether to hire you again. *Are you applying for full-time or part-time work?* If you are still in school, you will probably apply for part-time work. Click the button next to "part-time." *What days and hours are you available?* Be as **specific** as possible when filling in this information. *What date are you available to begin work?* Answer this carefully. If you already have another job, you should give your employer two weeks' notice before taking a new job.

4. Fill in the name and address of the last school you attended, and give the months and years you attended. Tell whether you graduated. Some applications have space for four or five schools. Fill in your own school history, listing the most recent school first.

5. In the sample applicaton on page 94, you are asked to list your most recent employer first. If this is your first job, leave this section blank or write "Does Not Apply." If you have worked before, type in the company name, address, and telephone number. Fill in the job title you had and the months and years that you worked for the employer. In the box next to *Responsibilities*, give a brief description of the tasks you performed. In the box next to *Reason for Leaving*, be brief, as well as honest.

6. Most online job applications have sections such as this. In this agreement, you declare that the information you have provided on the application is true. You also give the company permission to double-check the information. Before you submit your application, reread it. Did you leave out any information? Make sure there are no mistakes. Check your spelling. When you are finished, click "Agree" and "Submit."

[8]You're done! That's all there is to filling out a typical online job application. When you begin a job search, the first step will be easy—right?

○ **AGREE**   ○ **DISAGREE**

96

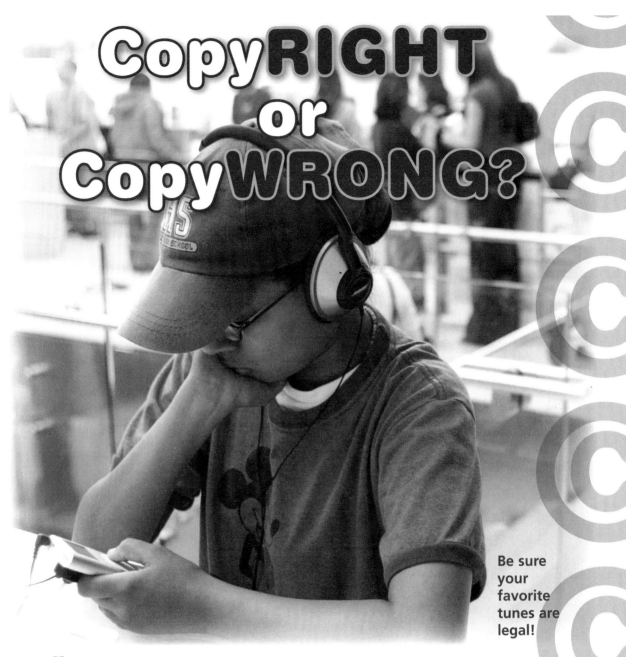

CopyRIGHT or CopyWRONG?

Be sure your favorite tunes are legal!

[1]**Y**ou're walking down the sidewalk. You've got your earbuds in and your **audio** player on. You're listening to a great new song by your favorite artist. Your legs move to the rhythm of the music. Suddenly, you feel a tap on your shoulder. You stop walking and turn around. It's your friend Kelly. "Hey!" she says. You remove the earbuds. "That music you're listening to—where did you get it?"

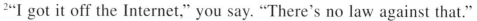

[2]"I got it off the Internet," you say. "There's no law against that."

[3]"Yes, there is," says Kelly. "You'd better make sure you got it legally, or else you could be in trouble."

[4]"What?" you reply. "You mean, I could get in trouble if I just **download** some tunes?"

[5]Kelly is right. Nowadays, it's illegal to download some types of music from the Internet.

It's the Law

[6]Copyright laws protect artists, writers, and musicians from others who might try to steal their work. For example, when a musician writes a song, that song becomes the artist's property. The musician owns the legal right to earn money from the song—from sales of CDs, from radio play, from concert play, and in other ways. No one else can make money from the song without the permission of the artist. Often, a musician will sell permission to a music company.

[7]In the late 1990s, a computer file format called MP3 made it possible to copy music files and post them on the Internet. MP3 compresses sound data so that it can be transferred. Several Web sites copied music and made it available to everyone.

[8]The Web sites did not charge money for the music. Many people began downloading music instead of buying it in stores. This meant that musicians and music companies lost money. Music artists and recording companies claimed that downloading the music was against the copyright laws.

Napster Changed Everything

[9]In 1999, an 18-year old student created a new type of computer program. He called his program "Napster." This was the student's nickname in high school. Napster made it possible to transfer MP3 files directly from user to user. This meant that MP3 files were no longer stored on a Web site. People could trade files with one another. As you might guess, downloading files from Napster became very

98

popular in a very short time. Napster led to a huge increase in music file sharing. It also had a huge impact on music sales. And it prompted a lively debate about the copyright laws.

[10]A national law passed in 1992 made it legal for people to buy recorded music and make a few copies for themselves and their friends. They could not sell the copies, though. The thinking behind the law was that making a few copies of music for private use would not hurt record sales.

[11]That was not the case with Napster, though. When Napster became popular, sales of recorded music went way down. This had serious **consequences** for musicians and music companies. They blamed Napster. They felt that access to Napster files **deprived** them of income they deserved. Fewer people than before were paying for the music.

Some music can be downloaded legally.

[12]Napster users claimed that the 1992 law made music file sharing legal. They were not paying for the music. Napster was not getting money that would otherwise have gone to musicians and record companies.

[13]Before long, the debate ended up in the courts. First, both sides argued their case. Then the courts decided that using Napster to transfer music files among individuals was against the copyright laws. The court said Napster had to stop free file transfers. Downloading the music for free was the same as stealing. After that, record companies warned those illegally downloading music to **anticipate** lawsuits.

[14]Finally, by 2002 Napster had changed its way of operating. It began selling music downloads. Napster charges a monthly fee. Musicians and music companies receive payment from Napster. Other Internet sites offer similar services. Research is now showing that more people are willing to pay for music downloads.

Legal Downloading

[15]Paying money for music files from Napster or other Internet sites is legal. You can also download free music legally in some cases. Sometimes musicians and music companies allow people to download music for free. This is a way to introduce new artists. People will often buy other songs by an artist after getting a free sample.

[16]And, yes, some Internet sites are still breaking the copyright laws. They offer downloads or make it easy to share files illegally. This is where you could get into trouble. The music companies will take people to court if they can prove that they downloaded music files illegally from one of these sites.

[17]You may already know how to import music from a legal Internet site and download it to your computer and **digital** audio player. If not, follow these simple steps to get your legal tunes.

- First, go to the Internet site and search by musician or song title for the music you want.
- Then, fill out the form for payment information.
- Next, download the music. The site will make it easy for you to do. It takes just one or two clicks of the mouse.
- After the download is complete, the music is on your computer.
- Next, you can transfer the music from the computer to your MP3 player. The software that came with your player will help you create a list of music files you want to transfer.
- Then, plug your MP3 player into your computer.
- Finally, click to transfer the music files to the player.

[18]That's all there is to it. Now you're ready to carry a concert with you wherever you go!

Unique records
and stereos can
be found on
eBay®.

A Store the Size of Earth

[1]**W**here on Earth can you buy a drum set, a tractor seat, and an office building—all at the same store? You can find these things, and many, many more, at eBay®, "the world's online marketplace." The site has transformed selling and buying. Begun in 1995, eBay is open 24 hours a day, 7 days a week. More than 100 million people around the world buy and sell everything from anchors to zithers on eBay. At any given moment, there are more than 10 million items for sale at this site.

[2]Want to buy a camera? eBay has jillions. How about sports cards, computers, or pet supplies? There are plenty to choose from. Do you have something unusual to sell? One seller sold a jar that was said to contain a

ghost. Another sold a plastic cup that Elvis Presley supposedly drank from. A buyer paid $455 for it. A Christmas pudding that belonged to the Queen of England sold on eBay.

[3]People who offer unusual items for sale on eBay usually have interesting stories connected with the items. A woman who sold a magician's wand on eBay claimed that the magician used the wand to make himself disappear. Only the wand was left. Some people sell unusual services on eBay. A man in Omaha sold advertising space on his forehead.

eBay celebrates its 10-year anniversary in 2005.

Getting Started on eBay

[4]It's easy to register on eBay. First, you must be 18 years old or have the permission of a parent. Then you need to fill out an online form. The form asks for your name, address, date of birth, telephone number, and e-mail address. eBay honors your privacy. You register at a confidential, secure site, which means that your personal information is protected.

[5]Next, you agree to eBay's terms for buying or selling items. Then, you have to choose a user name and a password. Your user name is a name you use online. Most people do not use their real names. The password is a word or set of letters and numbers that only you know. The user name and password are used when you buy or sell items on eBay.

Buying on eBay

[6]Buying and selling on eBay are simple. Let's begin with buying. Every page on eBay's Web site has a search box. You type in the name of the item you want to buy and click on the "search" button. The more specific your search term, the faster you'll find what you want. A list of these items will appear. When you click a link for an item on the list, you'll be taken to a Web page, where you can read more about the item and place a bid.

[7]Bidding follows three steps. Just for fun, let's imagine that you want to buy something unusual—how about an African djembe drum?

- Type "djembe drum" into the "search" box. You may find hundreds of these drums for sale. Look through the listing on the first few pages, and check the prices. Click on the links for a few and read about them. You'll see the current price being bid for each drum.
- Once you've found the drum you want, click the "Place Bid" button. You'll be taken to a sign-in page. Sign in, using your password.
- On the next screen, you type in your bid. That's all there is to it.

[8]Any other eBay user can also bid for the drum. Whoever places the highest bid for an item gets it. If your bid is highest, you're expected to pay for it, so make sure that you really want an item before you bid on it.

[9]So, what if your bid on the drum is highest? The seller will send you an e-mail with payment instructions. Most sellers accept checks and credit cards. You will exchange addresses with the seller, and then you'll send your payment. Within a week or two, your doorbell will ring, and a delivery person will hand you your African djembe drum!

djembe drum

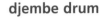

Selling on eBay

[10]First, you need to describe your item online. Be honest about its condition. You might want to include a picture of the item. To do this, you must use a digital camera. You will also need a computer program that makes the picture the right size for a computer screen.

[11]Next, you must fill out online forms for the item. You can choose to put the item on sale for three, five, seven, or 10 days. For an extra fee, you can add more than one picture of the item. You can list your item in bold type to make it stand out. After filling out the forms, you click a final box. Now your item is for sale. You'll want to check the site often to see whether anyone has bid on it. When the sale ends, you will send the highest bidder an e-mail with the final price and shipping costs. After the buyer pays you, you will ship the item.

[12]The eBay site is designed to be easy and fun. It can be a great place to buy a gift or find a collector's item. It can also be a good way to clean out a closet and make money at the same time.

Online auctions can be fun and a good way to sell your old treasures.

Expedition 7

MONEY MATTERS

- What are the advantages and disadvantages of buying on credit?
- What are different ways you can pay for things?
- What hidden costs go into making a single product?

¹**O**ne day you will have a job. You'll work hard for your money, and you won't want to waste it. Here are some **precautions** that will help you avoid giving too much of your money away.

Banks and Check-Cashing Shops

²Suppose that on your first payday at your new job, your boss hands you a check for $120. During your lunch break, you walk to the bank across the street to cash your check. You hand the check to the bank teller. "I'd like to cash this check," you say. The teller asks whether you have an account at this bank. You explain that because the bank requires account holders to keep at least $50 in their checking accounts, you'd prefer to open an account elsewhere.

³"But my employer has an account at this bank," you say. You point out that the bank's name is on the check. The teller can easily determine whether there's enough money in your employer's bank account to pay your check.

⁴"I'm sorry," the teller responds. "If you don't have an account here, you'll have to pay a $5 fee to cash this check. It's a **policy** at this bank. Of course, if you open an account here, we'll cash your check for free."

⁵Now what can you do? You remember the shop down the street. It cashes checks too. "I'd be happy to cash your check," the clerk at the check-cashing shop says. "It'll cost you 10 percent of the amount of the check." You didn't anticipate paying this much to cash your check. Do you really want to give up $12?

⁶You thank the clerk and leave with your check. Now you're beginning to think that it makes more sense to open a checking account rather than cash your paychecks each week. If you have to keep $50 in the account, at least it's still your money. In contrast, the money you pay to a check-cashing shop is gone for good.

⁷You decide to hold on to your check for now. During tomorrow's lunch break, you'll open a bank account. Maybe you can find a bank that doesn't require a minimum balance.

Payday Loans

[8]Now you've set up a checking account at a bank, but your account is empty. Luckily for you, the bank doesn't charge a **penalty** when your balance is zero. Payday is next week, but your favorite band is coming to your city tomorrow, and you need to buy a ticket today. The tickets cost $35.

[9]Most check-cashing shops give loans. You write a check from your account, using the date of your next payday. Another requirement is that you show the shop a pay stub or other proof that you have a job. The shop will give you the money you need. They will wait until the date on your check to cash it, because by then, you will have put your paycheck into your account.

[10]Sounds easy, doesn't it? Here is the catch: there's a fee for the loan. For example, if you want $35, the shop might ask you to write a check for $45. It will give you $35 and will keep the other $10 as the loan fee. The greater the amount of the loan, the higher the fee. Now you see the consequences of not planning ahead. You promise yourself to make a **budget** and stick to it.

"Floating" Your Own Loan

[11]You might know people who intentionally write checks before they have enough money in their accounts to cover them. Knowing that they'll receive a paycheck in a few days, they think they will be able to put money into their checking accounts before the bank receives the checks. This is called "floating" checks. Years ago, this often worked. Checks were taken in person or mailed from a store to the store's bank. Some checks also had to go from the store's bank to the customer's bank. This took several days.

[12]Now, however, because of computers, banks can transfer money more quickly. If you write a check, the bank will probably subtract the money from your account within one day. If you don't have enough money in your account to cover the check, the check will "bounce." The bank will send the check back to the store. Then both the store and the bank will charge you an expensive fee.

[13]Getting a paycheck is great, but it comes with **responsibilities**. Be smart about managing your money. Don't give it away in fees or penalties, if you can help it. Remember: You worked hard for the money, so you're **entitled** to keep as much of it as you can!

CHARGE IT!

[1]Your friend Henry has offered to buy you and two other friends dinner. The four of you order hamburgers. When it comes time to pay, Henry digs into his pocket. Uh-oh. He doesn't have enough money to pay for the food. Luckily, the rest of you come up with enough change to pay for the meal. Henry is embarrassed. "I wish I had a credit card," he says.

[2]Having a credit card is convenient. When you don't have enough cash with you, you can use the card. This is both the benefit and the potential danger of using credit cards. The average American family has *eight* credit cards, and owes about $8,000 to credit card companies. Many people are deep in debt because of the way they use, or **misuse**, credit cards.

How Credit Cards Work

³When you use a credit card, you're getting a loan. You're asking the credit card company to pay for what you're buying—for now. The company is happy to do so. It will send you a bill each month, which lists all the purchases you made during the month. The total amount you owe will also appear on the bill.

⁴Some people pay the total amount each month. By doing so, they avoid paying a fee to the credit card company. This seems like a shrewd thing to do, doesn't it? But a credit card company doesn't want its cardholders acting so rationally. It doesn't make any money from people who do this. In fact, it calls them "deadbeats," a term that used to mean "people who do not pay their bills." Now, to credit card companies, deadbeats are people who *do* pay their bills!

⁵Most people pay only part of their credit card bill each month. A credit card company **calculates** a minimum amount that each cardholder is required to pay. About one out of every three cardholders pays only the minimum amount, which could be around 2 percent of the total bill. For example, if the total owed is $1,000, the minimum payment might be $20.

Paying the total on your credit card bill will avoid interest charges.

How Credit Card Companies Make Money

⁶Are you beginning to see why a credit card company is eager to loan you money? When you pay only part of your bill, the company makes money. It charges interest on the unpaid portion of the bill. Interest is a type of loan fee. It's a percent of what you owe the company. The interest charged is often 18 to 20 percent of the bill. Sometimes it can be much higher. In fact, there's no limit on the amount of interest a company can charge. That's a

good reason to find out a company's interest rate *before* you accept its credit card.

[7]Let's imagine that your friend Henry *does* have a credit card. In one month, he manages to charge $500 worth of clothes, meals, and concert tickets. You can see the attraction of buying on credit. Having the card makes it easy to give in to the urge to buy what you want when you want it.

[8]A few weeks later, Henry's credit card bill arrives. The minimum payment is $10. The yearly interest rate is 18 percent. Henry pays the company $10. This means that he owes the company $490, plus interest. In this case, the interest, figured at an annual rate, is $7.35. Henry is starting to catch on. He wisely decides not to use his card during the next month. When his next bill arrives, he owes $490 + $7.35, or $497.35.

[9]If Henry pays only the minimum amount each month, it could take him several *years* to pay back the original $500. During that time, he could end up paying the company a total of about $930. That includes $430 in interest! And that amount doesn't include any new purchases Henry might make.

[10]There's more bad news for Henry. Many credit card companies charge a yearly fee for the privilege of using their card. They also charge a late fee if payments aren't made by a certain date. There could be another penalty for late payments; the company might raise its interest rate even further. Some companies even charge interest whether or not a cardholder pays the total bill amount.

Other Ways to Pay

[11]Henry is now rethinking the whole idea of using credit cards. But how can he make purchases and not pay all those fees? What advice would you give him? Perhaps he should **postpone** buying things until he has saved enough money to pay for them. "That's fine," says Henry. "But I don't want to carry around a lot of cash."

[12]Henry could get a debit card. It looks much like a credit card. But it differs from a

Debit cards automatically subtract money from your account.

credit card in an important way. To have a debit card, Henry would need to have money in a checking account at a bank. When he uses his debit card, the amount of the purchase would be subtracted from his checking account right then. He'd pay no interest because he's using his own money. He's not taking out a loan. Many banks provide free debit cards. Some charge a small fee for each use of the card.

[13]Using a debit card is similar to writing a check. In both cases, money is taken out of a checking account. With a debit card, the money may be subtracted more quickly than when you use a check. Using a debit card prevents you from spending money you don't have. You don't **accumulate** debt.

[14]Your friend Henry wants to buy a CD player that costs $150. He's trying to decide the best way to pay for it. Let's help him make a decision. The chart below shows three ways to pay for the CD player.

	credit card (2% payments)	debit card	cash
cost	$150	$150	$150
18% interest	$404	none	none
other fees	?	$1	none
total	$554	$151	$150

[15]If Henry already has $150 in a checking account, the choice is easy. He should use cash or a check to buy the CD player. Using a debit card also makes good sense.

[16]Some day, Henry may have an **actual** credit card. He'll need **discipline** to avoid going into debt and paying huge fees. Do you think Henry can handle the responsibility of having a credit card? Could you?

Is It Real or Counterfeit?

not legal tender

¹**D**o you have a dollar in your pocket? If so, take it out and look at it carefully, front and back. Is it real or is it counterfeit—a fake? How do you know for sure?

²Fortunately, it's not that easy to make and distribute counterfeit money. Otherwise, it might cause problems with a country's **economy**—its money system. Citizens might lose faith in the value of their paper money. Stores might refuse to accept cash. This could have far-reaching effects.

Dollars and Change

³In fact, in the 1800s, counterfeiting was a huge problem. There were about 7,000 types of real money and 4,000 types of counterfeit money. During the Civil War, about one-third of all money was counterfeit. If you had three bills—pieces of paper money—in your wallet, one was likely a fake.

⁴Up to 1863, states had been able to print money. After that time, though, the U.S. government began printing all of the nation's

Printed paper money goes through careful inspection to meet government standards.

113

money. Paper money began to have a more standard, or widely known, look. However, counterfeiting remained a problem. To help stop this practice, the government set up the United States Secret Service.

[5]In 1996, the government changed the look of paper money to make it harder to duplicate. Then, in 2003, the government made additional changes to discourage counterfeiting. A new $20 bill was introduced with even more features. You'll read about these features below.

[6]Even with these precautions, some people **endeavor** to get rich by printing their own money. The government makes sure to **enforce** laws against counterfeiting. Punishment for this crime is a minimum of 15 years in jail. Counterfeiters are usually caught the first time they try to spend the money they print. Fake bills are often easy to **detect**. Many people are on the watch for this "money," including store clerks, bank clerks, Secret Service officials, and ordinary citizens.

What's the Difference?

[7]Why is it easy to catch counterfeiters? For one thing, when you look carefully, fake money looks different from real money. Sometimes the difference is obvious, but other times it's **subtle**. The color may not seem quite right on a false bill, and the images may not be clear. Most printing and copying machines cannot show fine enough detail to make fake money look real. They cannot duplicate very thin lines, for example. A copied row of thin lines looks like a solid stripe.

Counterfeit   Real

[8]Compare these two pieces of the bill. The image on the right is part of a real bill, and the image on the left is part of a counterfeit bill. Notice the differences in detail between the two bills.

[9]Not only does artificial money look different from real money, it also *feels* different. Ordinary paper is made from wood chips. Real money is made from cotton and linen fibers. These fibers make "rag paper." You can use a special marker to see if a bill is real or not. The colors that the marker makes on real money differ from those it makes on ordinary paper.

[10]Rag paper also includes tiny red and blue fibers that cannot be printed onto ordinary paper. And rag paper is much thinner than paper made from wood chips.

[11]Why don't counterfeiters use the same kind of paper that the government uses for money? It's nearly impossible to buy this paper. One counterfeiter tried to get around this problem by using actual money. He used household bleach to remove the numbers from real $1 and $5 bills. Then he changed the numbers to 20 and 50.

[12]This man was caught. How? The ink he used made his money feel different. In time, people noticed this difference. Secret Service officials were able to trace the fake money back to the counterfeiter.

More Changes

[13]Among the changes made in 1996 and 2003 was adding small print to the bills to make them harder to copy. There are other features that make newer bills harder to counterfeit. All newer bills now have the same bank seal instead of different seals from different national banks. Hold a new bill up to the light, and you'll see another change. Do you see a faint picture of the same person who is pictured on the bill? This hard-to-see picture is called a "watermark." A missing watermark is proof that the bill is a fake.

[14]Newer bills also have a stripe woven into the paper. The placement of the stripe differs on bills that have different values. A special light makes this stripe glow red. This is another way to tell how much the bill is really worth, even if its numbers have been bleached off and changed.

[15]Another feature of the new bills is color-shifting ink. On a $20 bill, the number 20 in the lower right corner is printed in this type of ink. Its color changes from copper to green when you move the bill in front of you a little.

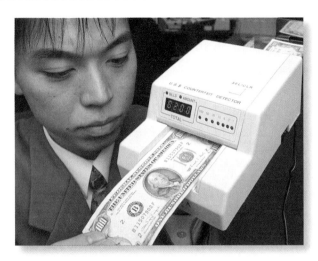

Some banks use scanners to detect counterfeit money.

Some of the ink on real bills is also magnetic. Why? This allows vending machines and bill-changing machines to identify real bills. If a machine doesn't detect magnetic ink, it refuses to accept the bill. Vending machines also have other ways to identify fake money. What are they? They're secret.

[16]These features make counterfeiting difficult. Even so, people try to get away with making fake money. The government **enlists** many people to spot counterfeit money. What can you do to help? Here are a few tips.

- Look closely at paper money you receive. Do the bills look or feel strange? If so, ask to have them replaced, or take them to a bank to be checked.

- Do not accept "old" money. Most of the real money printed before 1996 has been destroyed. Old money has fewer safety features. It's harder to tell if it's counterfeit.

- Check for color-shifting ink and a watermark. If they're present, the bill is most likely real.

JEANology

¹**W**ant to get confused in a hurry? Go shopping for a pair of jeans. In one store, you find jeans that cost $80. In the next, you find a pair that looks pretty much like the $80 pair. The price is $45. That's a little more than half the cost of the other jeans. In yet another store, you find a pair on sale for $30! This pair is similar to the first two.

²The sensible thing to do is buy the cheapest pair—right? But what if they're shoddily made? Will they last as long as the more expensive jeans? And while we're on the subject, why does one pair of jeans cost so much more than another?

[3]Differences in the prices of jeans are mainly the result of differences in production costs. A jeans manufacturer will figure out every single expense that goes into making a pair of jeans. This even includes the cost of advertising the jeans. Then the company will add to that total. It wants to make a profit. Profit is the money a company makes after all its expenses are paid. The cost to make the jeans, plus the company's profit, equals the price tag on the jeans in the store.

Paying Workers

[4]A big part of the production cost is payment for the workers. Workers receive hourly or weekly pay. Many of them also receive benefits. These can include vacation leave. They can also include paid sick leave and health insurance. You're helping to pay for these when you buy a pair of jeans. So, that's one reason that you may pay less for one pair of jeans than for another pair. The workers who make the jeans are being paid less. They may have fewer benefits than other workers too.

[5]In some countries, millions of people need jobs. Available jobs are **sparse**. With jobs in short supply, people are willing to work for low pay. Companies in these countries cannot afford to pay workers much. For example, the average pay in Chinese factories is very low. It's only 64 cents per hour. This amount includes any benefits. Chinese workers have to accept this pay because companies are unable to pay more.

[6]In contrast to this, workers in factories in the United States earn much more. Their average pay is around $22 per hour. That rate includes the cost of benefits for the workers.

[7]Let's say that it takes two hours to sew one pair of jeans. In China, those two hours cost the manufacturer $1.28 in wages for one worker. In the United States, the two hours cost the manufacturer nearly $44 in worker's wages.

Protecting Workers

[8]There are other costs that you help pay for when you buy a pair of jeans. For example, many countries have laws that protect their workers from accidents. Companies must put into place **procedures** that help keep workers from getting hurt. One specific law might require that a workplace be clean and safe. The United States has established such a law. Workers in the United States use safety equipment. They're also given adequate space in which to work safely. A jeans company has to pay for these protections. You share in this cost when you buy jeans made in the United States.

[9]Also, many U.S. workers belong to special groups called labor unions. Unions help their members get better pay. They also promote better working conditions. For example, a union might make sure that members are paid for overtime, or working more than their usual hours. This can affect the price of jeans too.

Other Costs

[10]In addition to the cost of paying workers and protecting them, companies must pay for the **fabric** and other materials that jeans are made from. They have to pay for the tools and machines the workers use. Also, they must pay for the costs of the buildings where the work is done and the warehouses in which materials are stored.

[11]What about the cost of getting jeans from the factory to the stores? Shipping can be expensive—especially between countries and continents. China is halfway around the world. So, shouldn't jeans shipped from China cost more than jeans made in New York? In general, shipping jeans from far away does cost more. But remember that workers' pay is much lower in Chinese factories than U.S. factories. Jeans **imported** from China will still probably cost less than those made in the United States.

[12]Many countries, including the United States, have laws to protect natural resources too. Companies here must not dump harmful wastes into the air, rivers, or lakes. Getting rid of these wastes safely can be expensive. Once again, this cost is added to the price of a pair of jeans.

What About the Materials?

[13]Companies can charge less for their jeans by using cheaper materials. However, the jeans probably won't last as long as those made with better materials. As a **consumer**, you want to make wise choices. Should you pay less for a pair of jeans made of cheaper materials? They may last only six months. Or should you buy a more expensive pair made of better materials? These might last a year or longer.

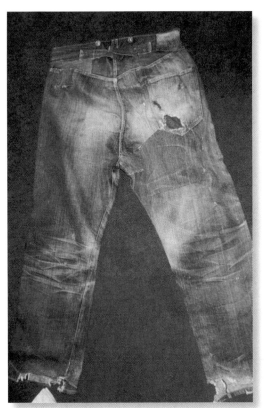

This pair of Levi's® 501 jeans is 100 years old!

What's in a Name? Brand Names and Designer Labels

[14]Here's something else that affects the price you pay for jeans: the name on the label. One pair of jeans may cost the same to produce as another pair. But if one pair has a **popular** brand name, it will cost more than the less popular brand. Or, if the jeans are made by a well-known clothing designer, the jeans will cost more. Sometimes they'll cost a *lot* more. Many customers will pay more for brand names and designer labels, even if the quality of the **apparel** isn't any better than lesser-known brands. That might mean, for example, that a company that sells its jeans for $80 can make as much as $10 profit on every pair of jeans. Multiply that times millions of pairs of jeans. You can see that making and selling jeans is a good business.

Rich and Famous

[1]We live in a society dazzled by wealth and fame. Don't believe it? Look at magazines on newsstands. Check out programs on TV. Glance at billboards along highways. Sometimes the image of a person who is rich and famous seems to shout, "Envy me!"

[2]But why should we envy people with money and fame? After all, envy has some unkind thoughts connected to it. Can't we *admire* them—or at least some of them? If so, what qualities are worth admiring? Here are the stories of three people who became rich and famous. What can you find to admire about each one? How are these people alike? In what ways are they different from one another?

Robert
Rodriguez

Robert Rodriguez, Movie Director

[3]Robert Rodriguez was born in Austin, Texas, in 1968. He was one of 10 children. Robert's mother loved motion pictures and took her children to see at least one movie every week. While Robert watched the action on the screen, he would say to himself, "I can make a movie like that!"

[4]One day Robert found his family's old movie camera. He began filming movies at home and around town. He enlisted members of his family to act in his movies. Soon his friends asked to be in the movies too. Robert's father could see that his son had talent, so he found a way to buy Robert a video camera and a VCR. After that, Robert made movies from morning until night. At school, he was even allowed to submit movies instead of written papers. Before long, he began winning awards for his movies.

[5]In 1992, Robert had an idea for a movie about a guitar player who is mistaken for a criminal. He needed money to make the movie, though, so he became a volunteer in a hospital study. The study paid him $7,000. Robert used the money to make *El Mariachi*. The movie became a big hit, and Robert soon became famous as a director.

[6]After a few years, Robert had become best known for making good movies with low budgets. Big companies usually spend millions of dollars to make a movie. Unlike them, Robert spent only thousands making movies such as *Spy Kids*.

[7]Nowadays, Robert could spend millions on a movie, but he prefers to keep the costs down. For example, he recorded the music for the second *Spy Kids* movie in his own garage. What matters most in making a great movie? To Robert Rodriguez, it's not the money—it's having a great idea.

Wally Amos

"Famous" Amos, Cookie Maker

[8]Wally Amos was born in Florida in 1936. At age 12, he moved to New York City to live with his Aunt Della. She taught him how to bake cookies. This simple act changed Wally's life. After serving in the Air Force, Wally started making and selling cookies. He had a small store in Hollywood, California. Just 10 years later, the Famous Amos Cookie Company was worth $10 million! Part of Wally's success was that his cookies were very good. He believed in his product. The other part of his success was that Wally believed in himself.

[9]Wally sold his cookie company. His new "business" is helping others recognize and develop the best in themselves. He has appeared on hundreds of radio shows and on television with his message.

[10]Wally did not graduate from high school. Instead, he earned his diploma while he was in the Air Force. Now he's the national spokesman for the Literacy Volunteers of America. Through this group, he helps people across the nation learn to read. He has also written a children's book in which the characters encourage children to learn to read.

[11]Wally travels around the country giving speeches. He urges people to believe in themselves and to make their dreams come true. He has used his fame—and his money—to inspire others. Wally Amos has been rewarded in many ways for his success. But the reward he values most is seeing others achieve success.

Oprah Winfrey, Talk Show Host

Oprah Winfrey receiving the Hall of Fame Award at the NAACP Awards in 2005

[12]Oprah Winfrey was born in Mississippi in 1954. She lived on a farm with her grandmother until she was three. Next, she moved to Milwaukee to live with her mother. After that, at age 13, Oprah went to live with her father in Tennessee. Her father was very strict. He expected Oprah to work hard. For example, she had to read at least one book a week and write a report on it. Oprah's early life was unsettled and difficult.

[13]When Oprah was 19, she became a television reporter. Just four years later, she became the host of a TV talk show in Baltimore. And just a few years after that, Oprah had become the host of one of the top talk shows in the nation. During this time, she discovered that she had a talent for acting. She appeared in the movie *The Color Purple* and was nominated for an Oscar for Best Supporting Actress for her role. Since then, Oprah has acted in several movies and now has her own movie company.

[14]At age 32, she began hosting "The Oprah Show." Oprah Winfrey was the first woman to own and produce her own talk show. Her program continues to attract millions of viewers. Oprah has earned many millions of dollars, but she doesn't feel that her success entitles her to special treatment. She remembers her past. This inspires her to help others—especially women—rise above troubled childhoods to make the most of their lives.

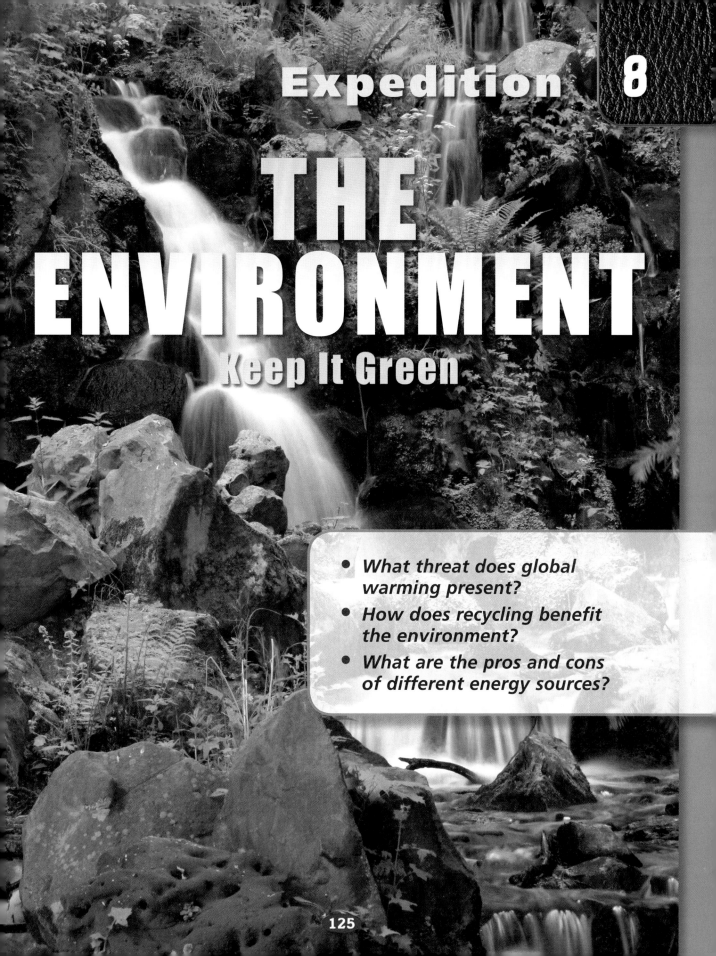

Expedition 8

THE ENVIRONMENT
Keep It Green

- **What threat does global warming present?**
- **How does recycling benefit the environment?**
- **What are the pros and cons of different energy sources?**

Fill Up, Then Pay Up

If gasoline prices were high enough, would Americans give up their cars?

¹I'd like you to meet my friend Harold. He's the maintenance person at our apartment building. Harold fixes leaky faucets and tends the flower garden and does a thousand other things. Why do I want you to meet him? Because he's someone worth knowing. He's got integrity; that is, his deeds match his words. And he illustrates a point I've been trying to make for a long time: We have *got* to use fossil fuels more responsibly.

²For the past three years, Harold has ridden a bicycle to work. He owned a car once, but when the price of gasoline reached $2 a gallon, Harold sold the car and bought a bike. "It wasn't just gas prices that got to me," he says. "I realized that if I went around claiming to care about the planet, I had to *show* it." I like to think that all of us would react as Harold did, sooner or later—especially the people who drive those stupid SUVs.

Hooked on Oil

[3]Our appetite for petroleum is shameful. We should use less gas. All of this use is hurting our planet and weakening our integrity. There's that word again: integrity. It means "honesty." What's my solution? Tax gasoline till it hurts—up to $10 a gallon. *Now* have I got your attention? Then, use the tax money to pay off the country's debt and improve schools. Anybody not in favor of *that*? We'll be forced to drive less or drive smarter.

[4]How is our appetite for gas hurting the Earth? For one thing, it's causing a climate crisis. Many scientists think that burning fossil fuels has caused warmer global temperatures, which can cause changes in rainfall patterns and increases in sea levels. Crops and food supplies can be affected. Every living thing on this planet is affected by these changes.

[5]The burning of fossil fuels harms the quality of the air we breathe. There are about 800 million cars in active use in the world, which produce a lot of smog. And experts say that 50 years from now, three billion cars will be in use. That's a figure to choke on.

[6]How is our dependence on oil weakening our integrity? The U.S. has about 5% of the world's known oil reserves, which means that we have to buy oil from other countries. So, what if a country we buy oil from is ruled by a cruel leader? By supporting that country's money system, aren't we in effect supporting the mistreatment of its people? We're a nation "conceived in liberty," so how can we support governments that withhold people's liberties? I don't want to have to be nice to a bully, just because he has something I need.

Alternatives to Gas

[7]What about cleaner, less gas-hungry cars such as hybrids, which run on both electricity and gas? According to a noted car magazine, hybrids get 40 to 50 miles to the gallon. Car makers are also working on the use of hydrogen fuel cells to power cars and buses. Like electricity, this is also a cleaner energy source. These are steps in the right direction.

The Other Side of the Issue

[8]I can hear some of you now, though: "Ten dollars a gallon for gas? Taxpayers won't stand for it!" Maybe not, at first, but we could **implement** the increase gradually. And did I hear some of you say there's no evidence of a climate crisis? Hundreds of respected scientists would argue otherwise.

[9]I've heard some say that the world has an **infinite** supply of fuel, so there's no need for **restraint** in our use of it. They argue that using less fuel isn't the solution. Instead, we should make the fuel we burn less harmful. The truth is, experts are divided on how much oil there is. So, just to be safe, let's conserve what we know is there.

[10]There's also the argument that if people have to pay high prices at the pump, they'll have less money for important things such as housing and health care. There's no **basis** for this argument. When prices are higher, people quit spending money on *less* important things like dining out and going to movies.

[11]Will people with lower incomes suffer the most from high taxes on gas? That's a valid point. Maybe we could reduce other types of taxes for these people.

A Problem We Can't Ignore

[12]We can't keep ignoring this problem. It's only going to get worse. America could be a leader in solving the climate crisis. We could become stronger and cleaner by reducing our use of oil. Let's face it, though—most of us don't change bad habits just because someone tells us to. Our **tendency** is to make changes when the squeeze is on.

[13]So, I challenge our government to raise gas taxes, and I urge citizens to take action now. Don't wait for the squeeze. Take the bus or subway to work. Better yet, ride a bike or walk. If you care at all about our **fragile** planet, show some integrity, like my friend Harold.

ALL-TERRAIN VEHICLES
All Too Common

The popularity of ATVs is growing—and so are the dangers that go with them.

[1]**"T**he woods are lovely, dark, and deep," wrote Robert Frost in one of his best-known poems. I was remembering this line one recent morning as I set out on a hike through the forest. The sky hung cloudless above the trees, and sunlight dappled the forest floor. The temperature was slightly cool. I could sense the first faint signs of fall in the air. Soon, I could sense the first faint signs of something else in the air: the distant buzz of a gas-powered engine.

129

A Good Hike Spoiled

[2]I knew what I was hearing. It was the sound of ATVs—all-terrain vehicles. And I knew that the noise would continue and even increase for the rest of the day and into the night. I turned around, hiked back to my car, and went home.

[3]What's wrong with us? Have we lost our appreciation of silence and slowness in nature? Whatever happened to lacing up hiking boots and heading on foot into the woods? Or going swimming and picnicking? Instead, we rip through the **landscape** on motorized vehicles. It's just plain wrong.

ATVs Are Big Business

[4]The sport of riding ATVs is growing fast in Wisconsin and everywhere in the U.S. There are more than a quarter million registered ATV users in our state. **Nonresidents** bought more than 4,000 trail passes last year. In the entire U.S., about 15 million people ride ATVs. Sales of these vehicles, which cost up to $8,000 each, have increased fivefold in the past dozen years.

[5]Motor sports bring in a lot of money for states. A 2004 survey shows that the average ATV user spends a little more than $500 per trip. ATV riders bring in close to $300 million a year to our state.

On and Off the Trails

[6]There are 1,800 miles of trails for ATV riders in Wisconsin, during spring, summer, and fall. In winter, some snowmobile trails open for ATVs too. On the basis of these figures, you'd think that would be enough riding room. But more and more riders are ignoring these trails and crossing into fragile wetlands or onto private land. "The dry land isn't challenging enough," says one rider. Some even try riding on state highways. Not long ago, one rider tried to cross a four-lane highway and was hit by a car. Amazingly, he survived.

Dangers to the Environment

[7]ATVs are tearing up our land. Trails in one forest in our state have sunk more than a foot since 1986 because of ATV users. These machines create mud holes and gullies that increase erosion and runoff. They widen and create ruts in forest roads. This increases sediment—stones, sand, dirt, and other matter—in streams, which can affect fish.

[8]Riders go "mudding" through wetlands. Some of them drive their ATVs from mudding sites into shallow lake water to clean off their vehicles. Oil and gasoline get into the water. Riders have damaged trees and other vegetation. They disturb nesting areas for birds and **displace** animals such as deer from their habitats. And I'm willing to bet that they create more smog than cars.

Dangers to the Riders

[9]In 2002, there were more than 600 ATV-related deaths in the U.S. About a third were children under the age of 16. A lawyer for a national consumer group says that the **trend** toward more injuries and deaths is a "public health crisis" in this country. State governments need to implement laws to protect children. A particular problem is that many children ride adult-sized ATVs. Children don't have the strength, motor skills, and judgment to drive ATVs. These vehicles can exceed speeds of 70 miles per hour. If we don't allow 9-year-olds to drive cars, why do we allow them to drive ATVs?

[10]Many ATV owners say that most riders are careful. They point out that ATV safety education courses are required of anyone who rides on public land in the state. They say the dangers of the sport is overblown. "This is a healthy, family sport," claims a mother of two sons who ride ATVs. She says that with proper education, riding ATVs can be safe. "Accidents occur when parents aren't out there watching," says the woman. But the statistics are alarming. And many accidents have happened, even when parents are around.

[11]"It's fun, fast, and the scenery is pretty cool up here," says a teenage rider. "It's safe, if you watch what you are doing," he adds. Another rider, now 16, has a different point of view. Three years ago, he hopped on his ATV to ride to a friend's house—without a helmet. He crashed. The boy was flown by helicopter to a local hospital. He survived, but with head injuries that left him blind. Now what's his opinion of ATVs? "They're fun," he says. "But they are dangerous."

More Views from the Other Side

[12]ATV owners **portray** riding as a basic right. "We deserve places to ride in the forests," says one ATV fan. "We're only using a limited area. There's still plenty of land for hikers and birdwatchers." He claims that the forests exist for everyone to enjoy. He's right about that. But I say the forests deserve to be protected more than ATV riders deserve to go through them, gunning their engines and gouging out the land.

[13]Some say that the solution is to set aside more land for ATV use. Does this make sense? These vehicles are ripping up our land, and we want to provide *more* land for them to ruin?

[14]For their part, manufacturers of ATVs claim to be working to help protect nature. They say that they're making ATVs cleaner and quieter. How can this be possible, if ATVs are getting more powerful each year?

What's to Be Done?

[15]If it were up to me, I'd do away with ATVs. In fact, I'd be happy if the state would **prohibit** all motor sports. But that's not going to happen. So let us work together to protect the unspoiled land left in our state. By "us" I mean state forest officials, ATV riders, and those of us who like to meet nature on its own terms. Let's make sure that riders stay on the trails set aside for them. Maybe we could have "quiet zones" in state forests, where ATVs wouldn't be allowed. Let's find ways to keep the woods lovely, so that the poets will continue to write poems about them.

GOOD NEWS ABOUT RECYCLING:
IT'S WORKING

Recycling is an important
way to cut down on waste.

*The following is an open letter to the citizens of Parkdale.
It was printed in the local newspaper.*

Dear Citizens:

[1]Do you get a little tired of rinsing out those glass jars? How about
hauling those used newspapers to the curb each week? Do you sometimes
feel that one person's efforts can't make much of a difference? If so, I've
got some encouraging news. Your efforts are making a huge difference
in our city. As Parkdale's recycling coordinator, I'm pleased to announce
that our city has received the state Green Arrow Award for its recycling
program. That's two years in a row.

Less Trash, More Benefits

[2]Each person in the United States throws away an average of about four pounds of garbage every day. A study done by our department shows that each Parkdale citizen throws away two pounds of trash a day. That's half of the national average! I can say with **assurance** that every glass jar, aluminum can, and plastic milk carton you recycle helps reduce the city's average waste per person.

We're Saving Natural Resources and Energy

[3]Each year, 850 million trees are cut down to make paper products in the United States. This takes a heavy toll on our forests. It means less oxygen in the air. It also means fewer homes for forest animals. Our office estimates that the people of Parkdale saved more than 80,000 trees by recycling paper this year. You also saved millions of gallons of water. How? It takes water to make paper. About 400 gallons of water are needed to turn wood chips from one tree into paper pulp.

[4]And more of you are recycling your used motor oil. This helps protect our lakes, rivers, and streams. It also protects our groundwater. Used motor oil is taken to our city's reprocessing **facility**. There it's made into fuel that can warm our homes in the winter. It can keep us cool in the summer too. Recycled oil is burned in our local power plant. This produces electricity for all of us.

[5]More than three quarters of the aluminum cans that Parkdale residents use are being recycled. These are cans that would otherwise sit in our landfill for hundreds of years. This type of recycling saves energy. It takes 20 times as much energy to produce a ton of aluminum from newly mined ore as it does to produce a ton of aluminum from scrap metal. How much electricity do you think you save when you recycle just one aluminum soda can? Enough to light a 100-watt bulb for 3-1/2 hours or run a TV for 3 hours.

Recycling Helps Our Economy

[6]Your recycling efforts helped create 121 new jobs in our city this year. We've needed more people to collect and sort used paper, cans, glass, and other items. Companies that make some of these items into various products have needed more help. So have companies that rework and repair products that can be reused in their original form. In fact, we estimate that total **revenue** from recycling reached nearly $13 million this past year. And here's another savings. Recycling in our city has reduced the need for a new landfill. This has saved us millions of dollars.

Precycling

[7]It's clear that many more of you are "precycling." What's precycling? You're probably already doing it. This means reducing waste before it occurs. More citizens in our area are buying products in containers that can be reused, recycled, or refilled. City supermarket managers say that more customers are choosing products packaged in materials that biodegrade—or are broken down—easily. And more of you are bringing your own shopping bags to the store. This saves trees. It keeps more plastic out of our landfills. And it sometimes keeps us from buying more food than we need.

Thanks to You

[8]So, I hope I've helped you see that rinsing bottles and putting newspapers on the curb makes a difference. In fact, it's doing a world of good. And I hope that I've inspired others to join our city's recycling program. It's not just a good thing to do. It's the right thing to do.

Maria Loza
Parkdale Recycling Coordinator

PAPER OR PLASTIC?
IT DOESN'T REALLY MATTER

The following is a letter to the editor of the local newspaper.

Dear Editor:

[9]I have one question. If I don't recycle things, does that make me a bad person? You'd think so, the way some of my neighbors glare at me when I wheel my two garbage bins to the curb every Wednesday morning. Besides, what's the difference if one person isn't recycling? Plenty of other people are.

A Waste of Time

[10]Is the trouble it takes to recycle things worth it? You have to scrub glass bottles and jars, and shove a week's worth of newspapers into a *paper* bag—heaven help you if you put them in a *plastic* bag. You have to rinse tin cans until they're spotless, and you'd better make sure you recycle the *right* kind of plastic—the kind with a number 1 or 2, or whatever, on the bottom. Woe unto you who put the *wrong* plastic in the curbside bin!

[11]I'm not trying to portray myself as an expert on these things, but it doesn't take a genius to see that recycling is a burden on people. What's the payoff? So you save a little landfill space. Big deal. There's plenty of land for new landfills. We shouldn't be wasting valuable time on the latest do-gooder trend.

Just a Fad

[12]I think this recycling movement is just a passing fad that's a **remnant** from the hippie years. I've often **speculated** about what we'd learn if we took a serious look at the costs and benefits of recycling. Then maybe we'd stop this foolishness.

Landfill Crisis: It's a Myth

[13]Everybody's hollering about a landfill crisis. The **geoscientists** have got us all worked up. "Ooh, it's hurting Earth!" "There's no more room for trash!" "The sky is falling!" Well, just take a drive around the city. You'll see a lot of land that's not being used. There are hundreds of acres of forests east of town. Why not put a landfill there?

[14]"What!!?? Cut down trees?" I can just hear the tree-huggers. They have a tendency to react with shock and horror at the thought of a fallen tree. I'm willing to bet that we're growing as many trees as we cut down each year. Haven't you heard of tree farms?

Let's Rethink Recycling

[15]I could go on, but I think you get my point. Recycling takes too much time, and the effort isn't worth it. In fact, it probably costs more to recycle stuff than it does to make new stuff. So let's stop the madness. Come on. I dare you: Toss that soda can into the trash.

Sincerely,

Henry Howard

Aluminum cans are the most recycled item in the U.S.

POWER FAILURE

[1]Our government is talking about building more nuclear power plants. This makes us mad enough to explode. Our group—Citizens Against Nuclear Power (CAN)—strongly opposes the use of nuclear energy. Why? Here are some of the reasons:

- The risks to the environment and to public safety are too great. Accidents in the past—in the United States and in other countries— have taught us about the dangers of using nuclear energy.
- The costs of building nuclear power plants are too high. The benefits are not worth the expense.
- The waste from nuclear energy plants can cause harm for hundreds of thousands—maybe millions—of years.

[2]Creating nuclear energy produces radiation—**particles** and rays that can be very dangerous. Radiation released from accidents at nuclear power plants has caused serious illnesses and even deaths.

[3]We say, why go nuclear when you have choices such as these:

- solar energy
- **biofuel**, such as wood
- wind energy
- geothermal energy

[4]We don't need any new nuclear plants. There are already 103 in operation in America. That's scary enough. For all of these reasons, we're spending *our* energy to keep the world safe. Won't you join us? Together, we CAN make a difference.

We CAN find safe energy sources.

Citizens Against Nuclear Power

The Wrong Picture of Nuclear Energy

[5]This letter is in response to an advertisement that appeared in your magazine in June of this year. The ad was produced by a citizens' group that seeks to prohibit the use of nuclear power. I am very concerned about some of the misinformation that is being spread about nuclear energy. This ad is yet another example of that kind of misinformation, especially the picture that accompanied the ad.

[6]First, I should identify myself. That way, you'll know up front which side of the debate I'm on. My name is Frank Seely. I work for a power company that owns and operates a nuclear power plant. I have been employed in the nuclear energy business for more than 15 years. I believe in the value of nuclear energy. And I believe in taking good care of the planet. That includes human life. Those two beliefs don't **contradict** each other, from my point of view.

Let's Set the Record Straight

[7]We all know that "one picture is worth a thousand words." The photograph that accompanied the anti-nuclear ad says a lot. And what it says is wrong. So, I have a few words of my own to say about the picture. First, it's misleading to **associate** nuclear power with the explosion of an atomic bomb. Creating electrical power and exploding weapons are two completely different enterprises. One is a peaceful use of nuclear energy. The other is a wartime use of that energy. A *reactor* is a device where nuclear energy is produced and controlled. The reactor in a nuclear power plant cannot explode and cause the kind of destruction shown in the photograph.

[8]The decision by the group to use that photograph in the ad was very clever. These people know how powerful images can be. Many readers of your magazine will now link a safe energy source with the death and destruction caused by an atomic bomb.

The Safety Issue

[9]So let's talk about the safety issue at nuclear plants. It's true that there have been dangerous accidents at nuclear power plants. No one can forget the terrible accident at Chernobyl in 1986. But we haven't had a major accident in more than 20 years. Our routine safety measures in the United States have greatly reduced the chances of a serious accident. No one can give absolute assurances that accidents won't occur at nuclear plants. But new designs can better handle any problems that might occur. Nuclear power plants are far safer and cleaner than they were years ago. And scientists are working to make future nuclear power plants even safer. Some scientists are exploring the idea of building nuclear plants underground.

The Costs of Nuclear Plants

[10]Right now, about 20 percent of America's power supply comes from nuclear energy. Operating these nuclear plants is not as costly as operating our natural gas and coal plants. Nuclear power plants may be expensive to build, but the power they produce is cheaper than power produced in other ways.

[11]We haven't built any new facilities since the 1970s. This is due to the concern for public safety. Instead we've concentrated on making sure that existing plants are in good working order. But we will have to think about adding more plants as our energy needs increase.

Thinking Ahead

[12]In many ways, I think the question comes down to this: Do you want global warming or do you want nuclear power? If we keep burning fossil fuels—coal, oil, and gas—we're going to put more harmful gases into the

atmosphere. These gases trap heat and bring more climate changes. These climate changes will affect life throughout our **hemisphere** and around the globe. Nuclear power is simply the best way to reduce pollution.

[13]As populations grow in countries all over the world, the need for energy also will grow. How are we going to meet the energy needs of the developing world? How will we protect the environment at the same time? We've got to look ahead. Oil resources are not infinite. Also, by the middle of this century, drilling for oil might be too expensive.

[14]Nuclear energy is becoming more accepted as a source of electricity. In 1995, 46 percent of Americans favored nuclear energy. Today, that number is 70 percent. Right now, about 20 percent of America's power supply comes from nuclear energy. In the next 50 years, half of our energy could be produced in nuclear plants.

[15]In the meantime, the debate over nuclear energy is **liable** to continue. I'd like for us to be reasonable in this debate, and honest. We don't need scare tactics to get our ideas across. Let's all use our energy wisely.

A nuclear power plant near a rural field

| Hamilton Daily Sun | Opinions and Editorials | Section B, page 3 |

¹ am Julie Tran. I own The Wheel Deal bicycle shop here in our city. I'm a cyclist, as you might guess. And I'm strongly in favor of using bicycles for transportation instead of cars. But that's not why I'm writing this. My reason for writing is to convince our city council and the public to support the development of bicycle lanes in our town.

²You should know something before I make my argument. I own a car. And I use it, when I have to. I'm not trying to persuade everyone to give up their cars and switch to riding bicycles. This is just not practical in a town of our size. I simply want the town government to recognize that there are cyclists among the motorists. There are quite a number of them, in fact. And they deserve recognition. They also deserve protection on city streets.

The Two-Wheeled Point of View

³When was the last time you rode a bicycle in your community? Did you drive on city streets? If so, did drivers seem to be aware of you? Did they share the road? Did you feel safe? Would you want your children riding bicycles on city streets? Why or why not?

⁴My experience as a cyclist on city streets has varied. I have found, on the whole, that many drivers are mindful of cyclists. They politely share the

road. Some drivers, though, seem not to notice two-wheeled vehicles in their midst. It's as if bicycles are invisible to them. Perhaps they're distracted by thoughts of ever-increasing gas prices. Perhaps smog is clouding their vision. And, sad to say, a few drivers seem annoyed that cyclists are on the road. They honk their horns, yell insults, and use their cars as weapons to bully bicyclists. "Might makes right," they seem to say.

[5]Hundreds of bicyclists are killed on streets and highways in our country each year. Thousands more are injured. Some are the result of careless motorists. Some are the result of careless cyclists. I often see riders who are not wearing helmets. The good news is that the number of these deaths and injuries each year is falling. These numbers are liable to fall even further as more communities create bike lanes.

Benefits of Bike Lanes

[6]Bike lanes encourage bicycling. Bicycles are more Earth-friendly than cars. A bicycle doesn't put harmful gases into the air. A car does. And operating a bicycle isn't harmful to the pocketbook, but operating a car is. Gas prices are going up by the week.

[7]Bike lanes clearly show which part of the road belongs to motorized vehicles and which belongs to bicycles. They encourage cyclists to follow traffic rules, such as riding *with*, rather than against, the flow of traffic. They reduce the chance of a driver straying into the path of a cyclist.

[8]Many cities and communities across the nation have made their streets more "bikeable." They have put in place excellent bicycle safety programs. These places are recognizing that bicycles are a lawful means of transportation. They are also recognizing that bicyclists, like drivers, have a right to the road.

Opposing Views

[9]One city official has told me that adding bike lanes is too complicated. He fears that the city will spend thousands of dollars on studies and planning that could take years. I explained to him that, thanks to the work of officials in other cities, planning doesn't have to be complicated.

[10]For example, the city of Chicago has published a 48-page guide to planning and creating bike lanes. The guide contains detailed information on marking bike lanes. It tells how to deal with intersections and bus stops, and how to use signs for motorists and cyclists. This guide is promoted as "a report that addresses every reason, fear, excuse, or other barrier to getting bike lanes on your city's streets."

[11]Philadelphia is another city that promotes bicycle use. A decade ago, the city set up a bicycle safety task force. It is now working to establish a network of bicycle routes that include lanes for cyclists.

[12]Some people opposed to bike lanes say that these lanes are dangerous. They claim that they encourage drivers to make right turns in front of cyclists. An alert cyclist can see a motorist begin a right turn and can escape danger by also turning right. So this is not a problem.

[13]Another argument is that bike lanes encourage both drivers and cyclists to believe that cyclists don't belong on regular roads. I happen to believe that the opposite is true. Setting aside part of a road for cyclists shows that bicycles have as much right to the road as do cars, trucks, and buses.

[14]Some critics of bike lanes say that the lanes *increase* bicycle accidents rather than reduce them. They cite so-called studies that show increases in accidents. But these study results aren't convincing. The opinion that bike lanes raise the risk of accidents goes against all common sense.

Continue a Tradition of Friendliness

[15]In spite of certain risks associated with bicycling, it's a healthful, safe, fun activity. Have you noticed, while riding a bike, that you see many things in the nearby landscape that you might've missed if you were rushing by in a car? Many more people in this country die from health problems related to lack of proper diet and exercise than from bicycle accidents. Ours is a health-conscious town. Wouldn't we all want to promote cycling as a way to stay healthy and fit?

[16]Cyclists will continue to share the road with drivers, whether or not we have bike lanes. We might as well make our roadways safe for everyone. Our town is known for its friendliness. It seems entirely fitting, then, that we develop bike-friendly streets. Let's begin by creating bike lanes.

DISEASES
Tiny Killers

- *What can result from a single mosquito bite?*
- *How is our government involved in fighting disease?*
- *What are some unusual ways of treating diseases?*

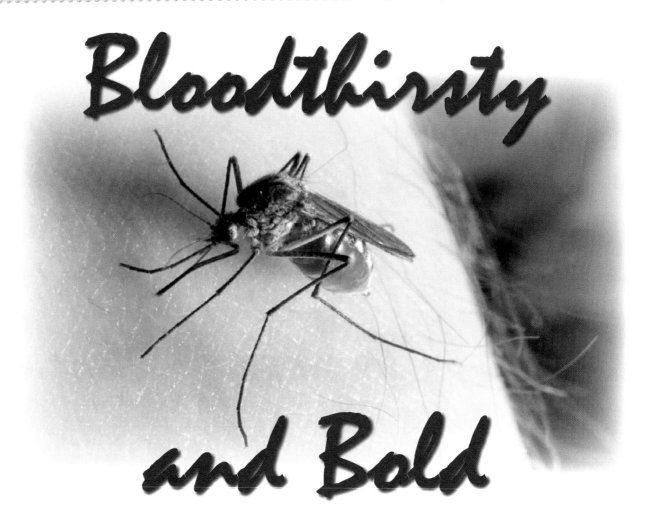

Bloodthirsty and Bold

What's that Buzz?

¹The sun has set, and it's a nice evening. You and your cousin are relaxing in the backyard. All of a sudden, there is a whining sound in your ear. Ouch! You feel a sting on your arm. A red bump appears there. There is the whining sound again. This time you feel a sting on your leg. A red bump appears there too. Then, the awful itching begins.

²What's going on here? You are being bitten by mosquitoes. These are insects that find human blood **irresistible**. They are small and hard to see. In fact, the word "mosquito" is Spanish for "little fly," but there is nothing little about this creature's sting. A swarm of these hungry insects can cause even the nicest person to become **disagreeable** as a result of the itchy bites. Mosquitoes are definitely bugs with an attitude.

You Can Run, but Can You Hide?

[3]Mosquitoes have been around for about 30 million years. So they've had time to become experts at finding clever ways to find you.

[4]A mosquito has three kinds of special sensors. The first is a chemical sensor. Human skin produces certain chemicals. These chemicals are different in everyone. Mosquitoes choose the ones that make the best snack. While mosquitoes **bombard** you, your cousin isn't bothered at all. Why is this? Some people attract mosquitoes while others seem to repel them. The second sensor is a visual sensor. Wearing brightly colored clothing and moving around helps make you an easy target for mosquitoes. The third sensor is a heat sensor. Because warm-blooded mammals—like you—give off heat, they attract the pesky mosquitoes.

Why Do They Bite?

[5]Female and male mosquitoes aren't exactly alike. Only the females have the long mouth part used to suck blood. Consequently, they are the only ones that bite. The female lands on your skin and punctures it. Because of a substance in her saliva, your blood does not form a **clot**. Her long mouth part **penetrates** the wound and sucks your blood. She has a special sensory nerve in her abdomen that tells her when she has reached full capacity. Without this nerve, the mosquito would drink blood until she burst. Blood from her unwilling victim supplies protein for the female's eggs.

[6]A mosquito bite causes skin irritation. The area around the wound swells. This is a type of allergic reaction, so the skin itches. As long as saliva remains in the wound, there is itching. Even after the swelling goes away, the bite itches for a time.

[7]Some researchers use their own bodies in mosquito experiments. They enter a room with hundreds of mosquitoes and then count the number of bites in a certain amount of time. One study reported over 9,000 bites per minute. There was a frightening conclusion from that study. With constant biting by enough mosquitoes over a period of two hours, you could lose half your blood! That would cause you to die.

Is the Bite Really Worse than the Buzz?

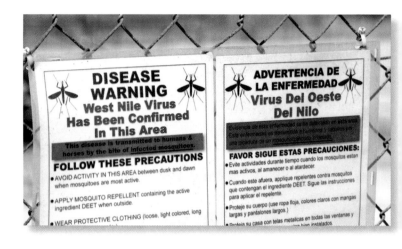

[8]Scientists believe mosquitoes are the worst disease carriers ever. This is because mosquitoes can carry deadly germs and viruses in their bodies. It is important to remember that not every mosquito carries a disease. When mosquitoes cause illnesses in people or animals, scientists call these illnesses mosquito-borne diseases. Because these kinds of illnesses often spread rapidly from person to person, **epidemics** can occur. Thousands of people can become ill or even die. Diseases caused by mosquitoes include yellow fever, malaria, and West Nile virus. Symptoms of these diseases include high fever, chills, nausea, aches and pains, and a very tired feeling.

[9]Long ago, doctors weren't sure how to treat patients with these life-threatening diseases. Consequently, many died. Today, doctors can vaccinate people and animals against some mosquito-borne illnesses.

What Can Be Done About These Flying Nightmares?

[10]Prevention and protection are keys to solving the mosquito problem. The best thing to do is to discourage mosquitoes from coming into your yard in the first place. Fountains, wading pools, and bird baths are popular mosquito hangouts. Since all mosquitoes lay their eggs in water, standing water is a mosquito breeding ground. Old tires, pet dishes, and even watering cans could become mosquito daycare centers, so they should be removed from yards. Eliminating standing water can help eliminate mosquitoes. If you have mosquitoes, keep them outside. Make sure that all house screens are tight and without holes.

[11]Mosquitoes tend to swarm at dawn or dusk. Staying inside during these times of day can prevent bites. If you must go out then, pick a windy day, since a strong breeze can keep mosquitoes away. Here are some other helpful ideas. Apply safe bug repellents to your skin before you go outside, and cover up with protective clothing.

[12]Why all this fuss about mosquitoes? First, a mosquito bite is no fun! Second, you don't know which mosquito is carrying a disease and which is not. One bite by the wrong mosquito and you might end up really, really sick.

Is There Anything Good About Mosquitoes?

[13]Mosquitoes are an important part of the food chain. The eggs provide food for certain kinds of fish. The adult mosquito is food for birds such as swallows, purple martins, bats, and even for other insects. Keep these things in mind the next time you're scratching that itchy red bump.

Lizards and bats feed on mosquitoes.

Attack of the Body Invaders

[1]**"W**e're under attack by hostile life-forms!" the Captain of the Defenders shouts at his troops. "We must find and destroy the aliens. All defense units and squads report for duty. The T-Unit will find the enemy. They will send a message to the B-Unit to lock on the target. Then the Z-Squad will attack and destroy. The Phantom Squad will patrol the secret tunnels and devour any enemies that sneak through. These aliens have attacked before. But their assaults have only made us faster and stronger. If we stick together, victory will be ours. There is no turning back!"

[2]This might sound like a cool video game, but it is not a game at all. This is your immune system at work.

The Security Areas

[3]Your immune system is made up of tissues, organs, and special cells. These all work together to defend your body against germs. Billions of germs bombard your body every day. These tiny invaders are so small that you need a microscope to see them. But they can cause big problems. If the wrong germ manages to get inside you, it can make you very sick.

[4]The good news is that most germs are stuck on the outside because they cannot penetrate your skin. Your body even has ways of keeping germs from sneaking into the openings in your skin. Germs have a hard time entering your nose, eyes, or mouth because they get trapped in sticky fluids. Some of the parts of your body that you use to breathe are covered with many tiny hairs, so germs are captured before they can do harm. Your digestive system contains acids. Consequently, if a germ gets to your stomach, the acid kills it.

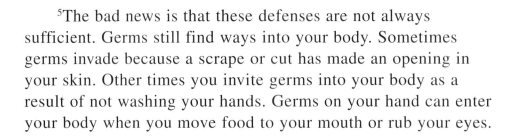

[5]The bad news is that these defenses are not always sufficient. Germs still find ways into your body. Sometimes germs invade because a scrape or cut has made an opening in your skin. Other times you invite germs into your body as a result of not washing your hands. Germs on your hand can enter your body when you move food to your mouth or rub your eyes.

The Defenders

[6]Even when germs manage to invade, the battle is not over. Your body has other ways to fight germs. The first line of defense is your immune cells, or white blood cells. These cells find and kill germs as soon as they enter your body. Your body makes a lot of these cells and stores them in your organs until you need them. When it's time for battle, these cells travel through your blood to wherever the germs are attacking.

[7]These amazing cells can remember how they fought an enemy. If the cells detect a germ they have faced before, they strike with greater speed and strength. As a result, a germ attacking your body a second time can be wiped out before you get sick. When this happens, your body has become immune. Have you ever had chicken pox? If so, you probably won't get it again because your body has learned how to fight it.

[8]There are different kinds of white blood cells. Each has a different job. Some are helper cells. Others are killer cells. Some recognize previous invaders and send messages to the other cells. Others roam around your body and chew up any invaders they find. Some cells lock onto germs, while others kill them.

The Invaders

[9]Just as there are different types of white blood cells, there are different types of germs. Bacteria are one type of germ. They can live in many places. A table or doorknob is as good a home as your hands or your stomach. Some

152

bacteria can make you very sick. Others may not affect you at all. Still others help your body work right. Therefore, your body actually needs these helpful bacteria to stay healthy.

[10]Viruses and parasites are other types of germs. Viruses attack healthy cells and trick them into making more viruses. Then the new viruses attack other healthy cells. As a result, the viruses **persist** and multiply. Parasites are tiny germs that live by eating cells in your body. Germs such as bacteria, viruses, and parasites can cause a simple illness such as a cold or a deadly epidemic such as yellow fever.

[11]Not everyone's immune system reacts to germs the same way. Some people seem never to get sick. Others seem to be sick all the time. Babies get sick more often because their bodies have not learned to fight off very many germs. People come into contact with more and more germs as they get older. As a result, their bodies learn how to fight off more germs and they get sick less often. For example, teenagers and adults get fewer colds than young children. That's because their bodies know how to fight the viruses that cause colds.

The Helpers

[12]A healthy immune system is important because your body is always under attack from germs. One way to help your immune system stay healthy is to avoid germs so you don't get sick in the first place. Doctors are **unanimous** in their belief that one of the best ways to avoid germs is to wash your hands. It may seem **tedious** to wash your hands all the time, but it kills germs before they can invade your body. To be **absolutely** certain that you have killed as many germs as possible, scrub your hands with soap and warm water for at least 10 seconds. Another way to help your immune system is to eat healthful foods. Some people take a **vitamin** tablet every day to make sure their diet is well balanced.

[13]Sometimes your immune system needs a little help, so your doctor might **prescribe** antibiotics. This medicine kills germs that cause infections. Antibiotics have saved millions of lives, but you have to be careful. These medicines kill good bacteria as well as bad bacteria. You might be at greater risk of another infection due to a lack of good bacteria. Another problem is that antibiotics can be used too often. This gives bacteria a chance to get used to the medicine. Over time, the bacteria become so strong that the medicine no longer works.

[14]Remember, germs are so small that they can sneak into your body without your noticing. Once there, they can cause all kinds of problems. Your mission, if you choose to accept it, is to help your immune system defend *you* from these hostile aliens. With the help of the Captain of the Defenders, you can beat germs before they beat you.

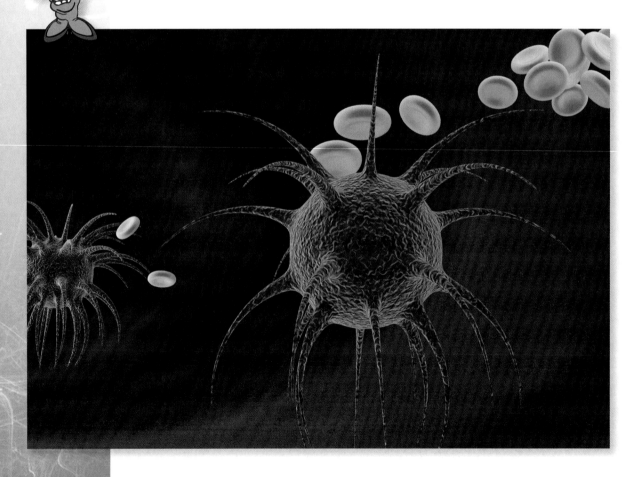

CREEPY MEDICINE

[1]The basement room had no windows. A dim light bulb hung from the ceiling. The cool air smelled like moldy bread. "This is more like a cave than a doctor's office," the patient thought. He glanced at the open sore on his left leg. It looked awful. The entire leg was swollen. He could barely walk. He had tried 10 different doctors and dozens of medicines, but nothing worked. The wound refused to heal. He was beginning to feel hopeless. Then his regular doctor sent him here. "It's your last hope," the doctor had said. "If this doesn't work, we will have to cut off your leg."

[2]The door creaked open. A woman in a white coat entered. She was carrying a large glass jar. "The doctor, at last," the man thought. The doctor sat the jar on the table next to the man. "Are you ready?" she said. The man thought he saw something move in the jar. He quickly turned away and stared at the ceiling. "Let's get it over with," he said. The doctor opened the jar and scooped out what looked like a handful of rice that had somehow come to life. Hundreds of tiny creatures wriggled and squirmed in the doctor's hand. The patient was horrified! He closed his eyes and waited. He could not watch as the doctor placed the maggots on his open sore. She carefully wrapped gauze around the man's leg so the maggots could not crawl away. The man felt something wriggle inside his wound. He felt like screaming.

[3]This isn't a scene from a horror flick. It is a treatment that doctors turn to when other medicines do not work. The government has approved the use of "living medical devices" like maggots and leeches to treat patients. The government has also allowed some companies to grow the creepy critters for doctors.

Leeches

[4]A leech is a type of worm that sucks blood. It has suction cups at each end of its body. The front cup has three Y-shaped jaws and hundreds of teeth. The rear cup helps the leech move and cling to people or animals as it feeds. A leech has 32 brains and five pairs of eyes. There are more than 300 types of leeches. They can be as long as 18 inches, but most are only a few inches long.

[5]Healers have used leeches for thousands of years. Doctors once thought that when people got sick, bad blood was a major **factor**. Therefore, doctors figured that the best way to make people well again was to remove the bad blood. And what better way to remove blood than by attaching a blood-sucking worm? It made sense at the time.

[6]Doctors used leeches to cure everything from headaches to **cancer** and many illnesses in between. Because leeching was so popular, doctors needed a lot of the little bloodsuckers. Some people were desperate for money, so they would stand in lakes until their legs were covered with leeches. Then they would pull the leeches off and sell them to doctors. In the 1800s, doctors kept leeches in fancy jars with tiny air holes. At one point, leeches almost became extinct because doctors were using so many of them. **Eventually**, new treatments made leeches less useful. As a result, doctors stopped treating patients with leeches.

Maggots

[7]Maggots are flies that haven't yet grown wings and legs. Doctors found maggots useful because the little critters love eating rotten or dead flesh. During a war in the early 1900s, doctors noticed that bad wounds healed faster if they were covered with maggots. Doctors figured that this was because maggots cleaned the wounds better than medicine. In

the 1920s one doctor began promoting the use of maggots for injuries and wounds. Thousands of doctors followed his advice. By the 1940s, doctors had developed new drugs and treatments that did a better job than maggots. As a result, doctors used maggots less and less.

Bloodsuckers and Flesh-Eaters

[8]Before long, it was hard to find a doctor who used leeches and maggots. People thought of leeches and maggots as nothing more than examples of the crazy ways doctors once treated patients in the distant and dark past. But today, leeches and maggots are back in style because they do some things very well.

[9]Take leech spit, for example. Leech spit has special chemicals that keep blood flowing. Since the blood cannot clot, leeches can feed for hours at a time. Leeches can drink up to 10 times their weight in blood. These bloodsucking skills come in handy when doctors perform **microsurgery**. This is a special operation on body parts that are so small that doctors have to use microscopes. Doctors use this type of operation to reattach toes, fingers, and other body parts that have been sliced off. The tiny, fragile veins inside the appendage can be hard to find and reattach. As a result, blood can gather and clot in the body part. This can cause the body part to die. Leeches help prevent this because they can keep the blood from clotting until the body can reattach the tiny veins on its own.

[10]Maggots love to chow down on dead, rotting flesh, so they are great at cleaning wounds. While eating, maggots **sterilize** wounds by leaving behind a germ-killing substance. This maggot spit kills germs as well as alcohol, only it doesn't sting as much. As a result, maggots can help wounds heal faster than many modern medicines.

[11]Today, doctors have developed an **arsenal** of medical techniques to cure injuries and diseases. Maggots and leeches are two promising weapons for people like the man with the swollen leg. He has a disease called diabetes. He had always been afraid of worms, so he had to get over his phobia before he would let the doctor treat him. He had faced a difficult choice. He could let the doctor use maggots, or he could lose his leg. He chose the maggots, and he has no regrets. Today he has two healthy legs with no open sores. Faced with a similar situation, which choice would you make?

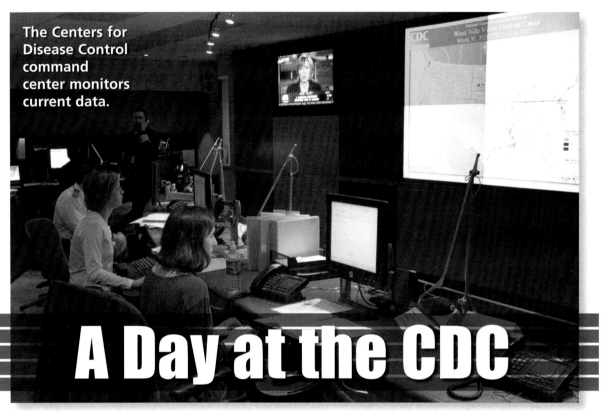

The Centers for Disease Control command center monitors current data.

A Day at the CDC

¹The director walks through the security gates of a large building in Atlanta, Georgia. She wonders what the day will bring. The dangers are always there. She looks forward to them. She has faced many challenges. She will face many more in the coming days. Facing **obstacles** is part of her job. She is the director of the Centers for Disease Control and Prevention, also known as the CDC.

²The government started the CDC in 1946 due to an outbreak of malaria. This deadly disease is spread by mosquitoes. It had been killing people for thousands of years. The CDC gathered doctors and scientists to find ways to treat and prevent the disease. As a result of their work, malaria is no longer the problem it used to be.

³Since the CDC did such a great job, the government decided that the centers should continue to work for the **welfare** of people everywhere. Today the centers work to prevent and treat all kinds of diseases. The centers also work to reduce injuries, guard against terrorists, and clean up dangers to the environment. Because the centers have so many tasks, they work closely with other groups that share the **objective** of caring for public health and safety.

The Centers at Work

[4]The centers' doctors, scientists, researchers, and students are trained to learn everything they can about threats to public health and safety. Then they share this information with everyone. As a result, people know how to avoid diseases and how to prevent accidents at home and at work. Because it is easier to prevent diseases than cure them, the centers also work on treatments and help prepare immunizations. The centers also work to protect people from hazards caused by dangerous chemical spills.

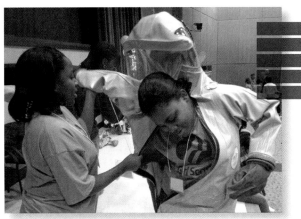

Girl Scouts try on lab suits at the CDC in Atlanta, Georgia.

[5]Natural disasters and epidemics can put many people in danger. Therefore, workers at the centers spend hours planning the best way to handle emergencies. But they are not worried only about natural disasters. They also must plan for intentional disasters. Deadly viruses and bacteria can be used like weapons, so some groups might try to spread them on purpose to make people afraid. Consequently, the workers spend a lot of time getting ready for these kinds of attacks.

The Field Teams

[6]This morning, the director is worried about the two calls she received on her way to work. As she walks to her office, she passes a group of people carrying special gear. She knows what's inside the containers because of the first telephone call. This is a field team on its way to clean up a chemical spill. No one knows what chemical was spilled, so the team has to be ready for anything. There might be no **casualties**, or there could be hundreds of injured people. The area might need to be evacuated.

[7]When the field team arrives at the site, the workers will begin a tedious job. First they will put on bulky clothes that will protect them from the chemical. Then they will carefully clean the site with special equipment. As they work, they will take samples of the chemical. Later, they will take the samples back to the centers so scientists can study them more closely.

[8]The director turns a corner and passes another field team. This group is going to an office building. The building is filled with sick people. That was the second call she received. No one knows why the people are sick, so the team has special gear to test water, food, and air. They will set up a tent to test the samples for clues about why the people are sick. The field team must learn where the people became ill. So they use maps and charts to find out who is sick, where they live, and when they first started feeling bad. As a result, the field team will decide the best way to treat the sick people. When they are finished, they will take the samples back to the centers so the laboratory teams can study them.

The Laboratory Teams

[9]The director walks down a long hall. She passes labs with heavy doors and small glass windows. She cannot enter these labs because scientists are studying smallpox and anthrax, two deadly diseases. The scientists must wear special suits while they **isolate** and study these diseases. The suits must cover every inch of their bodies because even a small hole can let in a deadly disease. Some diseases float in the air, so scientists must breathe through a hose that sends fresh air into the suit. The hose also helps keep the inside of the suit cool and comfortable. Vents let out old air so the fresh air doesn't blow up the suits like balloons.

[10]One group of scientists is studying anthrax. This rare and deadly disease is caused by bacteria that form spores. Spores are like sleeping cells. These spores can wake up and make many people sick. Different types of the disease attack different parts of the body. One attacks skin. Another attacks

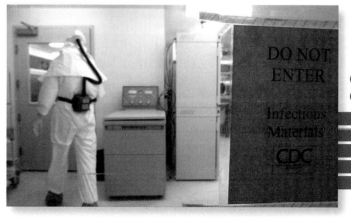

CDC lab in Fort Collins, Colorado

lungs. A third attacks the intestines. The disease does not spread from person to person, so you can catch it only by touching or breathing the spores. Because the disease is so deadly, doctors must quickly treat people with antibiotics.

[11]Another group is studying smallpox. This deadly disease is caused by a virus. You catch smallpox from someone who is already sick. The disease causes tiny swollen bumps to cover your entire body. There is no treatment for smallpox, so people must recover on their own. However, not everyone recovers. Therefore, doctors try to prevent the disease by giving people shots.

[12]The lab teams study the diseases with microscopes. They write reports about what they learn. Then they send the reports to the research teams.

The Research Teams

[13]The director walks through the research area. The area has libraries and hundreds of computers. Researchers are busy writing reports about the best ways to stay safe and healthy. They also study reports from the labs and field teams. As a result of this work, the centers can help doctors find out what illness a person has. The centers also can give doctors **instructions** about the best way to treat the illnesses. The researchers also watch out for outbreaks of diseases, terrorist attacks, and environmental hazards around the world. Because of their hard work, the centers are ready to respond at a moment's notice.

[14]The director finally reaches her office. She sits at a desk piled high with urgent messages. Like every work day, this day will be challenging and exciting. In other words, it will be a typical day.

CDC director, Dr. Julie Gerberding, speaks at a news conference.

The Centers for Disease Control and Prevention

Atlanta, Georgia

When Your Body Attacks

[1]**Y**our ears itch. Your head hurts. Your eyes are red and watery. You can't stop sneezing. It feels like someone has shoved an orange into the space behind your throbbing nose. You have already used up a whole box of tissues. If you don't get more quick, you are going to have to start using your sleeves. What in the world is happening to you?

[2]The problem is your immune system. It's usually your best friend, fighting off germs that can make you sick. But now it has turned on you. Your best friend has become your worst enemy. As a result, you are in the middle of an allergy attack.

What Is It?

[3]An allergy happens because your immune system mistakes something harmless for a dangerous intruder. As a result, your body goes into seek and destroy mode. The foreign invader must be defeated, so the body system starts producing chemicals. One of these chemicals is called histamine. When

162

this chemical is released into your blood, it causes your body to have an allergic reaction. Doctors say there is no cure for allergies. Therefore, the best you can do is treat the symptoms.

[4]Two common allergic reactions are hives and hay fever. Hives are ugly red bumps that itch like crazy. They can be as small as a pencil eraser or as large as a dinner plate. They can appear and disappear for no apparent reason. Hives usually last less than a day. In some cases they last for weeks or even years. Hay fever is caused by powdery stuff called pollen that is released into the air by plants. Pollen can cause watery eyes, sneezing, a runny nose, and a scratchy throat.

What Causes Allergies?

[5]Anything that causes an allergy is called an allergen. There are several different types of allergens. Breathing dust, mold, or pollen from plants such as ragweed can make many people feel sick. Others are allergic to certain foods. Nuts, shellfish, eggs, or milk might make these people feel sick. Sometimes people are allergic to certain drugs, like antibiotics or other prescription medications. Toxins from bee stings, household cleaners, or pesticides are also common allergens.

[6]Your immune system has a great memory, so it always reacts the same way when it runs into the same allergen. These reactions can be mild. They might cause you to feel tired or cranky. You might even feel a little sick. When allergies cause a condition called asthma, however, the result can be dangerous. Asthma is an allergic reaction that causes inflammation and swelling in a person's airways. As a result, breathing becomes very difficult. An asthma attack can kill you, so it must be treated at once. Other types of allergies might make it hard for you to swallow. Or they might make your lips, tongue, or throat swell terribly. These symptoms can be very dangerous, so they require immediate treatment by a doctor as well. You might even have to stay in a hospital.

[7]Different people are allergic to different things. A cat jumps into Jasmine's lap. As a result, Jasmine spends the rest of the day sneezing and wiping her puffy eyes. Jeff plays with the same cat and has no reaction at all. Jeff's ears turn red and feel itchy because he eats one bite of pizza. Jasmine eats an entire pizza with no reaction at all, except a very full stomach. Why are some people allergic to one thing and not another? Doctors think this is because people inherit their allergies from their parents. If one of your parents is allergic to something, you probably will be too.

What Can Be Done?

[8]Drugs that can be bought without a doctor's permission can help mild symptoms. As a result, some people can find what they need at the local drug store. Others, however, might need a doctor to prescribe stronger drugs. These people often turn to special doctors called allergists. These doctors know more about allergies than regular doctors. Since different allergies are treated in different ways, the doctor must be absolutely sure about what is making you allergic. Sometimes they can figure this out by asking questions. Often, they have to test you by putting tiny bits of different allergens on your skin. Then they watch to see if you have a reaction. Once doctors know what is causing your allergies, they can decide how to make you feel better.

[9]Often the best treatment is to avoid the thing that makes you allergic. You might be allergic to dander, the dry skin cells that flake off of furry animals like dogs and cats. Consequently, your doctor's instructions would be to avoid animals. Or you might have to avoid eating shrimp or lobster because you are allergic to shellfish. Or maybe dust makes you sneeze, so you have to keep your room spotless. At least that would make your family happy.

[10]Other allergens are harder to avoid, so they have to be treated with medicine and allergy shots. Even in these cases, doctors say you can reduce the amount of allergens you have to deal with. If you are allergic to pollen, for example, your doctor might tell you to watch TV before you go outside. Because so many people are allergic to pollen, many TV weather shows tell their viewers how much pollen is in the air. If the pollen count is high, you might want to stay inside so you can avoid an allergic reaction.

[11]Allergies certainly are nothing to sneeze at. If you have allergies, you have a lot of company. More than 50 million people in America suffer from allergies. Because so many people have allergies, scientists are working hard to understand why the immune system misbehaves in the first place. As a result, doctors might someday come up with a way to prevent allergies.

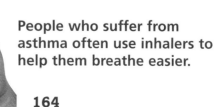

People who suffer from asthma often use inhalers to help them breathe easier.

164

TECHNOLOGY
Keeping in Touch

- *How does the cellphone change the way we communicate?*

- *What technologies have been used in history to communicate?*

- *What communication devices came from the discovery of electricity?*

The Gutenberg Bible on display

THE PRINTING PRESS

An example of raised lead type for printing

¹If you had been born 600 years ago, you probably would have lived your whole life without ever learning to read. Even if you could read, you were still out of luck. Back then, books were rare because they were so hard to make. And because they were rare, books were so expensive that only the richest people could afford them.

²That all changed thanks to an **industrious** man named Johann Gutenberg. Gutenberg came up with an idea to make books faster and cheaper. He spent years working out all the details of his idea. When he was finished, he had invented something that would change the world. Before long, there were plenty of books and plenty of people who could read them. Gutenberg had turned the world upside down.

Blending the Ideas of Others

A printing press at the Gutenberg Museum in Mainz, Germany

³Gutenberg was born about 600 years ago in Germany. At that time, most books were copied by hand. A scribe sat at a desk for days copying books one letter at a time. A short book would take months to finish. A Harry Potter book would take years to copy.

⁴Gutenberg figured he could make books faster and cheaper with a machine. He knew that people in China had been printing for centuries. They carved words or pictures into a block of wood, then rubbed ink on it and pressed it against a sheet of paper. But this method wasn't much faster or cheaper than a scribe. A new block had to be carved for each page, and the soft wood quickly wore out or split.

⁵Gutenberg found solutions for these problems by looking at the world around him. He got one idea from a tool used by people who made bowls and plates out of silver and gold. They marked their work with a small metal tool that had a raised symbol on one end. Gutenberg decided to make a metal stamp for each letter in the alphabet. All of the letters had to look exactly right, so **precision** was important. Gutenberg carefully made hundreds of small metal stamps, each with a raised letter, number, or punctuation mark. These metal stamps, called "type," were much harder than wood. They could be used over and over again without breaking or wearing out. Better yet, the metal type could be rearranged into a new page. This was much faster than carving a new page out of wood.

⁶To hold the type together, Gutenberg built a frame about the size of a sheet of paper. Then he carefully placed his metal type in the frame, spelling out words as he went. Once the entire page was assembled, he had a metal version of the woodblocks used in China.

⁷Then Gutenberg had to make the right kind of ink. If the ink was too thin, it would drip off his letters and mess up his printed pages. If it was too thick, the ink would clog up his letters and make the printed page hard to read. Gutenberg tried different inks until he got it just right.

[8]Gutenberg had one more problem to solve. He had to find a way to press the inked letters evenly against the paper. If he pressed it by hand, he might press too hard on one side. Then the letters on that side would be printed too dark. Gutenberg **analyzed** machines used to flatten paper and studied other machines used to squeeze juice from grapes. Then he put all these ideas together and made his printing press. When everything was working just right, he started printing books.

A Bestseller

[9]Gutenberg used his printing press to make 180 copies of the Bible. Then he took the copies to a book fair. He needed to sell the books to pay back the money he had borrowed to build his press. The books were a huge hit. One man who saw the books was very excited. The man wrote a letter to his boss, who wore glasses. The letters in Gutenberg's book were printed so clearly, the man wrote, that his boss could read them without his glasses. Gutenberg's Bible cost as much as the average scribe earned in three years, but he sold every single copy.

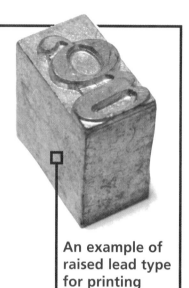

An example of raised lead type for printing

[10]Despite his success, Gutenberg never got rich or famous. Today, inventions are protected by **patent** laws that make it illegal to use an invention without paying the inventor. In the 1400s, there were no such laws. Gutenberg's only hope was to keep his invention a secret. But good ideas are hard to hide. Soon people were replicating Gutenberg's press and printing books without paying him a cent. Before long, there were thousands of printing presses in hundreds of towns. Though his invention had spread all over, Gutenberg received little **acknowledgement**. It was only after his death that people gave him credit for inventing the printing press.

Changing the World

[11]The printing press has been called the most **influential** invention in history. It changed almost everything about the world. Books that cover every topic under the sun were now available to almost everyone. With books came education, and with education, people could improve their lives. And, best of all, now you don't have to wait years for your copy of the latest Harry Potter book!

COMMUNICATING TO WIN

Al Gross, inventor of the walkie-talkie

¹**A**rmy leaders are always looking for ways to beat the enemy—more soldiers, better weapons, smarter planning. These things usually add up to victory. But they are all useless if an army can't communicate. Generals need to monitor battles to see if their tactics are working. Soldiers need to know when to change these plans. And leaders back home need to know how the war is going.

²The main goal of military communication is to share information as quickly as possible. Ancient armies had a simple solution. Someone took a message, jumped on a horse, and galloped off. If the message had to be carried a long way, the rider would change horses at posts set up along the way. This system allowed armies to send messages across long distances with surprising speed.

³But horses could be slowed down by a rocky mountain or a muddy road. A large body of water could stop a horse in its tracks. These were the problems faced by a warrior named Genghis Khan about 800 years ago. His solution was "for the birds." Khan strapped his messages to the leg of a homing pigeon. These amazing birds would fly straight back to their homes, even if they started out

Today, soldiers continue to use pigeons to send and track messages.

hundreds of miles away. They were no faster than a galloping horse, but they had one huge advantage. When a pigeon came to a mountain, it could simply **elevate** higher into the air and fly right over it. And these pigeons didn't have to wait around for a boat to carry them across rivers and oceans.

[4]Khan's pigeon messengers helped him conquer many lands. As his empire grew, he needed a way for his pigeons to cover more land. Like the ancient leaders before him, Khan set up a series of posts. When an exhausted pigeon reached a post, it would land. There, the message was transferred to a rested pigeon. That pigeon would fly the message to the next relay station. This system helped Khan build one of history's greatest empires.

[5]Hundreds of years later, pigeons were still delivering messages for armies. But they were **beneficial** in other ways, as well. In World War I, one army used pigeons as photographers. Pigeons would fly over enemy positions. Cameras strapped to the pigeons' bellies would photograph the positions below. Another army had more than 30,000 pigeons. Anyone who interfered with the flight of these pigeons could be sentenced to death. During one bloody battle, an American pigeon saved an entire battalion. The pigeon carried 12 messages across enemy lines, dodging bullets and bombs the whole way. It delivered its last message despite being shot in one leg. For its **historical** feats, the pigeon was awarded a medal.

Sending Messages over Wires

[6]In the 1840s, a new invention made it possible to send messages thousands of miles in an instant. Horses and pigeons seemed to take an **eternity** by comparison. This invention, called the telegraph, sent its messages through wires. People could not talk over these wires like we talk over telephone wires today. Instead, the telegraph used a code made up of short and long pulses that stood for letters. During the Civil War, both the

Telegraph machine

North and South armies used the telegraph to send messages. Wagon trains of workers strung telegraph wires wherever they were needed. Armies were able to send messages faster than ever.

[7]But there was one big problem. When one side found a telegraph line used by the opposing side, the soldiers would simply cut it. Wires were also brought down by bombs. When a wire was damaged, armies had to go back to slower messengers. But once again, technology came to the rescue. This time, it was the invention of the radio. Radios sent messages over the air. Since they didn't need wires, it was harder to cut off the messages.

[8]By the First World War, it was obvious that radio had one serious problem. The enemy could listen to messages sent over the radio as easily as you can listen to music on your radio at home. To keep the enemy from hearing their messages, armies came up with secret codes. The enemy could hear the message, but they had no idea what it meant.

[9]Another problem with radios was that the sets could not be moved easily because they were too big and heavy. Their antennas were so large that the enemy could easily tell where the radios were. Once they knew its location, the enemy could blow up the radio. Scientists worked hard to make radios and their antennas smaller. They also had to improve the radio's **reception**. Messages were often lost in all the popping and crackling that came out of radio speakers.

Coded Messages

[10]By World War II, radios were smaller and delivered clearer messages. They became an important way for soldiers to talk to one another. To keep their radio messages secret, armies spent a lot of time and effort coming up with new codes. The Germans had a machine that came up with a new code every day. Even if someone could break the code, this precision instrument

Hedy Lamarr with soldiers at the Hollywood Canteen during WWII

would come up with a new one the next day. The English faced a terrible problem. They would probably lose the war if they didn't figure out how to read the German messages. English scientists and mathematicians worked on this vital task night and day. Their industrious efforts paid off. They figured out how the German machine worked, then came up with a way to read the messages. They also invented a computer that helped them read other secret messages. The Germans thought their machine was perfect. They never knew that the English could read all their messages.

[11]It wasn't only scientists and math whizzes who contributed to the German defeat. In 1941, movie star Hedy Lamarr and her friend invented a machine that could send secret messages over the radio without even using a code. Her **gadget** kept radio messages secret by constantly changing how they were sent. Imagine your favorite radio station constantly changing where it was located on the radio dial. The only way you could listen to a song would be if you knew the order in which the radio station's location was changing. Lamarr's invention did more than protect messages from the enemy. It eventually led to the invention of today's cellphones.

The Future

[12]Good communication is so important that armies never stop trying to improve it. Today's soldiers use the Internet and wireless satellites to send messages. Tomorrow's soldier will be even more hooked in. Right now, the U.S. Army is working on a wireless, space-based system. When it is finished, every soldier in the army will be able to access information and send messages from any place on Earth.

James E. West's invention is used in many products you see every day.

Rocking the Microphone

¹**Y**our favorite singer belts out her latest hit as she dances and whirls across the stage like a tornado. Your seat is so far away that she seems to be about a foot tall. But thanks to the tiny microphone on her headset, you can hear every word she sings.

²The telephone rings. It's your friend calling from his new home in a neighboring state. Though he has moved hundreds of miles away, his voice sounds as clear as a bell. It's as though he is sitting right next to you.

³You whisper to your little brother that your grandmother's biscuits are as hard as hockey pucks. Grandmother's ears aren't as good as they used to be, so you think she can't hear your **criticism**. But thanks to her new hearing aid, you find yourself in big trouble.

173

[4]These things may not seem to have much in common, but they do. They can all be traced to the work of James West and his fellow scientists more than 40 years ago. Their **alliance** resulted in a new kind of microphone. It was better, smaller, lighter, and cheaper than most people could have ever imagined.

A Curious Child

[5]West was born in Virginia in 1931. As a child, he loved to take things apart and figure out how they worked. "Anything that had screws in it, I could open up," West says. "I was always fascinated by how things work and why things work." His brother remembers West's early learning methods. "He used to take my toys to pieces," Nathaniel West says. "He took his grandfather's watch and left it in pieces and couldn't put it back."

[6]West's curiosity often got him in trouble. Once, when he was about 10 years old, he found an old radio that someone had thrown away. He decided to take it home and plug it in to see if it worked. As soon as he stuck the plug in the electric outlet, he realized why the radio had been thrown away. Electricity surged from the radio, into his fingers, and down to his toes. "My whole body was rattling," he remembers. "I got hung up. My brother had to push me away." The shock didn't hurt West. Instead, it sparked his interest in electricity. "I had to learn more about that," he said.

[7]His opportunity came two years later. His cousin needed someone to help him install electricity in some houses. West was eager to help, even if it meant crawling under houses pulling wires from one room to the other. "As a result of that training," West says, "I learned how electricity behaves."

A Change of Course

[8]After high school, West tried to put aside his interest in electricity and follow his parent's wishes. They wanted him to be a doctor, so he enrolled in college and started studying medicine. "In those days in the South, the only professional jobs that seemed to be open to a black man were a teacher, a preacher, a doctor, or a lawyer," West says. "My father introduced me to three black men who had earned doctorates in chemistry and physics. The best jobs they could find were at the post office. My father said I was taking

the long road toward working at the post office."

[9]It didn't take West long to figure out that he wasn't interested in medicine. He couldn't shake his interest in electricity and in how things worked, so he decided to quit medical school and study physics. His parents were upset. They thought physics would never lead to success and **prestige**. So they stopped paying for West's education. "I guess I learned very early in life that in spite of the punishment, I was going to do what was most important to me," West said. "My parents were tough on me, but boy, do I appreciate that now. I've never forgotten the discipline and other things important in life." To help pay for college, West took a summer job at a laboratory. That summer job turned into full-time work.

Smaller, Better, Cheaper

[10]In the mid 1950s, West and a group of scientists at the laboratory were studying how the human ear worked. They needed microphones that could capture very tiny changes in sound. The microphones in use at the time were not nearly sensitive enough. They also required huge batteries that made them hard to use. West was asked to help solve the problem.

[11]Rather than try to improve the old microphone, West and another researcher named Gerhard Sessler developed an entirely new kind of microphone. It used a thin film coated with metal on one side. This film could capture the small sounds that the scientists wanted to study. West and Sessler even found a way to store energy in this thin film. That meant that their new microphone would not need a big battery. Better yet, it was the size of a shirt button and cost much less than the old microphones.

[12]These advantages made the new microphones beneficial in many ways. Without large batteries, for example, the new microphones were perfect for hearing aids. Soon these new microphones were showing up in a wide variety of gadgets, such as telephones, tape recorders, camcorders, and even talking dolls. Today, 90 percent of the microphones in the world are based on the work of West and Sessler.

[13]West didn't stop there. During the 40 years he worked at Bell Labs, West received more than 250 patents for his inventions. His four **decades** of work earned him many awards. In 1999 he was honored with a spot in the National Inventors Hall of Fame, beside **prominent** inventors like Thomas Edison and Alexander Graham Bell. "These were people that, when I grew up, I wanted to be like them," West says.

No Slowing Down

[14]West retired from his job at the lab in 2002, but he didn't give **boredom** a chance to set in. He immediately took a job as a college professor. "I'm having such a great life," West says. "Being allowed to be what I wanted to be has been worth far more to me than I ever imagined."

[15]Today, West is as busy as ever. He has his own lab at the college, where he is studying ways to send sound over the Internet. He has even found a way to contribute to the field his parents wanted him to enter—medicine. The thin film he used in his microphone might help doctors measure blood flow in their patients. West won't be slowing down anytime soon. "My hobby is my work," he says. "I have the best of both worlds because I love what I do. Do I ever get tired of it? Not so far."

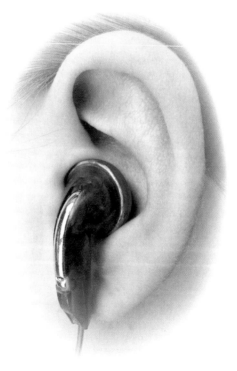

Letters at the Speed of Light

¹It wasn't always so easy to keep in touch with your friends. Three hundred years ago, sending a letter to a friend in another city was a major pain. First, you had to find paper and a pen and write your letter by hand. Then you put your **correspondence** in an envelope and addressed it. There was no post office, so you had to find a neighbor who was traveling to the city where your friend lived. Once you found someone, you gave him or her the letter and hoped for the best. If everything worked out, your friend would get your letter in a couple of weeks—unless your friend lived across the ocean. Then the letter would have to go by ship, which could take months!

Even then, there was no **guarantee** that your friend would ever get your letter. The person carrying your letter could lose it. Or he or she could decide that there were better things to do than deliver letters. Or the ship he or she was on could sink, taking your letter down with it.

[2]If the letter actually got to your friend, it would take just as long for his or her reply to get back to you. By then, you might have forgotten what you were writing about in the first place. As you can see, this system made it pretty hard to get a group of friends together for some pizza.

[3]By the 1970s, things were a lot easier. Three decades ago, a letter could get across town in a day or across the country in a few days. If you planned ahead, you could get your friends together for a pizza party without much trouble. Mail was pretty fast, but it was about to get a lot faster.

Mail in the Blink of an Eye

[4]Today, you can carry a computer in your backpack. In the 1970s, however, a single computer could take up an entire room and was far too expensive for ordinary people to buy. Back then, computers were mainly used in offices. The big computer was kept in a room by itself. Wires snaked out of the computer room to every desk in the office. Each desk would have only a screen and a keyboard. If you needed to write a memorandum to someone in the office, you would type it into your computer screen. Then you would leave it in a special place on the big computer. This method of communicating came to be called e-mail, short for "electronic mail."

[5]Today, e-mail is the most common way people write letters to one another. Every day, there are billions of e-mails sent over the Internet. You can send an e-mail to a friend on the other side of the world and get a response in seconds. Now you can procrastinate until the last minute to start organizing your pizza night. You might even be able to order your pizza by e-mail.

The Advantages of E-mail

[6]The most obvious advantage of e-mail is speed. Even today, a letter dropped in a mailbox takes a day or two to be delivered. E-mail, on the other hand, is so fast that people started calling the old way of sending letters "snail mail." To understand why, just watch a snail moving inch by inch across a floor. Compared to e-mail, snail mail seemed to take an eternity.

[7]E-mail is also easier. There's no hassle of finding paper, an envelope, and a pen. You don't have the **inconvenience** of buying a stamp or finding a mailbox. Just type into your e-mail program, hit "send," and get on with your day. You don't even have to be around a computer. These days, you can even send e-mail from your cellphone.

[8]E-mails make it easier to send a message to a lot of people. You can type an e-mail once and send it to a thousand people. With snail mail, you would have to make a copy for each person on your mailing list. You can also send things by e-mail that won't fit in a regular envelope. Songs, movies, and even video games can be attached to an e-mail. Also, letters from people with poor handwriting can be hard to read. E-mails appear in neat, legible type.

Some Problems with E-mail

[9]It's true that e-mail is fast and convenient, but it has problems too. Two big problems are spam and viruses. Spam is junk mail that you might get after visiting a fake Internet site. The site might offer you a free **subscription** to an online magazine about the products or services you were searching for.

With e-mail, you can send a letter to a friend on the other side of the world in seconds.

179

When you sign up, you are really giving your e-mail address to a spammer. The magazine that was promised never shows up but tons of junk e-mail does!

[10]Viruses are harmful computer programs that are attached to e-mails. If you open an e-mail that has a virus, it can destroy all the information on your computer. It can even cause your computer to crash. Many viruses get into your e-mail address book. Then they send themselves to all your friends and cause them trouble.

[11]If you get a virus or receive too much spam, there are solutions. You can install programs that protect your computer. These programs will take care of most of the problems, but not all of them. A few junk e-mails or a new kind of virus might slip through.

[12]There are other problems that can't be solved by computer programs. One big problem is that not everyone has e-mail. To use e-mail, you have to have a computer. You also have to have e-mail software and a phone line or cable connection. If you or the people you want to contact don't have these things, e-mail is useless.

[13]Another problem is that e-mail is hard to keep private. A computer screen is easy for others to see. They can just look over your shoulder as you read or type. People who share your computer might also look in your mailbox. They might see e-mail messages you have sent or received. Maybe that doesn't matter to you. But if you're sending a message that is personal, it might be best to use snail mail. E-mail isn't very good at keeping secrets!

[14]Some people also worry that e-mail is making people bad spellers. People like to type a message as quickly as they think of it. Spelling shortcuts make typing a message faster. One popular shortcut is spelling words **phonetically**. Spelling a word the way it sounds instead of the way it is spelled in the dictionary can save time. For example, typing "becuz" instead of "because" saves two keystrokes. Using short, incorrect spellings can quickly become a habit.

[15]For many people, the advantages of e-mail far outweigh the problems. E-mail is a fast, easy, and cheap way to stay in touch with friends and family. It's not likely to go away anytime soon.

Telephones to Go

[1]When your grandparents were expecting an important telephone call, their lives came to a stop. They sat by a telephone wired into the wall and waited. And waited. And waited. And if they left the house for a minute, that, of course, is when the phone would ring.

[2]That might seem unimaginable today, when many people walk around with a telephone in their pockets. Over the past two decades, cellphones have become as common as ants at a picnic. People no longer have to wait for a call at their house. Now the call comes to them wherever they are.

Once a luxury owned by only a few, cellphones have become a necessity for millions of people.

Martin Cooper pictured with his cellphone invention

The History of Cellphones

[3]The technology for cellphones has been around since 1947. It was used mainly in police cars. These early phones were as big as a suitcase and ran off a car battery. Rather than sending a person's voice over wires, car phones sent voices over radio waves to towers. With car phones, people no longer waited around their house for calls. But they had to wait around in their cars.

[4]That all started to change in 1973, when a man named Martin Cooper made the first call from a truly portable cellphone. "People want to talk to other people—not a house, or an office, or a car," Cooper says. It took 10 more years and millions of dollars before portable cellphones were ready to be sold to the public. First, cellphones had to be tested by small groups to make sure they worked. Then cellphone companies had to build towers to handle all of the cellphone calls.

Big Phones, Big Prices

[5]The first cellphones sold to the public were nothing like today's sleek models. They were bigger than a brick and weighed more than a pound. They also cost almost $4,000! Obviously, they weren't for everyone. By 1985, phone prices had dropped to $1,000, and there were about 200,000 users in the whole world. Two years later, cellphone users passed the one million mark. Today, more people have cellphones than home phones. Cellphones can fit in a pocket and weigh just a few ounces. And they cost a lot less too. In fact, many companies give new customers a cellphone for free.

[6]Cellphones may be the most popular gadget in history. Today there are four times as many cellphones sold as television sets. According to one report, by 2009 there will be one billion cellphones sold every year. One reason cellphones are so popular is that they do a lot more than simply let

people talk. People can use them to play video games or listen to music. They can watch movies or surf the Internet. They can send e-mails and even take pictures. The cellphone that fits in your pocket today can do much more than a computer could when your parents were your age.

The Effects of Cellphones

[7]Cellphones have proven to be beneficial in many ways. Some advantages are easy to guess. People no longer have to suffer the inconvenience of waiting around the living room for important calls. Also, people can quickly call for help in an emergency. Other effects are not so easy to guess. Here are a few.

[8]**Helping Poor Countries:** Some countries are so poor that they cannot afford to run telephone lines to everyone's houses. The cellphone is helping those countries catch up. Even in villages with almost no modern conveniences, people have cellphones. Doctors use them to call ambulances. People use them to talk to family members far away. Cellphones have provided people with new ways to make money. Farmers and fishermen use them to help sell goods. One woman in a village without electricity makes money by recharging cellphones for her neighbors with a car battery.

[9]**Waste Not, Want Not:** In 2004, the state of California started worrying about what happened to all the old cellphones that people no longer used. People throw away about 25,000 cellphones a day in California alone. Very few were recycled, and many ended up in landfills. Cellphones contain

Cellphones were essential after Hurricane Katrina to communicate disaster relief.

dangerous materials. When they are buried in landfills, these materials can leak into the water we drink. So California passed a law. Now all cellphones must be recycled. Many are given to people in poor countries.

[10]**Passing Time:** Since people now can do so many things on their cellphones, waiting around is a lot easier. One person might play a video game while waiting for a movie to start. Another might send e-mails while waiting in line at the grocery store. A third might listen to music while a friend tries on clothes at the store.

[11]**Wasting Time:** There is a down side to all the fun you can have with a cellphone. Some people find themselves wasting time playing with their phones instead of studying or doing their jobs. If you're not careful, you might find yourself getting bad grades or even losing a job because of your cellphone.

[12]**Social Insecurity:** Some people worry that cellphones cause people to talk less to the people around them. Instead, they play video games or send e-mails to friends in other places. In South Korea, for example, kids take their cellphones to dance parties. Rather than dance to the same music, they all dance while listening to their own music on their cellphones.

The Future of Cellphones

[13]It's hard to guess what the cellphones of tomorrow will be like. Maybe they will fit on your wrist. Maybe they will control all of the appliances in your house. Maybe you will use them to pay for things instead of using money or credit cards. Some people even think that everyone will be given a cellphone number for life when they are born. Whatever happens, you can bet that tomorrow's phones will be as different from today's as today's are from your grandparents' telephone.

A 1954 telephone with a crank handle

CAR CULTURE

- In what ways have cars changed people's ways of living?

- What features make a car appealing?

- How do people use cars for entertainment?

A Fast Argument

Fans of both stock car racing, left, and open-wheel racing think their sport is the best.

¹**C**ar racing is one of the most popular sports in the world. Millions of people all over the world watch drivers test their mettle in dangerous, high-speed car races on television. Millions more attend car races. Perhaps the only thing these fans love more than car racing is arguing over what kind of **vehicle** makes the best racer. The two most popular types of car races involve stock cars and open-wheel cars. Stock cars look like souped-up versions of the cars you see on the streets. Open-wheel cars, also called Formula One cars, look more like rocket ships with wheels attached to their sides. The two types of racing have a lot in common. Both involve racing four-wheeled cars around and around a track. Both honor the winners of individual races and also crown an **annual** champion. But stock car and Formula One racing are different in many ways. The cars are different. The tracks are different. Even the fans are different.

The Cars

[2]Races sponsored by the National Association for Stock Car Auto Racing (NASCAR) feature vehicles based on regular cars. In the first NASCAR race in 1949, the drivers bought cars straight off local car dealer lots. They were the standard cars that regular people drove to work and to the grocery store. That's why they are called stock cars. *Stock* means "standard." But those days are past. Over the years, NASCAR has allowed the drivers to make minor changes to the cars. These changes have made the cars safer and faster. Today's stock cars share little with standard cars other than the basic shape. Only the metal roof, hood, and trunk are made by the companies responsible for the **production** of regular cars. Stock car engines are similar to engines in regular cars, but they are much more powerful. These engines can push cars as fast as 200 miles per hour.

[3]Formula One racing, on the other hand, features cars that look completely different from regular vehicles. These low-slung cars have narrow bodies with tires sticking out of the side. On a Formula One car, you can see the entire wheel. By contrast, NASCAR wheels are hidden partly by fenders. Unlike stock cars, Formula One cars were never available from your local car dealer. From the first Formula One race in 1950, the cars were built for racing only. Today's Formula One cars can go about 30 miles per hour faster than NASCAR vehicles.

[4]NASCAR and Formula One cars are similar in some ways, however. Both are designed, built, and maintained by a team of experts. Both also use a variety of specially designed tires. The experts decide which set of tires will work best in a given race. Some tires work better on rough roads. Some work better on smooth roads. NASCAR and Formula One cars are similar in another way. Both are laden with safety features designed to protect drivers in case of accidents. That's especially important when you consider how fast they go!

The Tracks

[5]Another big difference between Formula One and NASCAR is the racetracks. The only similarity shared by the two types of tracks is that they are paved. Formula One racetracks have as many twists and turns as a butterfly's flight pattern. The drivers often have to slow down to make

sharp turns to the left or to the right. Sometimes the turns are so sharp that the drivers end up going in the opposite direction! Some Formula One races are even run on regular city streets.

⁶NASCAR races, however, take place on tracks built especially for car racing. These tracks are usually shaped like the letter *O*. Unlike Formula One drivers, NASCAR drivers have to make only two wide, gradual turns on each trip around the track. And those two turns are always to the left.

The Champions

⁷Drivers of both types of cars strive to win every race they enter. Similarly, both keep their eyes on a more important goal: the overall annual championship. In both types of racing, drivers are awarded points depending on where they finish in each race. The driver that accumulates the most points during the season is named champion. Because of the point system, both types of drivers can win the overall championship without winning a single race.

The Fans

⁸Most NASCAR fans live in the United States. By contrast, most Formula One fans live outside the United States. That's easy to understand if you consider where the races **occur**. All 39 NASCAR races take place in the United States. Formula One races, however, take place all over the world. Only one of the 18 Formula One races takes place in the United States.

⁹Wherever they live, NASCAR and Formula One fans love to **debate** which type of racing is more exciting. NASCAR fans like the fact that drivers race in cars similar to the ones the fans drive. They also like the fact that the tracks have more straight stretches. That makes it easier for the leader to be passed by other drivers. Formula One fans disagree. As **evidence**, they say their cars are faster, and the twisting tracks prove their drivers are more talented. In the end, which type of racing is best depends on who you ask. Only one thing is certain: Racing fans will never get tired of the argument.

Drive Thru

Most drive-through window signs use the simplified spelling *thru*.

SERVICE TO GO →→→

¹**R**ed Cheney had a problem. It was 1947, and Red was opening a new restaurant on a highway in Springfield, Missouri. The 2,000-mile-long highway was filled with potential customers on long car trips. But many of the customers were in a hurry. They didn't have time to stop, go inside a restaurant, and sit at a table for a meal. Red needed a strategy, or a lot of customers would speed right past his restaurant.

²For years, restaurants had offered curbside service to customers waiting in their cars. Customers would park at the curb outside the restaurant, where waiters would take orders and deliver food. This appealed to customers because they could get food fast and easily. But curbside service could not help Red. The curb outside his restaurant was a busy highway filled with speeding cars. People couldn't park there and wait for food to be delivered.

³Other restaurants offered drive-in service. At a drive-in restaurant, customers parked in a paved area off the road. A restaurant worker would come to their cars and take their orders. When the food was ready, the worker would take it out to the car. Then the customers could eat their food in their cars or take it home. But drive-in restaurants needed big parking lots and a lot of workers to serve customers. Red needed a better idea.

⁴Then it came to him. Red realized that he didn't need a drive-*in*. He needed a drive-*through*. So he knocked a hole in the wall of his restaurant and installed a window. Customers could drive up to the window, place an order, get their food, and get back on the road in a hurry. It was perfect. One worker could handle all the car customers. Since the customers would drive away with their food, Red did not need a big area for people to park while they ate. Because of this imaginative solution, Red's restaurant became a popular—and fast—stop for hungry travelers in a hurry.

Serving Soldiers

⁵Drive-through windows solved problems for more than just hungry travelers, however. For example, in 1975 a restaurant in Sierra Vista, Arizona, was losing business because of an army rule. Soldiers from the local army base were not allowed to wear their uniforms into non-military businesses. This meant soldiers couldn't stop at the restaurant for dinner on

the way home. They would have to drive home and change clothes first. A lot of soldiers decided just to eat at home. That was costing the restaurant valuable business. To solve this problem, the restaurant installed a drive-through window. As a result, soldiers could get food without having to enter the restaurant or go home to change clothes first. Even people who weren't soldiers found the drive-through more convenient than parking and walking into the restaurant to place a "to-go" order. Because people could pick up dinner with **ease**, the restaurant had more customers than ever.

The Need for Speed

[6]Drive-through windows quickly proved their worth to restaurants by increasing profits. But there were still problems to be worked out. One was speed. To make more money, restaurants needed to serve the maximum number of customers in the **minimum** amount of time possible. With just a window, a restaurant could help only one car customer at a time. The customer would drive up to the window, look at the menu, place an order, and wait for the food to be prepared. The next customer had to wait through this process before driving to the window and placing an order. Sometimes customers got **impatient** and drove away. That meant lost business.

[7]Restaurants solved this problem by setting up a menu board several car lengths away from the window. A menu board is a lighted sign with a list of the food served at the restaurant. The menu board also had an intercom. An intercom is a speaker and microphone that allows the customer to talk to the restaurant worker. With this new system, customers could place their order at the menu board, then drive up to the window to pay and pick up their food. While that customer was paying, the next customer could order. By setting the menu farther away from the window, restaurants could work on several orders at once. As a result, the restaurants reduced the amount of time customers had to wait in line.

[8]Restaurants thought of other ways to increase the speed of their service. One way was to have two windows. Customers would pay at the first window and pick up food at the second window. This system allowed different restaurant workers to concentrate on one part of the process. As a result, they could deliver food faster. This system also helped reduce the number of mistakes made when filling customer orders.

Stress Reliever

[9]Drive-through windows became so popular that they created an unexpected problem. Sometimes customers were not sure what they wanted to eat. They would sit at the menu board trying to decide if they would **prefer** a hamburger or a chicken sandwich. Hungry customers waiting to order would become frustrated. The customers at the menu board would start to feel a lot of pressure to hurry up and order. This slowed the process and caused a **decline** in customer satisfaction. Restaurants worried that they might start losing customers.

[10]Restaurants solved this problem by adding a preview menu to the drive-through line. Since the preview menu was a few car lengths ahead of the menu board and intercom, customers could decide what they wanted before it was their turn to order. The result was faster service and less stress on customers. Drive-through windows became more popular than ever.

They're Everywhere!

[11]Today, drive-through windows are a huge success. The average American orders food from drive-through windows three and a half times a week. Restaurants with drive-through windows do about 60 percent of their business with customers who never leave their cars. Some restaurants serve 99 percent of their food through the drive-through window.

[12]Drive-through windows worked so well for restaurants that other businesses found ways to use them. Banks began offering drive-through windows so their customers could conduct business from their cars. People can pick up groceries, videos, laundry, drug prescriptions, library books, and even a cup of espresso without ever leaving their cars. There is even a drive-through window in Las Vegas where people can get married! Customers with active lifestyles depend on drive-through windows to help them take care of errands and get on with their busy schedules. The faster they can take care of their errands, the sooner they can get home to relax and **decompress**.

You Need This Car

Would I steer you wrong?

[1]**G**ood afternoon, and welcome to Crazy Carl's Car Corner! No, I'm not Crazy Carl. He's the owner, the big cheese, the head honcho. He's on vacation. My name's Al. What's your name? Felix, eh? My grandfather's name was Felix. I'm pleased to meet you, Felix. I can see by the mustard stain on your shirt that you've already taken advantage of our free hot dog offer. Do you mind if I ask you a couple of questions so I can better understand which cars to show you? First of all, what kind of car do you drive right now? A sports car, eh? What do you like most about your sports car? The powerful engine, you say? I like to drive fast too. But not too fast, right? Always obey the speed limit, I say, but it's nice to be able to get up to the speed limit as quickly as possible. Know what I mean? Let me give you my honest

opinion, Felix. I think that what you need is a brand new Panther LX. It's the perfect car for you for four reasons: power, style, safety, and economy.

Power

[2]You say you like your current car's powerful engine, Felix? Well, power is what makes the Panther the perfect car for you. The Panther is the most powerful car of its type. It goes from 0 to 60 miles per hour in 5 seconds flat! The only thing faster is a jet! The Panther is 30 percent more powerful than the car you drove in here. Just imagine how all that power is going to feel when you are cruising down the highway leaving all the other drivers in your dust. Now, our competition sells a similar car called the Tiger 200X. It's not a bad car, but it's no Panther LX. *Car Buyer* magazine tested the Panther and the Tiger, and the tests showed that the Panther was 19 percent more powerful than the Tiger. You'll feel that extra 19 percent of power every time you step on the gas of your new Panther.

Style

[3]But the Panther is not just powerful, it's also the most beautiful car on the highway. You don't just want to go fast, you want to go fast and look good while you're doing it. Style is the second reason the Panther is the perfect car for you. Just look at the Panther's sleek lines! And if this isn't stylish enough for you, the Panther is also **available** as a convertible. Just imagine cruising down the highway on a lovely spring day with the top down and the wind blowing through your hair. Some people might argue about the usefulness of style, but you and I know better. Style is what makes everyone stop and look at you and your sleek new Panther. Style is what will make your neighbors jealous.

Safety

[4]Another reason this car is perfect for you is safety. The Panther has airbags that inflate if you are in a head-on collision, but it also has side airbags in case someone runs into the side of your car. Are you a married

man, Felix? What's your wife's name? Victoria! What a coincidence! My sister is named Victoria! Now, you could save a little money by buying a Tiger 200X, but it doesn't have side airbags. Imagine that Victoria is driving down the street one day when some jerk runs a red light and—bam!—rams into the side of this cheap, flimsy Tiger. Think about how you would feel seeing your lovely wife at the hospital, her face all swollen and bruised from the accident. What are you going to tell her, Felix? "Well, honey, at least we saved a little bit of money." But that's not going to happen, because you're not the kind of guy who's going to risk your wife's safety just to save a few bucks, are you, Felix?

Economy

[5]I think I know you pretty well by now, Felix. You will not hesitate to spend a little extra money on a product that is of the highest quality, like the Panther, but you're not the type of guy who's going to throw money away. That's another reason why this car is perfect for you. The Panther gets an **estimated** 28 miles per gallon on the highway and about 15 miles per gallon in the city. The fuel tank has a **capacity** of 18 gallons, so with a full tank, you can drive more than 500 miles! Can you do that in your car now? I don't think so. To tell you the truth, Felix, I'm not sure that car of yours can go another 500 miles, no matter how much gas you put in it. I'm just kidding around with you, pal.

[6]Are you a football fan, Felix? Well, so am I, and we both know that one football fan would never steer another football fan wrong. I'll let you in on a little secret, Felix. Crazy Carl is the biggest football fan in the world. You might even say he's crazy about football—get it? So, as a football fan who works for a football fan, I'm telling you that this car is perfect for you.

Think About This . . .

[7]I know what you're thinking, Felix. You're thinking, "I don't need a fancy car. I'm just looking for basic transportation. I prefer a cheaper car, maybe something with a little less power and a little less style and a few more miles per gallon." Let me tell you something, Felix. Buying a new car isn't about what you think you need, it's about what you *know you want*.

Sure, you can buy a cheaper car, but you'll regret it every time you step on the gas and remember how the power of the Panther LX felt. You'll regret it every time you drive by your neighbor's house and see his shiny new Panther LX gleaming in the driveway. You'll regret it every sunny, spring day when you think about how nice the wind feels blowing through your hair.

[8]You don't want to live with all that regret, do you Felix? The Panther LX is the perfect car for you because it's powerful, stylish, safe, and economical. I'm not exaggerating when I say that the Panther is the greatest car ever made. Now, I don't want you to feel like there's any **pressure** on you, but there was another gentleman in here earlier today looking at this very car. It's the last Panther LX that we have on the lot, so you need to make a decision as soon as possible. If you take advantage of this **opportunity**, I guarantee that you will never regret it. If the Panther LX doesn't live up to everything I told you, you can return it to us, and Crazy Carl will personally refund every penny you paid. Now, what do you think, Felix?

How to Sweeten Your Ride

With a little effort, you can turn a beat-up old clunker into a sweet ride.

¹**M**y favorite thing in the world is jumping in my car, cranking up some tunes, and driving slowly with nowhere to go. In that way, I'm like a lot of kids my age. But there's a big difference. Most kids cruise around in cars that look pretty much like they did when they first rolled off the car lot. I just can't roll like that. My ride needs to be unique. It needs to reflect who I am. It needs to stand out in the crowd of cookie-cutter cars rolling down the street. That's why I drive a low-rider. Specifically, I drive a tricked out, modified 1968 Chevy Impala. It's painted a dark metallic blue with light blue geometric designs down each side. The **entire** hood is covered with a coiled up cobra.

197

[2]The first thing people ask me about my low-rider is, "Dude, where did you get that sweet ride?" They're shocked when I say, "I bought it at Dirt Dog's Junkyard for 500 bucks." But it's true. A year ago, my low-rider was a rusty pile of junk. The gas tank had a hole in it, and the engine was completely rusted together. I had to have it towed back to my house. Then I worked on it every spare moment for six months to turn it into the sweet ride you see before you today. The second thing everyone asks me about my car is, "Dude, will you show me how to make a low-rider?" That's exactly what I'm going to do in this article—tell you how I built my low-rider, from the first step to the last.

Find a Car

[3]The first step, of course, is to find a car. A lot of people buy used cars to turn into low-riders. Some people even buy new cars. But I didn't have that kind of money in the bank. Besides, I was going to change everything anyway. If a car is already running, what's the sense in fixing it? So I started hanging out at junkyards. Buying from a junkyard saved me tons of money. I also **recycled** something that would otherwise just rust away. Before you start visiting junkyards, check out some low-rider magazines or books and decide what kind of car you want.

[4]While you're looking, pay close attention to the condition of each car's body. The main thing you're looking for is a car without many dents. The engine and seats and stuff don't really matter. You'll probably want to replace them anyway. Finally, have your car towed to a place where you can work on it. It's best to have a place with a roof overhead to keep your work from being rained on. If you don't have a roof, cover your car with tarps when you're not working on it.

Tear It Apart

[5]Next, disassemble your car. First, tear apart the interior. Remove the seats and rip out the carpets. If the seats are in good shape, hang on to them. Some seats can be cleaned, and others can be covered with new material. In my case, I ditched the seats and bought some really cool replacements. Next, work on the

exterior. Remove the bumpers. Then take off all the insignias, like the hood ornament and the car company's name. After that, take off the trunk lid and the hood and set them aside. Then rip out the carpeting from the trunk, and check out the gas tank. If it's rusted out like mine was, remove it and install a new one. Next, remove the engine and all the parts under the hood. As you remove each part, look at it closely. If it's in pretty good shape, hang on to it. If it's not, get rid of it. Finally, haul all your trashed parts back to the junkyard.

Clean It

[6]The next step is cleaning all the parts you kept. Start with a trip to your local car parts store. There are several products that will degrease different parts of your car. Use one of these products to clean all the grease out of the engine compartment. Then use an electric sander to remove every last **layer** of paint from your car's body, including the hood and trunk. Cars have several coats of paint, so this might take a while. Once the entire car body is clean and free of paint, carefully spray everything with primer. This special type of paint will protect your car from rusting.

Paint It

[7]The next step is to paint the body of the car. In the factory, the car body is dipped in giant vats of paint so the paint is distributed **throughout** the entire vehicle. You probably don't have giant vats of paint, so your car will have to be spray painted. If you have the skills and want to do it yourself, go for it. Otherwise, I recommend hiring a professional painter. They have all the gear, and they know all the different painting **methods**. Your paint job is the most visible thing about your car, so you want it to be perfect. Hiring a professional will increase your chances of having a perfect paint job.

Put It Back Together

[8]While your car is being painted, get everything ready to put your low-rider together. Clean and repair all the parts you took off and saved. Buy all the new parts you will need. Since you're building a low-rider, you'll need a hydraulics kit. The hydraulics are the parts that make the front or back of your low-rider bounce up and down. You will also need a new suspension system that will let your car ride lower to the ground. After all, that's why it's called a low-rider.

[9]Organize everything neatly in your work area. After the paint on your car body is completely dry, start putting your low-rider together. Begin with the interior. First, put new carpeting in, then reinstall your seats. This is the point in my project when I installed my special steering wheel made out of chrome chain. When the interior's finished, install your hydraulics and your low-rider suspension. This will be easier without the weight of the engine. Then put all your engine parts back together and replace the trunk and hood. Next, replace the bumpers and insignias. Finally, mount some shiny new chrome wheels, and you're good to go. Now you can start saving money for that new stereo system.

[10]I hope this article has inspired you to get to work on your own low-rider. It won't be easy. It fact, it might be the hardest thing you've done in your entire life. You'll feel like giving up again and again. But if you stick to it, one day people will stop you on the street and ask, "Dude, where did you get that sweet ride?"

BIRTH OF THE CAR CULTURE

Cars were an important part of American life in the 1930s, but by 1950, they had become a necessity.

¹**A**merica's love affair with the car started a hundred years ago. And like any love affair, it has gone through stages. In the early years, people considered cars to be important, but not essential. Many people didn't even own cars. Instead, they used public transportation or their feet to get where they were going. Some even rode horses to school or to work. But after America and its allies won World War II, everything was different. Americans still loved their cars, just as they did before the war. But before the war, it was as if Americans were "dating" their cars. After the war, Americans "married" their cars. Before the war, few families owned more than one car. After the war, by contrast, two-car families were common. Unlike pre-war

times, it became more common for teenagers to own their own cars. Before the war, many people considered cars a luxury. After the war, however, most people thought of a car as a necessity, as important as a home or clothes. America's love for cars was similar before and after the war. What had changed was the ability of the average family to afford not just one, but two and sometimes more cars.

America Falls in Love

[2]A hundred years ago, automobiles were expensive playthings for the wealthy. Cars were made by hand in a process so difficult that only a few thousand were built each year. Then Henry Ford figured out how to make cars cheaper, so more people could afford them. By 1916, Ford had cut the cost of a car to about $360, and American car production topped 1 million for the first time. America was in love with the automobile. Over the next 13 years, the American economy boomed, and so did car sales. People were making more money, and more people were spending some of that money on cars. In 1929, the number of cars produced annually topped 4 million.

[3]Then it all came crashing down. In 1929, the American economy began to collapse. Millions of people lost their jobs. Banks ran out of money, and people lost their life savings. Americans still loved cars, but fewer and fewer people could afford one. Car production plummeted for the next few years and fell below 1 million by 1932. Things improved slowly over the next few years, but people soon had more important things to think about than cars. War was raging across Europe. America's allies called for help. When America joined the war, car production came to a complete halt. Companies stopped making cars and started making tanks, airplanes, bombs, and other

war supplies. People were asked to use less gasoline to save fuel for the war effort. America's love affair with the car was put on hold.

[4]In 1945, after America and its allies won the war, American confidence soared. So did the economy. America was now the richest country in the world. People were making more money, and after scrimping during the war, Americans were ready to go shopping. Companies started making cars again, cranking out a record 5 million cars in 1949. The next year, production shot up to 6.5 million. Making cars became America's biggest business. The car became a central feature of American culture.

America Moves to the Suburbs

[5]Before cars, Americans had to live close enough to their jobs to walk or take public transportation. That started to change in the 1920s as car ownership became more common. With a car, a family could live farther from work and school. Some moved to new neighborhoods called "suburbs" that were built just outside the crowded cities. Suburbs were relatively rare before the war.

[6]By comparison, suburbs grew so fast after the war that every major American city was completely surrounded by these new neighborhoods. After the war, home construction surged. During the 1950s, 13 million new homes were built, and 85 percent of them were built in suburbs. Without the huge increase in car ownership that occurred after the war, this would not have been possible. Early suburbs consisted mainly of houses. There were few places for people who lived in the suburbs to work or shop. Most jobs and shopping areas were still in the city, so people needed cars to get there.

America Buys an Extra Car

[7]Before the war, few families owned more than one car. However, that began to change after the war. One reason was that so many families moved into the new suburbs. The parent who worked in the city, usually the father, needed a car to get to work. The parent who stayed home, usually the mother, needed a car to go buy groceries and run errands. Since people were making more money in the post-war boom, it was easier for families to afford more than one car.

[8]The war changed America's car needs in another way. During the war, almost all of the soldiers were men. Many women contributed to the war effort by working in factories that built war supplies. Some of these women found that they enjoyed working outside the home. When their husbands returned, many of these women kept their jobs. With both parents working, families needed two cars. They also had more money, so they could afford an additional car. When their children got old enough to drive, many parents added a third car to the family driveway. The abundance of jobs in the post-war boom also meant more teenagers could afford to buy their own cars. As a result, the number of cars on American roads jumped from 40 million to 60 million during the 1950s.

[9]Today, there are more than 200 million cars on American roads. There are more cars than there are people with driver's licenses. In fact, the state of California has more cars than it does people, with or without licenses. More than 90 percent of American households have at least one car, and the average household has two cars. Americans take about 90 percent of their long-distance trips in cars, and they drive more than 1.5 trillion miles a year. America remains married to the automobile, and there's no end in sight.

CHANGES

- *How do people adapt to changes in their lives?*
- *Why might someone experience a feeling of loss?*
- *What are some ways in which people express their feelings?*

Long Distance Love

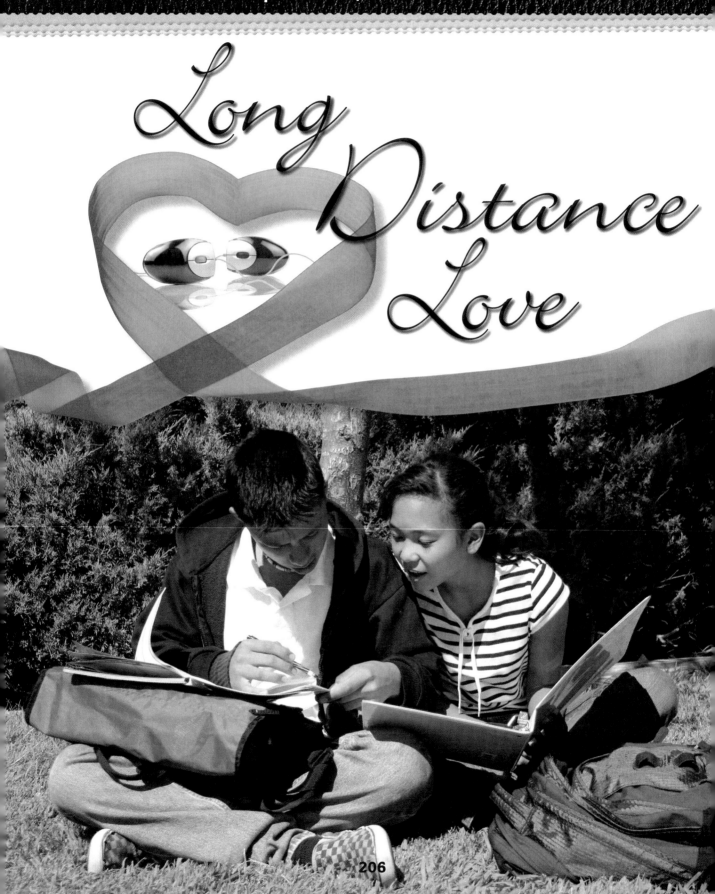

Dear Gaby,

[1] I can't believe you've only been gone for two weeks. Time has been dragging by since you left. So how's the big city? Full of interesting people and cool things to do, right? If I had super powers, I would **transform** this dull town into a place like that. Then maybe I wouldn't die of boredom.

[2] Speaking of boredom, I'm in study hall now. Coach Barnes is reading the paper, Jamal is sitting next to me snoring, and the clock is ticking so loud it's driving me nuts. Of course, since you left, everything about this place seems to bug me. It bugs me how the same old gang hangs out at the Frostee Freeze waiting for somebody to drive down Main, honking their car horn. Then everyone hollers and struts and puts on the same old show. It bugs me to flip through the lame collection of CDs at Frank's so-called music store. How about a little salsa or some hip-hop? And if I really want to get irritated, there's always our famous video store. I've memorized the *Die Hard* movies, and the rest of their selection stinks. I'm not going back there until they get some videos from this century.

[3] You can probably tell that missing you makes me pretty grouchy. Like yesterday when Uncle Carlos was helping me put new wheels on my skateboard, the drill slipped and he dinged the finish. I yelled and got really mad. You should've seen the look on my uncle's face. It was like I had punched him in the stomach. I felt like the lowest worm on Earth, so I got on my board and went riding down where the pavement is really rough. It rattled my whole body, but I couldn't shake the bad feelings. I rode out of town to Boot Hill and hiked up to that grassy spot under the trees that we like. That was a foolish move because the place was too quiet and lonely without you. I got depressed looking down at the town. I started thinking, "This is my prison, and I'm stuck here where nothing interesting will ever happen."

[4] I know it's a long way off, but my only way out is to get my driver's license and then get **access** to some wheels. I'm going to buy my cousin's truck, paint it black, and then put bright chrome wheels and really fat tires on it. I'll put in a sound system that will send the beat right through you too. When it's all fixed up, I'll come get you. So don't find anyone else before then. Promise?

Love, Mario

Dear Mario,

⁵I can't believe I haven't seen you for two whole weeks. It seems strange to think I really live here now. I keep thinking I'll wake up and be back in my old room with my friends and my old life and YOU! You can't imagine how much I miss everyone at Valley High. My new school is about five times bigger than Valley. There are so many kids that I don't see any of the same people twice in one day. Each class is a whole different group. I don't think I'll ever make friends. Back home I had a lot of **confidence**, but here I feel like such an outsider. I just act shy and keep to myself.

⁶Thinking of home makes a big lump swell up in my throat, then the tears just come spilling out. I never realized how lucky I was to have a whole **network** of friends and relatives around. It made me feel like I belonged— you know, like I mattered. I really miss that. Sometimes I just lie on my bed and daydream about being back home, doing familiar things and seeing familiar people. I picture myself riding through town with my cousins in the afternoons, and I can just hear the gang at the Frostee Freeze calling out and trying to get us to stop. Everybody on the street honks and waves at us like we're somebody. Here, when I walk down the street, I might as well be invisible.

⁷I love to imagine going downtown with you to all our favorite places— the park, the Frostee Freeze, the video store, and of course Frank's. It was so much fun joking with Frank about his ancient rock-and-roll CDs, the ones you called prehistoric. Is he still promising to order some salsa for you? Let me know if there's a **specific** CD you want, and I'll send it to you. There's a monster music store near here with the biggest **variety** of music in the city. It's two stories high and has glass booths where you can listen to CDs before buying them. I feel kind of lost in there, but they're sure to have any CD you want.

⁸It's getting late so I'd better stop and do my homework. I'd give anything to be at our spot on the hill watching the lights come on in town and enjoying the quiet. Please wait for me, and don't take anyone else to our special place. I'm trying to convince my parents to let me come back and live with relatives.

Love, Gaby

GAME DAY

[1]**B**ruce checked the hall clock and stepped into the school office. He waited for Mrs. Rocha to finish typing names from the small white attendance slips scattered over her desk. After several minutes, she looked up with a start.

[2]"Why, Bruce, you're late for the third day in a row!" she clucked, shaking her head. She moved to the counter and tore a pink sheet from a small pad. "What's the reason today?" she asked, peering over her reading glasses.

[3]"Same thing," he said in an expressionless voice. "I fell back asleep after my mom left for work."

[4]Mrs. Rocha looked at Bruce doubtfully, then filled out the **permit**. As Bruce reached for it, she leaned across the counter. Bruce braced himself for Mrs. Rocha's mother-hen routine. "This isn't like you, son," she said in a hushed, **confidential** tone. "Is something wrong?" She waited for an answer, but Bruce kept his eyes down and didn't respond.

[5]"Well!" she huffed, insulted by his refusal to speak. "I'm sure I don't know what's gotten into you."

[6]Bruce took the permit and left. He was surprised at how little Mrs. Rocha's disapproval bothered him. His life seemed like a TV show he was watching without much interest. Being tardy wasn't the only thing he had done differently this week, and he was getting used to people being upset with him. He had fallen asleep in class twice. Instead of eating in the cafeteria with friends, he had spent lunch period alone in the courtyard. He had pitched so badly in practice that the coach suggested he get his eyes examined. The weird thing was that Bruce didn't seem to care what people said. It was as if the kid he used to be had been swallowed up by a beast that was now in charge.

[7]The beast had moved in the day his father was deployed to Iraq. Since then, every day felt endless, boring, unimportant. Nighttime was a different story, though. At night, Bruce felt as if he were being buried alive, crushed under the weight of that strange, dark creature that was always with him now. He lay awake while TV news pictures flashed through his mind—pictures of explosions and rolling tanks, of soldiers taking cover behind crumbled walls, of wounded people with bloodstained clothes.

[8]As Bruce made his way through the crowded halls to his locker, his best friend Tyrone caught up with him. "Hey, Jackson!" he said enthusiastically. "Are you ready for the big game tonight?"

[9]"Not really," Bruce mumbled. He'd been trying not to think about the game because he didn't **anticipate** a win after the way he'd pitched in practice all week. Anyway, it was impossible to imagine pitching for the championship without his dad there. For a moment, he pictured his dad sitting in the front row cheering and twirling his lucky red bandana above his head. Bruce fumbled with his lock and blinked hard to stop the tears.

[10]Tyrone looked around uncomfortably then said, "Hey, I'm sorry your dad was deployed, but he's going to be OK. Before you know it he'll be back here watching you pitch your senior season."

[11]"Oh, yeah? How do you know?" snarled Bruce. Bruce could see the **impact** of his cold response in the hurt look on Tyrone's face, but the

avalanche of angry words continued. "You don't know anything about it, so just keep your mouth shut!" He slammed his locker and stormed off toward his math class.

[12]The rest of the day dragged by. When the final bell rang, Bruce took the back way out of the building, hoping he wouldn't see Tyrone. He walked along the athletic field where the JROTC was practicing for a drill competition. The cadets were in full dress uniform, and one was carrying a United States flag. The sight of the military uniforms and the flag led Bruce's thoughts far away. Then, suddenly, he realized he wasn't alone. Several guys had gathered nearby and were taunting the cadets.

[13]"Hey, G.I. Joe," yelled one. "Does playing dress-up make you feel like a big man?"

[14]"Oooh, look out," called another. "The enemy's right behind you. Too late—you're dead!" Then he grabbed his heart and made a face of mock pain.

[15]At that, the whole group burst out laughing. Bruce's blood boiled. Without a thought, he whirled and tackled the kid who was still hamming it up. Bruce pinned him down, but before he could land a punch, others in the group grabbed his arms and pulled him off.

[16]Coach Summers saw the scuffle from the coaching office and came rushing across the field like a shot from a gun. "What in the world **prompted** you to pull a stunt like that, Jackson?" he demanded.

[17]Coach Summers was an ex-Marine who took discipline very seriously. The other boys were obviously shaken by the coach's tone, but Bruce was defiantly silent. He kept clenching and unclenching his fists as he glared at his escaped victim.

[18]"You'd better go home and get your act together," warned the coach. "You have the **potential** to pitch a winner tonight, but not with this attitude. If you show up with this chip on your shoulder, don't expect to pitch the game."

[19]Bruce spent the rest of the afternoon in his room with his music turned up loud. He stared at the photographs on his walls. His dad was in a lot of them—catching for Bruce, standing outside the stadium with Bruce, holding up a trophy with Bruce. His dad had been his best coach over the years. He spent all his free evenings and weekends helping his

son become a great pitcher. Now Bruce felt that his reason for playing ball was gone.

[20]"Bruce!" called his mother as she came in from work. "Are you ready? It's nearly time to leave." She came into her son's room and turned down the music. One look at Bruce's face told her he was nowhere near ready to face a championship game.

[21]"Rough day?" she asked.

[22]"You might say that," said Bruce, avoiding eye contact.

[23]"Wait here," she said.

[24]A few minutes later she returned with a brown envelope. "Your dad wanted me to give you this before the game tonight," she explained.

[25]Bruce's heart pounded as he took the envelope. He reached inside and pulled out his dad's red bandana. For the first time in days, Bruce smiled.

[26]An hour later, he stood near the dugout scanning the packed stands. He spotted his mom sitting in the front row with Tyrone and Tyrone's dad like always. Bruce waved his hat at them and they waved back.

[27]When it was time to take the field, Bruce pulled out the red bandana, studied it for a moment, then tucked it back in his pocket. As he walked toward the mound, the weight in his heart lifted. For the moment, the beast was under control.

Blown Away

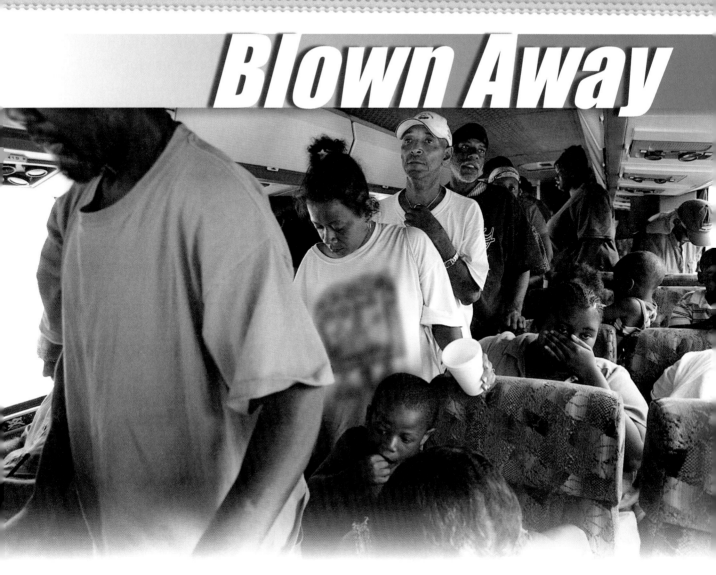

[1]**September 1, 2005**   It's Thursday afternoon—the fourth day of my bad dream. I want to write down everything that's happened so I can get it on paper and out of my head. On Monday, Hurricane Katrina hit New Orleans. Lots of people left town before then, but we stayed. Our neighborhood is on high ground, and my dad thought it would be safe from flooding. I trust my dad's judgment, so I wasn't worried, at least not at first. But the more I listened to the news, the more I worried that staying in our home might have terrible **consequences**. My dad, brother, and I all stayed glued to the TV news as the storm got bigger. The reporters could hardly keep from blowing away, and the wind turned their umbrellas inside out. Officials **classified** Katrina as a category 5 hurricane—one of the biggest storms in United States history!

[2]By the time the storm hit land, it was down to a category 4, but it was so strong that I wished we hadn't stayed behind. The sky turned kind of greenish, and the rain poured down. The wind whipped around our house and howled so loud that we had a hard time hearing each other talk. We heard loud clunks and crashes when the wind blew things against our house. Each time a big gust would come along, the house swayed back and forth, and I screamed. I kept picturing our roof turning inside out like one of the reporters' umbrellas. It was the worst morning of my life.

[3]The next day, we checked out the damage. It was unbelievable! The wind had pulled several huge trees right out of the ground, and one had fallen on our truck and crushed it! We all felt bad, but I was especially sorry for Deshaun. He just got his driver's license, and now there's nothing to drive. Two houses near us were completely flattened, and every **structure** in the neighborhood was damaged. The porch was missing from Mr. Rendon's store, and the roof of Willie's gas station had collapsed. The whole place looked like there had been an explosion. The streets and yards were littered with all kinds of things—a crumpled grocery basket, a car fender, pieces of houses, part of a billboard, a baby stroller. It made me feel kind of sick to see the neighborhood so destroyed and trashed out.

[4]All the streets lower than ours were filled with water. We thought the water would start going down right away, but instead it started rising. By the next morning, our street was gone! We were surrounded by water, and we couldn't figure out why. The power had been out since the storm, so we couldn't get any news. Dad got worried and told us to pack a bag so we could get to safety. We waded toward a nursing home that was a few blocks away. At times, the dark, smelly water was up to my shoulders. Yuk! When we finally got to the nursing home, the director told us the levee had broken and New Orleans was in big trouble. A bus was coming to evacuate the nursing home patients. We decided we'd better get on it, too.

[5]So that's why I'm on this bus that is half-driving, half-floating across New Orleans. It doesn't look like New Orleans anymore, though. It looks like a nightmare.

[6]**September 3, 2005**   It's too noisy to nap so I guess I'll write. I'm on a cot in the Astrodome in Houston, Texas, with thousands of other people who wish they were home. It's like a beehive here, with Red Cross workers passing out snacks and clothes, babies crying, people calling out names as

they search for lost family members, children squealing and running around, and lots of folks watching the giant TV to figure out what's going on back home. As crowded as this place is, I was glad to get here. We pulled in late last night, and volunteers came out to help us off the bus and get us settled in. A volunteer named Betty Jo took us under her wing right from the start. She gave me a big, warm hug and a paper cup of sweet lemonade. She made me feel better even though I was really tired and unhappy. The funny way she talks and calls everyone "honey" reminds me of Meemaw. When I asked her if I could get a toothbrush, she told me I was going to get the whole shootin' match. I wondered if she was saying I ought to be shot for asking. I figured out what she really meant when she came back with bags of supplies. Clothes, blankets, shampoo, soap, toothbrushes, and even dental floss—it was all there.

[7]We spent the next half hour wandering around with our things trying to find empty cots to sleep on. There were thousands of cots! When we finally found three together, Dad, Deshaun, and I took turns going to the showers while one of us kept an eye on our things. That was the most wonderful shower I have ever taken. The steam and hot water eased my tired muscles, and the sweet smell of soap replaced the stench of Katrina. I threw away my filthy, flood-soaked clothes and put on the new ones that Betty Jo had given me. It felt like heaven to lie down on soft, clean sheets and sleep.

[8]It was weird waking up in this huge place with people all around me today. It was like being onstage for anyone to look at. I want to be back home with my friends. What if they never come back to New Orleans? It feels like Katrina blew my whole life into pieces. Betty Jo tells me to keep my chin up. She keeps saying that with a good attitude, starting over will be just like falling off a log—whatever that means! Half the time I don't understand what Betty Jo is saying, but she does cheer me up.

[9]Right now, Dad's in line to talk to a social worker. He wants to find out if we're **eligible** for a government loan. On the news, they said that the hospital where Dad works is completely destroyed. He wants to find a job here now, so Betty Jo got him an **application** to fill out. A lot of companies are going to hold job **interviews** right here at the Astrodome. Betty Jo told Dad that misfortune can be a blessing in disguise and that he might just find a job even better than the one he had before. Dad says he'll settle for anything that keeps him from sitting around this place worrying all day. I know just how he feels.

THE LOSS OF LOVE

by Countee Cullen

In this poem, Cullen uses rich images, such as a crumbling house and decaying fruit, to describe the emotional pain he feels. The poem's traditional structure reflects Cullen's respect for romantic European poetry.

¹All through an empty place I go,
And find her not in any room;
The candles and the lamps I light
Go down before a wind of gloom.

²Thick-spraddled lies the dust about,
A fit, sad place to write her name
Or draw her face the way she looked
That legendary night she came.

spraddled:
spread in an ugly way

216

³The old house crumbles bit by bit;
Each day I hear the ominous thud
That says another rent is there
For winds to pierce and storms to flood.

ominous: warning that something bad is going to happen

rent: an opening made by a tear

⁴My orchards groan and sag with fruit;
Where, Indian-wise, the bees go round;
I let it rot upon the bough;
I eat what falls upon the ground.

⁵The heavy cows go laboring
In agony with clotted teats;
My hands are slack; my blood is cold;
I marvel that my heart still beats.

slack: hanging loosely

⁶I have no will to weep or sing,
No least desire to pray or curse;
The loss of love is a terrible thing;
They lie who say that death is worse.

Connect to the Author

In the 1920s, Countee Cullen was the most famous African American writer in the United States. Some biographers think that Cullen was born in Louisville, Kentucky, in 1903. But his birthplace is uncertain. When he was 15, Countee moved in with the influential Rev. Frederick A. Cullen, from whom he got his name. The Reverend lived in Harlem, New York, at a time when African American art and writing were beginning to flower into what became known as the Harlem Renaissance. The atmosphere in Harlem influenced Cullen profoundly. So did the poems he read in school. Cullen began winning awards for his poetry while he was still in high school. By the age of 25, Cullen was celebrated as one of the leaders of the Harlem Renaissance. In addition to poems, Cullen wrote a novel, plays, and stories for children. He also taught high school English, French, and creative writing. Cullen died in 1946.

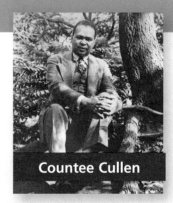

Countee Cullen

INVASION

¹One year ago, I lived in a different world. My life was going along just fine except for the occasional screaming match between my parents. They always seemed back to normal the next day, so I didn't worry about it much. Then one day, I found out those fights were a bigger deal than I thought. My mom's exact words are burned into my memory: "Carlos, your father and I have tried to work things out, but we can't, so we're getting a divorce. I want you to know that this has nothing to do with you."

[2]Nothing to do with me—yeah, right! It was only an end to life as I knew it. From then on, I lived in two places and moved my stuff back and forth every week. I felt like a yo-yo! At least they both promised to stay in Dallas so I wouldn't have to take an airplane back and forth. Unfortunately, they didn't promise to stay single. My parents both started dating, and that was totally weird. After a few months, my dad introduced me to Sara, the woman he was dating, and before I knew it, they were getting married.

[3]That's when my life got really complicated. Sara and her two little kids moved in, and Dad expected me to act all big brother and everything. Suddenly our house was overflowing with noise and toys and people I didn't even know.

[4]The noise always reminds me that invaders have taken over. For one thing, there is lots of lame music. You see, my stepmom sings golden oldies while she cooks, while she gets ready for work, even while she's driving. It never stops! Her daughter, Marisa, is even noisier. She is hooked on cartoons, and she has them blaring all afternoon. I hear her loud, goofy laugh the whole time the TV is on. As if that's not bad enough, each cartoon is followed by what I consider to be a kind of torture. Marisa corners me and makes me listen while she repeats every detail. ". . . and then the rabbit, he was hiding because he wanted to trick the duck, so he was hiding, hiding behind the tree. And then the duck tried to find the rabbit, but he couldn't because the rabbit was hiding behind the tree, and then . . ." It goes on forever!

[5]Only Luis, my new stepbrother, is quiet. Problem is that he's like a little shadow watching everything I do. I'm in my room repairing my radio-controlled plane when I get the feeling I'm not alone. I look up, and there's Luis, standing in the hallway watching me. I'm outside practicing end-overs on my skateboard, and there he is at the window—just staring at me. I'm tuning up my dirt bike in the garage, and suddenly I catch a glimpse of Luis in my rearview mirror. I nearly jump out of my skin! I'm starting to feel like I'm being haunted.

[6]The worst part is that Sara thinks Luis and I should be best buddies. "Why don't you see if Luis wants to go skateboarding with you?" she says to me, or "I'll bet you boys would have fun at the arcade together." It's like she can't see how different we are. Luis is a whole 5 years younger than I am,

and we don't like to do the same stuff. Heck, he still collects action figures!

[7]Last Saturday, I finally got to spend some time alone with my dad. His car had been running rough, and he was putting in a new carburetor. He always lets me help, because I love to work on engines. Anyway, we'd been working out on the driveway for about an hour when I notice Luis. He's just sitting on the front steps watching us.

[8]That's when Dad says, "Hey, Luis, come hand me that wrench, and I'll show you what we're doing." Well, the kid was on that wrench like a duck on a June bug. Dad started showing Luis stuff and telling him the name of everything under the hood, just like he did with me when I was younger. I got a little bent out of shape because I figured Luis was just acting interested to get my dad's attention.

[9]I was kind of mad at the world after that, so I went to my room to play video games. I'd been holed up there for a couple of hours when I thought I heard one of my friends coming up the driveway on a skateboard. When I looked outside, I realized it was Luis. He was on a cheesy little skateboard trying to do end-overs like he'd seen me doing. He was letting the nose go up too high so the turns weren't really working, but he wasn't giving up. He just kept on trying. I started to get the idea that maybe it wasn't Dad's attention he wanted after all.

[10]I was tired of playing video games, so I grabbed my board and an old one I don't use anymore. My old board is way better than the one Luis was riding. I went outside and handed Luis the old board and started doing end-overs up and down the driveway. At first he just stood by watching me, but I gave him some pointers and told him to try a couple. He started getting the hang of it right away.

[11]Luis is turning out to be an OK kid. I think he's got real potential as a skateboarder, but he's going to need a lot of lessons. I let him help me finish the repairs on my radio-controlled plane and told him he could come with Dad and me to fly it this weekend. Of course, Marisa is bugging me to come along, and Sara said she'd like to see it fly, too. I guess if Sara promises not to sing, that would be OK. Might as well let the whole . . . well, family . . . get in on the fun. As long as they don't expect me to hang out with them ALL the time!

LITERATURE AND LIFE

- *Why do we read stories?*
- *How is the setting important to a story?*
- *How can other people's stories affect our lives?*

from HOLES

by Louis Sachar

Stanley Yelnats is an overweight kid from a poor family. And he's being punished for a crime he didn't commit. The judge gave him an option: Either go to jail or go to Camp Green Lake. So Stanley chose Camp Green Lake. After a long, lonely ride on a bus with no air-conditioning, Stanley has arrived at camp. What he finds is nothing like what he expected.

¹**S**tanley felt somewhat **dazed** as the guard unlocked his handcuffs and led him off the bus. He'd been on the bus for over eight hours.

²"Be careful," the bus driver said as Stanley walked down the steps.

³Stanley wasn't sure if the bus driver meant for him to be careful going down the steps, or if he was telling him to be careful at Camp Green Lake. "Thanks for the ride," he said. His mouth was dry and his throat hurt. He stepped onto the hard, dry dirt. There was a band of sweat around his wrist where the handcuff had been.

⁴The land was barren and **desolate**. He could see a few rundown buildings and some tents. Farther away there was a cabin beneath two tall trees. Those two trees were the only plant life he could see. There weren't even weeds.

⁵The guard led Stanley to a small building. A sign on the front said, YOU ARE ENTERING CAMP GREEN LAKE JUVENILE CORRECTIONAL FACILITY. Next to it was another sign which declared that it was a violation of the Texas Penal Code to bring guns, explosives, weapons, drugs, or alcohol onto the **premises**.

⁶As Stanley read the sign he couldn't help but think, *Well, duh!*

⁷The guard led Stanley into the building, where he felt the welcome relief of air-conditioning.

⁸A man was sitting with his feet up on a desk. He turned his head when Stanley and the guard entered, but otherwise didn't move. Even though he was inside, he wore sunglasses and a cowboy hat. He also held a can of soda, and the sight of it made Stanley even more aware of his own thirst.

⁹He waited while the bus guard gave the man some papers to sign.

¹⁰"That's a lot of sunflower seeds," the bus guard said.

¹¹Stanley noticed a burlap sack filled with sunflower seeds on the floor next to the desk.

¹²"I quit smoking last month," said the man in the cowboy hat. He had a tattoo of a rattlesnake on his arm, and as he signed his name, the snake's rattle seemed to wiggle. "I used to smoke a pack a day. Now I eat a sack of these every week."

¹³The guard laughed.

¹⁴There must have been a small refrigerator behind his desk, because the man in the cowboy hat produced two more cans of soda. For a second Stanley hoped that one might be for him, but the man gave one to the guard and said the other was for the driver.

¹⁵"Nine hours here, and now nine hours back," the guard grumbled. "What a day."

¹⁶Stanley thought about the long, **miserable** bus ride and felt a little sorry for the guard and the bus driver.

¹⁷The man in the cowboy hat spit sunflower seed shells into a wastepaper basket. Then he walked around the desk to Stanley. "My name is Mr. Sir," he said. "Whenever you speak to me you must call me by my name, is that clear?"

¹⁸Stanley hesitated. "Uh, yes, Mr. Sir," he said, though he couldn't imagine that was really the man's name.

¹⁹"You're not in the Girl Scouts anymore," Mr. Sir said.

²⁰Stanley had to remove his clothes in front of Mr. Sir, who made sure

he wasn't hiding anything. He was then given two sets of clothes and a towel. Each set consisted of a long-sleeve orange jumpsuit, an orange T-shirt, and yellow socks. Stanley wasn't sure if the socks had been yellow originally.

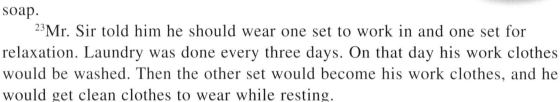

[21]He was also given white sneakers, an orange cap, and a canteen made of heavy plastic, which unfortunately was empty. The cap had a piece of cloth sewn on the back of it, for neck protection.

[22]Stanley got dressed. The clothes smelled like soap.

[23]Mr. Sir told him he should wear one set to work in and one set for relaxation. Laundry was done every three days. On that day his work clothes would be washed. Then the other set would become his work clothes, and he would get clean clothes to wear while resting.

[24]"You are going to dig one hole each day, including Saturdays and Sundays. Each hole must be five feet deep and five feet across in every direction. Your shovel is your measuring stick. Breakfast is served at 4:30."

[25]Stanley must have looked surprised, because Mr. Sir went on to explain that they started early to avoid the hottest part of the day. "No one is going to baby-sit you," he added. "The longer it takes you to dig, the longer you will be out in the sun. If you dig up anything interesting, you are to report it to me or any other counselor. When you finish, the rest of the day is yours."

[26]Stanley nodded to show he understood.

[27]"This isn't a Girl Scout camp," said Mr. Sir.

[28]He checked Stanley's backpack and allowed him to keep it. Then he led Stanley outside into the blazing heat.

[29]"Take a good look around you," Mr. Sir said. "What do you see?"

[30]Stanley looked out across the **vast** wasteland. The air seemed thick with heat and dirt. "Not much," he said, then hastily added, "Mr. Sir."

[31]Mr. Sir laughed. "You see any guard towers?"

[32]"No."

[33]"How about an electric fence?"

[34]"No, Mr. Sir."

[35]"There's no fence at all, is there?"

[36]"No, Mr. Sir."

[37] "You want to run away?" Mr. Sir asked him.

[38] Stanley looked back at him, unsure what he meant.

[39] "If you want to run away, go ahead, start running. I'm not going to stop you."

[40] Stanley didn't know what kind of game Mr. Sir was playing.

[41] "I see you're looking at my gun. Don't worry. I'm not going to shoot you." He tapped his holster. "This is for yellow-spotted lizards. I wouldn't waste a bullet on you."

[42] "I'm not going to run away," Stanley said.

[43] "Good thinking," said Mr. Sir. "Nobody runs away from here. We don't need a fence. Know why? Because we've got the only water for a hundred miles. You want to run away? You'll be buzzard food in three days."

[44] Stanley could see some kids dressed in orange and carrying shovels dragging themselves toward the tents.

[45] "You thirsty?" asked Mr. Sir.

[46] "Yes, Mr. Sir," Stanley said gratefully.

[47] "Well, you better get used to it. You're going to be thirsty for the next eighteen months."

Connect to the Author

Louis Sachar says that while he usually starts a book by thinking about the characters, he wrote *Holes* by thinking about the setting first. "The story began with the place, and the characters and plot grew out of it," says Sachar. "At the time I began the book, we had just returned from the relative coolness of a vacation in Maine to the Texas summer.

Louis Sachar

Anybody who has ever tried to do yard work in Texas in July can easily imagine Hell to be a place where you are required to dig a hole five feet deep and five feet across day after day under the brutal Texas sun." Into this searing landscape Sachar introduced Stanley Yelnats. "He's a kind of pathetic kid who feels like he has no friends, feels like his life is cursed. And I think everyone can identify with that in one way or another." Sachar was born in East Meadow, New York, in 1954. He now lives in Austin, Texas.

from

The Joy Luck Club

by Amy Tan

In 1937 a minor clash between Japan and China quickly grew into a full-scale war. To escape the bloody fighting, many Chinese people fled to Kweilin in southern China. Among them is the speaker in this excerpt, Jing-Mei Woo. Here, Jing-Mei explains why, despite the war, she started the Joy Luck Club. The four members of the club play an ancient Chinese board game called mah jong.

[1]"I thought up Joy Luck on a summer night that was so hot even the moths fainted to the ground, their wings were so heavy with the damp heat. Every place was so crowded there was no room for fresh air. **Unbearable** smells from the sewers rose up to my second-story window and the stink had nowhere else to go but into my nose. At all hours of the night and day, I heard screaming sounds. I didn't know if it was a peasant slitting the throat of a runaway pig or an officer beating a half-dead peasant for lying in his way on the sidewalk. I didn't go to the window to find out. What use would it have been? And that's when I thought I needed something to do to help me move.

[2]"My idea was to have a gathering of four women, one for each corner of my mah jong table. I knew which women I wanted to ask. They were all young like me, with wishful faces. One was an army officer's wife, like myself. Another was a girl with very fine manners from a rich

family in Shanghai. She had escaped with only a little money. And there was a girl from Nanking who had the blackest hair I have ever seen. She came from a low-class family, but she was pretty and pleasant and had married well, to an old man who died and left her with a better life.

3"Each week one of us would host a party to raise money and raise our spirits. The hostess had to serve special *dyansyin* foods to bring good fortune of all kinds—dumplings shaped like silver money ingots, long rice noodles for long life, boiled peanuts for conceiving sons, and of course, many good-luck oranges for a plentiful, sweet life.

4"What fine food we treated ourselves to with our **meager** allowances! We didn't notice that the dumplings were stuffed mostly with stringy squash and that the oranges were spotted with wormy holes. We ate sparingly, not as if we didn't have enough, but to protest how we could not eat another bite, we had already **bloated** ourselves from earlier in the day. We knew we had luxuries few people could afford. We were the lucky ones.

5"After filling our stomachs, we would then fill a bowl with money and put it where everyone could see. Then we would sit down at the mah jong table. My table was from my family and was of a very **fragrant** red wood, not what you call rosewood, but *hong mu*, which is so fine there's no English word for it. The table had a very thick pad, so that when the mah jong *pai* were spilled onto the table the only sound was of ivory tiles washing against one another.

6"Once we started to play, nobody could speak, except to say '*Pung!*' or '*Chr!*' when taking a tile. We had to play with seriousness and think of nothing else but adding to our happiness through winning. But

227

after sixteen rounds, we would again feast, this time to celebrate our good fortune. And then we would talk into the night until morning, saying stories about good times in the past and good times yet to come.

[7]"Oh, what good stories! Stories spilling out all over the place! We almost laughed to death. A rooster that ran into the house screeching on the top of dinner bowls, the same bowls that held him quietly in pieces the next day! And one about a girl who wrote love letters for two friends who loved the same man. And a silly foreign lady who fainted on a toilet when firecrackers went off next to her.

[8]"People thought we were wrong to serve banquets every week while many people in the city were starving, eating rats and, later, the garbage that the poorest rats used to feed on. Others thought

we were **possessed** by demons—to celebrate when even within our own families we had lost generations, had lost homes and fortunes, and were separated, husband from wife, brother from sister, daughter from mother. Hnnnh! How could we laugh, people asked.

[9]"It's not that we had no heart or eyes for pain. We were all afraid. We all had our **miseries**. But to despair was to wish back for something already lost. Or to prolong what was already unbearable. How much can you wish for a favorite warm coat that hangs in the closet of a house that burned down with your mother and father inside of it? How can you see in your mind arms and legs hanging from telephone wires

and starving dogs running down the streets with half-chewed hands dangling from their jaws? What was worse, we asked among ourselves, to sit and wait for our own deaths with proper **somber** faces? Or to choose our own happiness?

[10]So we decided to hold parties and pretend each week had become the new year. Each week we could forget past wrongs done to us. We weren't allowed to think a bad thought. We feasted, we laughed, we played games, lost and won, we told the best stories. And each week, we could hope to be lucky. That hope was our only joy. And that's how we came to call our little parties Joy Luck."

Connect to the Author

Amy Tan

Amy Tan's novels are inspired by her real life. They often explore the relationship between mothers and daughters who were raised in different countries, as she and her mother were. Tan, who was born in 1952 in California, never planned to become a writer. Her mother, who was born in China, wanted her daughter to be a neurosurgeon and concert pianist. Overworked, Tan turned to writing as a form of therapy. That strategy paid off in an unexpected way. Tan's very first novel, *The Joy Luck Club*, spent 9 months on the *New York Times* bestseller list. She has been a professional writer ever since.

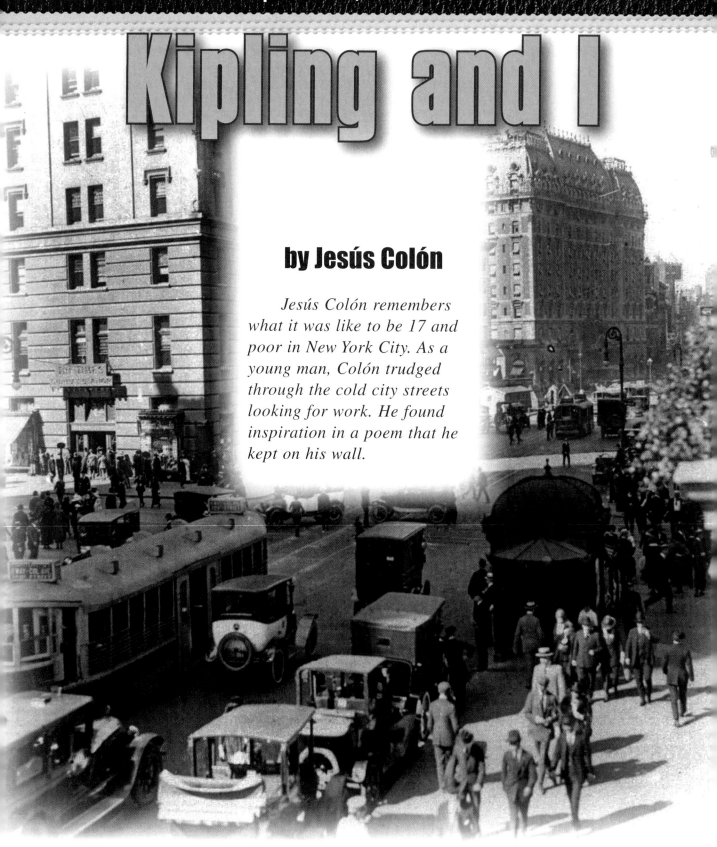

Kipling and I

by Jesús Colón

Jesús Colón remembers what it was like to be 17 and poor in New York City. As a young man, Colón trudged through the cold city streets looking for work. He found inspiration in a poem that he kept on his wall.

¹**S**ometimes I pass Debevoise Place at the corner of Willoughby Street . . . I look at the old wooden house, gray and ancient, the house where I used to live some forty years ago . . .

²My room was on the second floor at the corner. On hot summer nights I would sit at the window reading by the electric light from the street lamp which was almost at a level with the windowsill.

³It was nice to come home late during the winter, look for some scrap of old newspaper, some bits of wood and a few chunks of coal, and start a sparkling fire in the chunky fourlegged coal stove. I would be rewarded with an intimate warmth as little by little the pigmy stove became alive puffing out its sides, hot and red, like the crimson cheeks of a Santa Claus.

⁴My few books were in a soap box nailed to the wall. But my most prized possession in those days was a poem I had bought in a five-and-ten-cent store on Fulton Street. (I wonder what has become of these poems, maxims and sayings of wise men that they used to sell at the five-and-ten-cent stores?) The poem was printed on gold paper and mounted in a gilded frame ready to be hung in a **conspicuous** place in the house. I bought one of those fancy silken picture cords finishing in a rosette to match the color of the frame.

⁵I was seventeen. This poem to me then seemed to summarize, in one poetical nutshell, the wisdom of all the sages that ever lived. It was what I was looking for, something to guide myself by, a way of life, a compendium of the wise, the true and the beautiful. All I had to do was to live according to the counsel of the poem and follow its instructions and I would be a perfect man—the useful, the good, the true human being. I was very happy that day, forty years ago.

⁶The poem had to have the most **prominent** place in the room. Where could I hang it? I decided that the best place for the poem was on the wall right by the entrance to the room. No one coming in and out would miss it. Perhaps someone would be interested enough to read it and drink the profound waters of its message . . .

maxims: short sayings that express a truth

compendium: collection

counsel: advice

[7]Every morning as I prepared to leave, I stood in front of the poem and read it over and over again, sometimes half a dozen times. I let the sonorous music of the verse carry me away. I brought with me a handwritten copy as I stepped out every morning looking for work, repeating verses and stanzas from memory until the whole poem came to be part of me. Other days my lips kept repeating a single verse of the poem at intervals throughout the day.

intervals: times between one event and another

[8]In the subways I loved to compete with the shrill noises of the many wheels below by chanting the lines of the poem. People stared at me moving my lips as though I were in a trance. I looked back with pity. They were not so fortunate as I who had as a guide to direct my life a great poem to make me wise, useful and happy.

[9]And I chanted:

If you can keep your head when all about you
Are losing theirs and blaming it on you . . .

If you can wait and not be tired by waiting,
*   Or being lied about, don't deal in lies,*
Or being hated don't give way to hating . . .

If you can make one heap of all your winnings
*   And risk it on one turn of pitch-and-toss,*
And lose, and start again at your beginnings . . .

[10]"If —," by Kipling, was the poem. At seventeen, my evening prayer and my first morning thought. I repeated it every day with the resolution to live up to the very last line of that poem.

[11]I would visit the government employment office on Jay Street. The conversations among the Puerto Ricans on the large wooden benches in the employment office were always on the same subject. How to find a decent place to live. How they would not rent to Negroes or Puerto Ricans. How Negroes and Puerto Ricans were given the pink slips first at work.

[12]From the employment office I would call door to door at the piers, factories and storage houses in the streets under the

Brooklyn and Manhattan bridges. "Sorry, nothing today."
It seemed to me that that "today" was a continuation and
combination of all the yesterdays, todays and tomorrows.

¹³From the factories I would go to the restaurants, looking
for a job as a porter or dishwasher. At least I would eat and be
warm in a kitchen.

¹⁴"Sorry" . . . "Sorry" . . .

¹⁵Sometimes I was hired at ten dollars a week, ten hours
a day including Sundays and holidays. One day off during
the week. My work was that of three men: dishwasher, porter,
busboy. And to clear the sidewalk of snow and slush "when
you have nothing else to do." I was to be appropriately humble
and grateful not only to the owner but to everybody else in the
place.

¹⁶If I rebelled at insults or at a pointed innuendo or just the
inhuman amount of work, I was unceremoniously thrown out
and told to come "next week for your pay." "Next week" meant
weeks of calling for the **paltry** dollars owed me. The owners
relished this "next week."

¹⁷I clung to my poem as to a faith. Like a **potent** amulet, my
precious poem was clenched in the fist of my right hand inside
my secondhand overcoat. Again and again I declaimed aloud
a few precious lines when discouragement and disillusionment
threatened to overwhelm me.

> *If you can force your heart and nerve and sinew*
> *To serve your turn long after they are gone . . .*

¹⁸The weeks of unemployment and hard knocks turned into
months. I continued to find two or three days of work here and
there. And I continued to be thrown out when I rebelled at the
ill treatment, overwork and insults. I kept pounding the streets
looking for a place where they would treat me half decently,
where my devotion to work and faith in Kipling's poem would
be appreciated. I remember the worn-out shoes I bought in a
secondhand store on Myrtle Avenue at the corner of Adams

innuendo: a hint with an undertone of rudeness

amulet: item that protects against evil

declaimed: read or repeated from memory

Street. The round holes in the soles that I tried to cover with pieces of carton were no match for the frigid knives of the unrelenting snow.

[19]One night I returned late after a long day of looking for work. I was hungry. My room was dark and cold. I wanted to warm my numb body. I lit a match and began looking for some scraps of wood and a piece of paper to start a fire. I searched all over the floor. No wood, no paper. As I stood up, the glimmering flicker of the dying match was reflected in the glass surface of the framed poem. I unhooked the poem from the wall. I reflected for a minute, a minute that felt like an eternity. I took the frame apart, placing the square glass upon the small table. I tore the gold paper on which the poem was printed, threw its pieces inside the stove and, placing the small bits of wood from the frame on top of the paper, I lit it, adding soft and hard coal as the fire began to gain strength and brightness.

[20]I watched how the lines of the poem withered into ashes inside the small stove.

Connect to the Author

Jesús Colón arrived in New York City in 1918, when he was 17 years old. To get there, he had hidden on a boat leaving from his home country of Puerto Rico. Colón, who was of African descent, spoke only Spanish. He worked low-paying jobs to support himself. Meanwhile, he wrote articles for Puerto Rican newspapers. He soon became well known and respected in both New York and Puerto Rico

Jesús Colón

for his journalism. His 1961 book *A Puerto Rican in New York*, from which this story is taken, was one of the first works of Latino literature to talk about the experience of immigrants in this country. Colón died in 1974.

If —

Following is the poem about which Jesús Colón wrote in "Kipling and I." In the poem, Rudyard Kipling offers his definition of what it means to be an honorable man.

by Rudyard Kipling

²¹If you can keep your head when all about you
Are losing theirs and blaming it on you;
If you can trust yourself when all men doubt you,
But make allowance for their doubting too;
If you can wait and not be tired by waiting,
Or, being lied about, don't deal in lies,
Or, being hated, don't give way to hating,
And yet don't look too good, nor talk too wise;

²²If you can dream—and not make dreams your master;
If you can think—and not make thoughts your aim;
If you can meet with triumph and disaster
And treat those two imposters just the same;
If you can bear to hear the truth you've spoken
Twisted by knaves to make a trap for fools,
Or watch the things you gave your life to broken,
And stoop and build 'em up with wornout tools;

imposter: one who pretends to be someone else

knaves: dishonest men

235

[23]If you can make one heap of all your winnings
And risk it on one turn of pitch-and-toss,
And lose, and start again at your beginnings
And never breathe a word about your loss;
If you can force your heart and nerve and sinew
To serve your turn long after they are gone,
And so hold on when there is nothing in you
Except the Will which says to them: "Hold on";

[24]If you can talk with crowds and keep your virtue,
Or walk with kings—nor lose the common touch;
If neither foes nor loving friends can hurt you;
If all men count with you, but none too much;
If you can fill the unforgiving minute
With sixty seconds' worth of distance run—
Yours is the Earth and everything that's in it,
And—which is more—you'll be a Man my son!

sinew: tissue that connects bone to muscle

Connect to the Author

Between 1890 and 1920, Rudyard Kipling was the most popular writer in the English-speaking world. Kipling was born in India in 1865. His parents were English. When Kipling was six, his parents sent him and his sister to live with strangers in England. His parents wanted to keep him away from the illness that had killed his newborn brother. They also wanted him to get an English education. But Kipling's caretaker beat him, and he was often miserable. He returned to India when he was about 17 and began his writing career. He later traveled back to England and then to America. In his lifetime, Kipling published hundreds of short stories and poems. He is especially well known for his children's stories. He wrote *The Jungle Book* and *The Second Jungle Book*, stories of a boy named Mowgli who was raised by wolves, while he lived in the United States. The stories remain popular to this day. Kipling died in 1936.

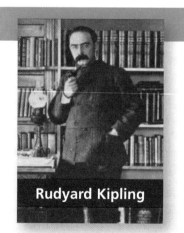
Rudyard Kipling

adapted from

THE CALL OF THE WILD

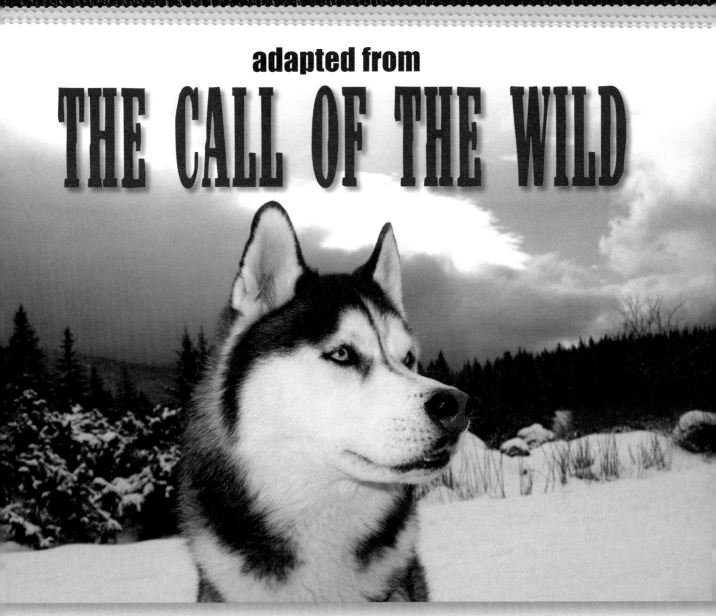

by Jack London

Buck is a cross between a Saint Bernard and a Scottish shepherd dog. He has lived the first four years of his life in the sun-kissed Santa Clara Valley of California. One day he is stolen and sold to a man who takes him to Alaska. Gold has been discovered there, and prospectors need dogs to pull sleds across the frozen tundra. In Alaska, Buck becomes a member of a dogsled team owned by Perrault and François. The team is led by Spitz, a fierce husky, and includes Dolly, Pike, and several other dogs.

¹**T**he wild beast was strong in Buck. During his terrible life on the trail, the beast grew and grew. But it was a secret growth. Buck avoided fights whenever possible. Spitz, on the other hand, sensed that Buck was a challenge to his leadership. He went out of his way to bully Buck, hoping to start a fight that could end only in the death of one or the other.

²One morning, as Perrault and François were harnessing the dogs, Dolly suddenly went mad. She let out a long wolf howl and lunged at Buck. He fled in panic with Dolly panting and frothing one leap behind him. Buck plunged into the woods and crossed the icy river with Dolly snarling at his heels. François called to him and Buck doubled back, gasping painfully for air. François held an axe. As Buck shot past him the axe crashed down on mad Dolly's head.

³Buck staggered over against the sled, exhausted, sobbing for breath. Spitz realized that this was no time for **restraint**. He sprang at Buck and sank his teeth into his helpless foe, ripping and tearing the flesh. Again, François came to his rescue, driving Spitz away with a whip.

⁴"Spitz is one devil," Perrault said. "He's going to kill Buck."

⁵"That Buck is two devils," François said. "Someday he'll chew Spitz up and spit him out on the snow."

⁶From then on, Spitz and Buck were at war. They were destined to fight it out for leadership of the pack. Buck wanted it. He wanted it because it was his nature. He wanted it because of the wild beast inside him.

⁷Buck began to openly challenge Spitz's leadership. One morning, after a heavy snowfall, Pike hid from François. Spitz, wild with anger, searched the camp. When he at last found Pike, Spitz flew at him to punish him for hiding. Buck flew with equal rage at Spitz and knocked him off his feet. Pike, who had been trembling with fear, took heart at this challenge and leaped on Spitz. François broke up the fight with his whip. Buck kept challenging Spitz, but he was careful to only confront Spitz when François was not around. The other dogs began to disobey Spitz, and there was constant fighting. Trouble was brewing, and at the bottom of it was Buck.

⁸One dreary afternoon the sled team pulled into the town of Dawson. The streets were filled with men and dogs hard at work. All day, sled teams pulled loads up and down the main street. At night, with the stars leaping in the frigid sky and the land numb and frozen under the snow, the dogs howled an eerie song of pain as old as their breed. Their wolf song stirred the wild beast in Buck, and he eagerly joined their howling. With each howl, Buck

moved further away from the warmth and comfort of his life in California and deeper into the wild beginnings of his breed.

⁹After resting in Dawson for a week, Buck and his sled team set out again, but the trip was troubled. The revolt led by Buck had destroyed the team's **discipline**. The dogs no longer feared Spitz, and challenged him at every opportunity. Many nights, the camp was a howling madhouse. François swore and stamped the snow in anger and beat the dogs with his whip, but it was no use. As soon as he turned his back, they were at it again.

¹⁰One night after supper, one of the dogs spotted a rabbit. In a second, the whole team was tearing across the barren **landscape** in full pursuit. The heat of the chase stirred the wild beast in Buck, and he whined eagerly as he bounded through the pale moonlight after the rabbit. He ran with but one thought, to kill the rabbit with his own teeth. Buck felt the beast surging inside him and howled the old wolf-cry.

¹¹There is an **infinite** joy that comes when one is living completely in the moment, with no thought for the past or the future. It comes to the artist caught up in fever of work and to the war-mad soldier fighting without mercy. It came to Buck, leading the pack, sounding the old wolf-cry, straining after the food that was alive and fleeing before him through the moonlight. He was seized by a surge of life, by the perfect joy of every muscle, of every joint, of everything that was not death.

¹²Spitz, cold and calculating even in sheer joy of the chase, saw his chance. He split off from the pack and took a shortcut. Buck did not know this, and as he rounded a bend he saw Spitz leap from a high bank into the path of the rabbit. The rabbit had nowhere to turn. As Spitz's white teeth broke its back, the rabbit shrieked as loudly as a man. At this sound—the cry of Life plunging down into the grip of Death—the pack at Buck's heels howled in wild, irrational delight.

¹³Buck did not howl. Instead, he threw himself at Spitz, shoulder to shoulder, so hard that he missed the throat. They rolled over and over in the powdery snow. Spitz scrambled to his feet, slashing Buck down the shoulder and leaping clear. Spitz snapped his teeth together twice, like the steel jaws of a trap, as he backed away for better footing. His lean lips curled back, baring his teeth.

¹⁴In a flash Buck knew it. The time had come. This was a fight to the death. The dogs circled each other, snarling, ears laid back. A ghostly calm came over the whiteness. The rest of the pack had made short work of the

rabbit, and now they circled Buck and Spitz, watching silently with gleaming eyes. Their visible breath rose slowly in the frosty air.

[15]Buck sprang forward, **endeavoring** to sink his teeth into Spitz's neck. Fang clashed against fang, and lips were cut and bleeding. Time and time again Buck lunged for the snow-white throat. Each time Spitz slashed him and leaped lightly away. Spitz was untouched, while Buck was streaming with blood and panting hard. The fight was growing desperate. And all the while the silent, wolfish circle waited to finish off whichever dog went down. With Buck winded, Spitz rushed him and knocked him off balance. Buck almost went down, and the circle of dogs started to close in. But Buck recovered in midair and landed on his feet. The dogs pulled back and waited.

[16]Buck possessed a quality that made for greatness—imagination. He fought by instinct, but he could use his head as well. Buck lunged for Spitz's throat, but at the last instant he dropped to the snow and clamped his teeth into Spitz's left foreleg. There was a crunch of breaking bone, and Spitz howled in agony. Three times Buck tried to knock Spitz over, then he repeated his trick and broke the right foreleg. Despite the pain and helplessness, Spitz struggled madly to keep up. The pack **detected** his fear. Spitz watched the silent circle closing in on him as he had watched similar circles close in on beaten dogs in the past. Only this time Spitz knew he was the one who was beaten.

Connect to the Author

Jack London was born in 1876 in San Francisco, California. He was an adventurer by nature. As a young man, London sailed to Japan and traveled widely throughout the United States. Then in 1897 he headed to Alaska in search of gold, but he got there too late. Most of the gold was gone, and London returned to San Francisco poorer than when he left. Though London didn't find gold in Alaska, he turned his adventures into gold. London's books and novels based on his experiences made him the highest paid writer in the United States. Among London's 50 novels are *White Fang* and *The Call of the Wild.*

Jack London

A Death in the Family

¹**C**atfish was a heavy sleeper. Somebody had to shake him awake every morning, and that morning it was my job. I shook him, hollered at him, kicked him playfully, but he wouldn't move. When I yanked his filthy woolen Army blanket off of him, I realized that Catfish wasn't ever going to wake up again. He lay face down, blood flowing from an ugly red gash on his temple.

²"Please," I thought, "let this be another nightmare." I had slept fitfully all night, scared awake by one bad dream after another. We usually slept outside, but Preacher knew about this abandoned farmhouse not far from where we had jumped off of the boxcar. It was already sprinkling, so a roof

over our heads seemed like a good idea. When we rounded a bend and I saw the house, though, I remember thinking that I might rather sleep in the rain. The whole place was overgrown with weeds, and the house looked like it might fall down any minute. The windows were shattered, the roof sagged dangerously, and the door hung on one hinge. When we walked in, I swear I saw a half dozen rats scurry for cover. The place smelled like death, and as it turns out, death was indeed spending the night there.

[3]I guess I should back up and tell you a bit about myself. My name is Jacob, and my folks were wheat farmers. Things started getting hard for us in 1931. Millions of people had lost their jobs, and wheat prices fell so low that we couldn't make our loan payments on the farm. The bank kicked us off our land and sent a bulldozer over to knock our house down. I can still see Pa's eyes filled with fear and guilt as he watched. We lived in our truck for a while, driving around and looking for work. But there wasn't much work to be had, and I figured Ma and Pa had their hands full feeding my little brothers and sisters. One morning I got up early, packed a few things, and started walking. I've been on the road ever since.

[4]The roads were filled with people in the same situation as me. We'd sneak rides on boxcars, traveling from town to town, looking for a day's work or maybe a bite to eat. We weren't welcome in most places, so we had to keep moving. The nicest thing people called us was "hobos," but most just called us "beggars" or "thieves."

[5]I joined up with Catfish and his group about three months ago. We took care of each other, sharing whatever food we came across. It was the closest thing to a family I'd had since I left Ma and Pa. Besides me and Catfish, there was Martino, Nick, Joe, and Preacher. That morning in that death-smelling shack, my first thought was that Martino had done it. Martino had a short fuse, and just a couple of days earlier, he and Catfish had gotten into a screaming argument over something Catfish had said. But it wasn't like Martino to sneak up on a sleeping man in the middle of the night. Martino

always fought people face to face, fair and square. Besides, as the guys gathered around Catfish's lifeless body, Martino looked as shocked as I did.

[6]"We should get the cops," I said.

[7]"No," Nick said softly.

[8]"He's right," Martino said. "Cops don't care nothin' about hobos, livin' or dead."

[9]Joe nodded and said, "We get the cops in on this, we'll all end up in jail."

[10]"Are you guys crazy?" I said. "One of us standing here is a cold-blooded killer. We can't just pretend nothing happened." I looked over at Preacher. He was the oldest and had been on the road the longest. He was as close as we had to a leader. "You know I'm right, don't you?" I said.

[11]"Yeah, kid, you're right, but so are the other guys," Preacher said. "We'll have to handle this ourselves. Grab some of them cans off that trash pile and let's go dig Catfish a grave."

[12]We found a nice place near some trees and started digging. The ground was pretty sandy, but digging a grave with nothing but tin cans still took most of the morning. We took turns digging and telling stories about Catfish. Nick, who had been with us only a week, seemed to be taking Catfish's death harder than the rest of us. You never know how people are going to react to a tragedy.

[13]When we finished digging, Preacher spread Catfish's blanket in the grave. We went back inside and split up Catfish's meager belongings, seeing as how he didn't have any use for them anymore. Martino got his shoes, Joe got his jacket, Nick got his knife, and I got his pocket watch with a jumping, twisting catfish carved into the hinged lid. It didn't work, of course, but it reminded me of Catfish, so I was glad to have it.

[14]Me and Preacher carried Catfish out and laid him in his grave. That's when I remembered the locket. Catfish had this heart-shaped locket that he always wore on a chain around his neck. Inside the locket was a picture of

his girlfriend, Tess, whom he hadn't seen since he and his family had been forced off their farm in Alabama. I had never seen Catfish take that locket off, but now it was nowhere to be seen.

[15]"Where's his locket?" I said. "We can't bury him without his locket."

[16]"Must have fell off when we was carrying him out," Preacher said.

[17]Everyone started looking around on the ground. Everyone, that is, except Nick. He just stood there, looking at his clinched fist and shaking his head slowly. His eyes looked just like Pa's the day our house was bulldozed. Nick opened his fist and a chain started slithering out. Then the locket fell to the ground.

[18]"Tess was my girl," Nick said. "I knew her back in Kentucky, long before she ever moved to Alabama. I'd stayed behind to make some money for us to get married, but when I caught up with her, she told me she had a new boy. That's when I hit the road. I never asked who her new boy was. I didn't think I cared. Then yesterday, Catfish showed me his locket."

[19]Nick fell to his knees, picked up the locket, and laid it on Catfish's chest.

[20]"I'm sorry, Catfish," he sobbed. "I'm so sorry."

[21]Nobody said anything. What was there to say? We all knelt around Catfish's grave and said a silent prayer. Then we pushed the sandy dirt over him. When we were done, Preacher put his hand on Nick's heaving shoulder.

[22]"Come on, Nick," he said. "We'd better get moving."

IMAGINE THE POSSIBILITIES

- *How can the work you do make a difference in the world?*
- *What barriers do people overcome to reach their dreams?*
- *What dreams do you have for your life's work?*

Dolores Huerta:
STRIKING FOR JUSTICE

United Farm Workers President Arturo Rodriguez, left, and union co-founder Dolores Huerta lead a march to the Capitol in Sacramento, California, in 2002.

[1]Dolores Fernandez Huerta is a living legend.

[2]She's been lionized in songs. She's been memorialized in paintings. She's been arrested more than 20 times and has been beaten almost to death by police. She was one of the most influential labor leaders of the 20th century. And she continues to work for justice in the 21st. Huerta has dedicated her life to the struggle for justice, dignity, and decent working conditions for the men, women, and children who pick the food we eat every day.

[3]Huerta was born in 1930, in the middle of the Great Depression, in a small mining town in northern New Mexico. After her parents divorced, her mother moved Dolores and her two brothers to California. Huerta's mother worked two jobs—literally day and night—to support her children.

⁴After high school, Huerta got her teaching certificate. But she wasn't satisfied teaching. "I realized one day that as a teacher I couldn't do anything for the kids who came to school barefoot and hungry," she says. After only a few months in the classroom, Huerta decided she should fight poverty more directly. She helped found a group to fight for the rights of Mexican Americans.

⁵As she became more active in social and labor organizations, her marriage **faltered**. "I knew I wasn't comfortable in a wife's role, but I wasn't clearly facing the issue. I hedged, I made excuses. I didn't come out and tell my husband that I cared more about helping other people than cleaning our house and doing my hair," she says.

⁶It was during her work for social justice that Huerta met Cesar Chavez. Chavez had worked in the California fields picking fruits and vegetables. He knew firsthand how hard it was to stoop over all day, gathering produce in the broiling sun, for just a few dollars. Though farm workers were crucial to the economy, they were treated terribly. They worked with no protection against the dangerous pesticides sprayed on the food they picked. Earning so little money, they were forced to live in shacks with no running water or electricity. Growers sometimes cheated them out of their wages. The farm workers were powerless to fight back.

⁷Huerta teamed up with Cesar Chavez in the early 1960s. "I think we really built on each other's strengths a lot," Huerta says. They worked together to form the National Farm Workers Association (later called the United Farm Workers). As second in command, Huerta led workers on strikes against growers. She organized a **boycott** too. In the boycott, she urged consumers not to buy grapes from growers who would not bargain with workers or protect them. Her efforts led directly to laws that allowed workers to bargain with growers.

⁸Huerta comments, "I think we brought to the world, the United States anyway, the whole idea of boycotting as a nonviolent tactic. I think we showed the world that nonviolence can work to make social change. . . . I think we have laid a pattern of how farm workers are eventually going to get out of their bondage. It may not happen right now in our foreseeable future, but the pattern is there and farm workers are going to make it."

⁹Though she is committed to changing the system with peaceful means, she herself has been the target of brutality. During a protest in 1988, baton-

wielding police beat her so severely she was rushed to the emergency room. The beating was captured on tape. The tape shows the officer hitting the small, 58-year-old woman with his baton again and again, though she was not threatening him. The officer broke her ribs and ruptured her spleen. Later, she reached a settlement with the police department. In addition to giving her money, they agreed to change their policy about how to control crowds during marches.

[10]Throughout her career, Huerta has worked long hours. Traveling often, she has had to spend much time away from her 11 children. Reflecting on the sacrifices her children have made for her political work, Huerta says, "I guess the political and the work has always come first with me and then I just tried to catch up on the other because I often felt that for every unmade bed and for every unwashed dish some farm worker got one dollar more in wages somewhere."

[11]In fact, Huerta believes that mothers have responsibilities to their children that go beyond cooking dinner and making the bed. In a 2005 editorial, Huerta urged mothers—and their children—to get involved in politics:

> The situation today for children and mothers in America is urgent.
>
> Asthma and autism rates in some places are up 400%; one of every six American moms has unsafe levels of mercury in their bodies; 200 species become extinct every day; our water, food and air are becoming more toxic instead of less for the first time since 1968; and more children fall into poverty and homelessness each year than ever since the Great Depression.
>
> Our children's future is bleak unless far more of us act now. Now more than ever is the time to get involved—and get our children involved with us.

[12]At age 75, Dolores Huerta continues her work. "We mothers have to help make the world safer not only for our children, but for other people's children too. Because if all children are not safe, no child is safe."

from A MIGRANT FAMILY

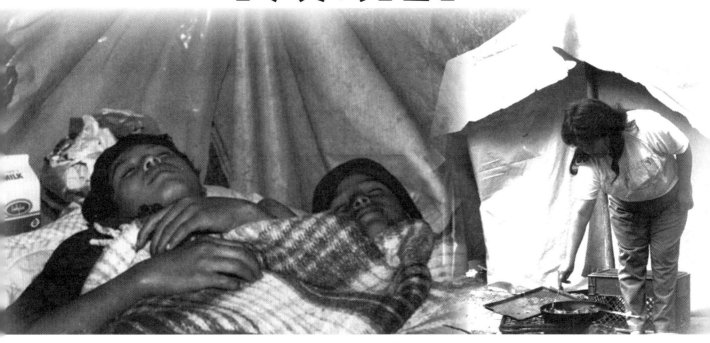

by Larry Dane Brimner

Twelve-year-old Juan Medina and his family live in a camp along a highway in Southern California. They share the camp with 300 other migrant workers. The houses in the camp are, at best, shacks, built with whatever plastic and plywood can be found. Sometimes the shelters are no more than plastic sheets draped over shrubs. The houses have dirt floors, no running water, and no electricity.

[13]**A**s darkness bleeds from the sky, Juan shivers at the 6:00 A.M. chill. The 12-year-old tugs at the blanket, wishing for a little more warmth and a few extra minutes of sleep. But it's no use. The blanket he shares with his brothers, eight-year-old Alejandro and four-year-old Martin, is just as quickly snatched back, so Juan stretches and gives in to another day.

¹⁴Juan Medina is used to getting up with the sun. "Es el reloj de alarma," he explains in Spanish. Then in English he interprets: "Alarm clock." He nods toward a **sliver** of sun peeking above the California hillside and buries his bare hands in his pockets.

¹⁵Juan is a **migrant**. He was born in Mexico, but he has lived in Indiana, Illinois, and Iowa, where his stepfather, Joel Ruiz, has worked on farms. For the last three years, however, Juan and his family have been in California. During the winter and spring, they stay in the coastal community of Encinitas, near San Diego. Juan's stepfather works as a day laborer—someone hired for one day's work at a time—in construction, harvesting flowers, or doing odd jobs. But when it's time to pick melons, tomatoes, and other crops, the family heads north to Fresno, a city in California's great Central Valley.

¹⁶Just as migratory birds fly north or south depending on the season and the weather, migrant farm workers have their own patterns of migration. For these people, it is the promise of earning minimum wages that keeps them on the move. Workers and their families **trek** to *el norte* (the north) as the days grow warmer and the crops reach their peak. There is food to be pulled from the ground or plucked from the trees and vines, and migrant farm workers provide the muscle to do the pulling and the plucking. When a job is done, they move on to the next crop and the next harvest in an annual cycle.

Connect to the Author

Award-winning writer Larry Dane Brimner is the author of more than 120 books for young readers. Born in Florida in 1949, Brimner spent his early years in Alaska. There, without television to keep him entertained, Brimner developed his love of reading and telling stories. In addition to being a writer, Brimner has worked as a waiter, ditch-digger, clothing model, teacher, interior designer, and house builder.

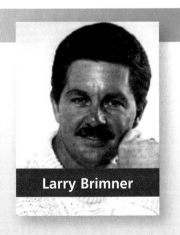

Larry Brimner

from Gig: Americans Talk About Their Jobs

To create the book Gig, *interviewers sat down with several dozen Americans and asked them about their jobs. They taped the interviews, transcribed them, and then cut them down to create personal essays. In this essay, Kysha Lewin describes her job at McDonald's.*

McDonald's Crew Member Kysha Lewin

[1]I'm 16 and a half. I go to Red Bank Regional High School in Little Silver, New Jersey. I'm in tenth grade. Last year I decided I needed a job because it's like only my mom, you know? She's trying to take care of the bills, and it's hard for her. So I don't get allowance, and I'm still a child, I want to have fun, to go out, not just sit on the porch crying. So when I turned fifteen, I decided that I wanted to work. I heard that McDonald's would hire you at fifteen and I came and talked to the managers.

[2]They asked what kind of things you do—do you communicate with people well? Are you good at talking to them, understanding what they're saying? You know? They asked me do I like kids because they wanted me to do birthday parties for little kids. I'm like the hostess sometimes. And I love kids. And I guess they liked me, because they hired me.

[3]It was kind of difficult at first. I had to get to know the register, to listen and concentrate on what the person's ordering and then find the buttons on the board—it took me like two days or so to really get to understand it. But everybody was very relaxed, kinda like, "It's just gonna take you some time to get used to it." They were very patient with me, even the customers were patient. And now it's a breeze. I just pick up stuff easily. I'm a good listener, a person that loves to follow directions.

[4]The only real thing with this job is you have to make sure you're always busy. Because McDonald's is always busy. Make sure everything is stocked, cleaned—if you don't have a customer to serve, maybe somebody else has a customer, try to help them out, back them up, get the food, you know? Look at the screen on their register and see what food they don't already have. Go get it. Work together.

[5]They have a lot of rules, but it's not like rule crazy. . . . It's really pretty straightforward, like with the balloon situation—we just always have to make sure there's balloons in the lobby 'cause, you know, we want to make the kids happy. And we have to sweep and mop every hour. And we have this thing, it's like a timer, and when it goes off, everybody in the place has to go and **sanitize** their hands. There's like a liquid that you rub on that dries off real quick. You have to make sure you go do that or you get in trouble.

[6]The other rules are basically you have to be on time, you have to stock, clean up, help out. They also have a rule for fries. You have to be sixteen to make fries. If you're fifteen you can only stuff 'em, you can't pick 'em up outta the fryer. I think it's a dumb rule—I mean, what are we supposed to do if it gets busy and there's nobody at the fries but you and you're fifteen? Sit and wait? Then the customer gets mad. Dumb rule, but whatever. Now I'm sixteen, so I make fries sometimes. I just started doing that. . . .

[7]Some of the customers can be friendly, some can just have an attitude, and some try to make you a fool. I've seen it many a time. Like, for instance, I was working the drive-through and the guy said he was missing his fries, right? So I gave him a fry. He came back into McDonald's and told the manager that he was missing his fries. He was trying to just get another fry for free. I went and told the manager. I don't know why they think they can get over like that. These people are crazy. They say the customer is always right, but personally, me, I don't let 'em get away with that. It makes me mad. I mean, it's costing the boss money and if he loses money then we lose money because we lose our hours and I can't have that.

[8]I work about twenty hours a week, after school and weekends. When I turned sixteen they wanted me to take more hours but my mom didn't want me to mess up my school. So I just stayed around twenty. With schoolwork, I guess it's a lot. But I got God in my life, I have a lot of faith, I'm not tired. I'm young and have a lot of energy.

[9]I make five-fifteen an hour and I give my mother about half of my check because it helps. I mean, I live with my eleven-year-old brother, my four-year-old sister, and my eight-month-old baby sister and we get along real well, but my mother works hard. I see how hard. . . .

[10]I got a lot of friends here. They're real cool to talk to, chill with, go out with. There's turnover—some people aren't used to working and they get lazy or they don't come to work and get fired, or if they don't obey the rules they have to go—but still, the majority of my friends work here. And cute boys come through the drive-through and flirt. Like you catch their eye or whatever and they ask you for your phone number. [Laughs] I don't ever give out my number. I ask them for theirs, and I decide if I want to call them or not. I'm not giving my number 'cause eehhhhh, you know, some people

like to play on the phone and some boys are just disgusting. But it's nice sometimes. It makes me happy.

[11]I know work won't be fun my whole life. 'Cause work is not always about fun and games. There comes a time when you have to be serious about what you're doing, you know? . . .

[12]But I'll always be grateful to McDonald's, you know? The majority of people I know first started here or some other kind of fast-food place before they got to a good job, a better job. I'd like to do something with hair or maybe clothes. Or I want to get a job working in the hospital—in the nursery with the little babies. I love little kids. I can't wait till I get older so I can have kids. I adore my sisters and my brothers, spoil them. So I'd like the hospital. But whatever happens, a year from now, I'm gonna have a better job. I have a lot of confidence in myself. There's nothing I can't do. I'm fine.

Connect to the Author

About 40 interviewers contributed to *Gig*. One of the interviewers was John Bowe, who also is an editor of the book. Bowe traveled around the country talking to a wide variety of people, including a carnival worker in Appalachia, a supermodel between flights at an airport, and truck drivers at a truck stop in Wyoming. The editors of the book wanted Americans to speak for themselves. "Our goal was to take accurate snapshots, person by person, of work as it is today in this country," writes Marisa Bowe, John's sister, another of the book's editors. "We were very moved by the wholehearted diligence that people bring to their work."

from

Keeping the Moon

by Sarah Dessen

Fifteen-year-old Colie Sparks is a loner. When her glamorous, outgoing mother leaves for Europe, Colie is forced to spend the summer with her oddball aunt Mira in the seaside town of Colby, South Carolina. There, Colie finds a job at the Last Chance Café. Her coworkers, Morgan and Isabel, teach her the ropes.

[13]**"M**ayonnaise," Morgan said, "is a lot like men."

[14]It was nine-thirty in the morning on my first day of work, but I'd been up since six. I kept thinking Morgan would forget me or change her mind but at nine-fifteen she pulled up in front of Mira's steps and beeped her horn, just as we'd planned.

[15]The restaurant was empty except for us and the radio, tuned to an oldies station. "Twisting the Night Away" was playing, and we were making salad dressing, both of us up to our elbows in thick, smelly mayonnaise.

[16]"It can," she went on, plopping another scoop into the bowl, "make everything much better, adding flavor and ease to your life. Or, it can just be sticky and gross and make you nauseous."

[17]I smiled, stirring my mayonnaise while I considered this. "I hate mayonnaise."

[18]"You'll probably hate men too, from time to time," she said. "At least mayonnaise you can avoid."

[19]This was the way Morgan taught. Not in instructions, but pronouncements. Everything was a lesson.

[20]"Lettuce," she announced later, pulling a head out of the plastic bag in front of us, "should be leafy, not slimy. And no black or brown edges. We use lettuce on everything: garnish, salads, burgers. A bad piece of lettuce can ruin your whole day."

[21]"Right," I said.

[22]"Chop it like this," she instructed, taking a few whacks with a knife before handing it to me. "Big chops, but not too big."

[23]I chopped. She watched. "Good," she said, reaching over to adjust my chops just a bit. I went on. "Very good."

[24]Morgan was this meticulous about everything. Preparing dressings was a **ritual**, every measurement carefully checked. Isabel, on the other hand, dumped it all in at once, knocked a spoon around, and came up with the same results, dipping in a finger and licking it to double-check.

[25]But Morgan had her own way.

[26]"Peel carrots away from you," she said, demonstrating, "and cut off the ends about a quarter inch each. When feeding them into the processor, pause about every five seconds. It gives a finer shred."

[27]I peeled, chopped, and stocked. I learned the perfect, **symmetrical** way to stack coffee cups and sugar packets, to fold rags at a right angle against flat surfaces, clean side up. Morgan kept the counter area spick-and-span, each element in its place. When she was nervous, she went around correcting things.

[28]"Take-out boxes on the *left*, cup lids on the *right*," she'd shout, slamming them around as she restored order to her universe. "And spoons are handle side *up,* Isabel."

[29]"Yeah, yeah," Isabel would say. When she was mad or just bored she purposely rearranged things just to see how long it took Morgan to find them. It was like a passive-aggressive treasure hunt.

[30]That first lunch, when Norman and I had stopped to pitch in, was a constant blur of people and noise and food. Everyone was screaming at each other, Isabel and Morgan running past with orders, Norman flipping burgers and yelling things to Bick, the other cook, who stayed stonily quiet and cool the entire time. I shoveled ice like my life depended on it, answered the phone and took orders although I knew almost nothing about the menu, and messed up the register so badly it stuck on $10,000.00 and beeped for fifteen

minutes straight before Isabel, in a fit of rage, whacked it with a plastic water pitcher. It was Us against Them, clearly, and for once I was part of Us. I didn't really know what I was doing; I had to go on faith. So I just handed out my drinks and grabbed the phone when it screamed, wrapping the cord around my wrist and stabbing the pen Morgan had tossed me in my hair, the same way Isabel wore hers, and fought on.

[31]"Last Chance," I'd shout over the din. "Can I help you?"

[32]And now, I was doing it every day.

[33]At first, just walking up to a table full of strangers had scared me to death. I couldn't even make eye contact, stuttering through the basic questions Morgan had taught me—*What would you like to drink? Have you decided? How would you like that cooked? Fries or hush puppies?*—my hand literally shaking as it moved across my order pad. It made me nervous to stand there so exposed, all of those people *looking* at me.

[34]But then, on about my third table, I finally got the nerve to glance up and realized that, basically, they *weren't*. For the most part, they were flipping through the menu, **extracting** Sweet'N Low packets from their toddler's grip, or so lost in their own conversation that I didn't even register: twenty minutes later they'd be flagging Isabel down, sure *she* was the one with their check. They didn't know or care about me. To them, I was just a waitress, a girl with an apron and a tea pitcher; they didn't even seem to notice my lip ring. And that was fine with me.

Connect to the Author

Sarah Dessen drew from her own experiences as a waitress to write *Keeping the Moon*. Dessen, who was born in 1970, worked as a waitress during college. Though she graduated with top honors, she continued to wait tables rather than find a corporate job. It gave her the time she needed to write. It also gave her a lot of material. For example, when a woman slapped Dessen's hand as she tried to remove her empty plate, Dessen immortalized her in a book as a bitter, nasty character. "I've learned that writing well can be the best revenge," Dessen says. Two of Dessen's novels were adapted into the 2003 movie *How to Deal*. In addition to writing novels, Dessen now teaches at her alma mater, UNC Chapel Hill.

Sarah Dessen

IndyCar® Rookie of the Year Danica Patrick races a go-cart in Union Square Park in New York City.

The Fast Track

[1]Race car driver Danica Patrick got her start almost by accident.

[2]When Danica was 10 years old, in Roscoe, Illinois, her sister Brooke wanted to race go-carts. Danica decided to give it a try too. While her sister soon lost interest, Danica was hooked. She found the thrill of racing to be **irresistible**. Within three months of taking up the sport, she broke the go-cart track record. Two years later, she was the national go-cart champion.

[3]By the time she was 16 years old, Danica had won three go-cart championships and was ready for racing bigger, faster cars against other top

young drivers. That meant moving to England and being **displaced** from her home and family. But the experience was worth the loneliness. "Going from [go-carting] to racing in England forced me to grow up very quickly," Danica says. "I had to learn to handle all kinds of situations." She continued her success, finishing second in the Formula Ford Festival in 2000. It was the best finish ever by an American.

[4]Former championship racer Bobby Rahal saw something special in the 5-foot 2-inch, 100-pound Danica. "She has desire, good judgment, and composure under pressure," Rahal says. "And she has that thing that only champions have, that chip on the shoulder that says, 'You don't think I can do it. Come out and take a shot at me.'" She also has another characteristic that is important to champions: confidence. "If I'm doing something, it's because I feel I can beat everyone; I feel like I can win," she says with **assurance**.

[5]Danica spent a couple of years driving cars in practice leagues, finishing in the top three several times. In 2004, she finished in third place in the overall championship standings. Rahal decided she was ready for big-time racing in 2005.

[6]Danica suffered a concussion when she crashed in her first big-time race in 2005, but she recovered in time for the next race. She improved with each race, even leading a race in Japan for 32 laps before finishing fourth.

[7]Next up for Danica was the biggest race in America, the Indianapolis 500. She stunned the racing world by posting the fastest speed during qualifying runs before the race. These qualifying runs decide the order in which drivers will line up at the start of the race. Danica qualified for the fourth position, the best ever by a woman driver at the Indy 500. She raced well, becoming the first woman ever to lead in that race. She might have won if she had not been forced to slow down near the end of the race to avoid running out of fuel. Still, her fourth-place finish was the best ever by a woman at the Indy 500.

[8]Danica finished her rookie season the same way she started it, with a crash. Despite this substandard finish, Danica had much to be proud of about her first year of big-time racing. She finished 12th in the overall standings and was named the Rookie of the Year. "I wanted more at the end, but I can walk away knowing that I accomplished many of the goals I set before the season," Danica says. "Now I have a year of IRL racing under me and we'll be ready for a good 2006 season."

Danica Patrick waves to the crowd during the Indy 500 Festival Parade in Indianapolis in 2005.

Making History at Indianapolis

[9]The 89th Indianapolis 500 was filled with firsts for Danica Patrick. It was the first time she had raced at the Indy 500. In fact, the 500-mile race marked the first time that she had raced more than 300 miles. Then, early in the race, Danica became the first woman ever to lead the Indy 500.

[10]*Four* was another important number for Danica in the May 29, 2005, race. She was the fourth woman ever to drive in the race. During qualifying runs before the race, she earned the right to start in the fourth position. And

after three hours and 500 miles of racing, she finished in fourth place. Her starting and finishing positions were the best ever by a woman in the history of the race.

[11]The Indy 500 is one of the biggest car races of the year. Drivers race around an oval track for 200 laps while some 300,000 fans scream in the stands. Finishing first in this race can do wonders for a driver's **revenue**. The winner earns $1.5 million. The potential for a big payday drew some of the best drivers in the world, and Danica was out to prove that she belonged among them. She posted the fastest speed of all the drivers during the qualifying runs before the race, causing many to **speculate** that she might win the prestigious event. Danica was confident going into the race. "I think I have a great chance of winning this race," she said.

[12]She almost did, but a couple of what she called "rookie mistakes" cost her dearly. In the 52nd lap of the race, Danica briefly took the lead. About halfway through the race, she was still hanging on to fourth place. Then she pulled off the track to get some fuel. As she hit the gas pedal to get back on the track, the car's engine stalled. That error dropped her back into 16th place. But Danica was **persistent**; she patiently worked her way back to seventh place before making another costly error. She spun out and bashed into another car, damaging the front of her car.

[13]But Danica stayed calm and pulled her car off the track. Her team replaced the broken parts, and she was back on the track in 60 seconds. The accident cost her only two positions, dropping her to ninth place with 41 laps remaining. But time was running out. Danica would have to take a risk if she had any chance of winning.

[14]When the eight cars ahead of her pulled off the track for a final refueling in the 172nd lap, Danica decided to keep driving, hoping that she would have enough fuel to finish the race. If she was right, she would win. If she was wrong, she would lose.

[15]While the other drivers refueled, Danica zipped back into the lead. She held the lead for 12 laps, averaging 225 miles per hour. But she could not lengthen her lead, and her fuel was getting dangerously low. She lost the lead briefly on the 186th lap, but then charged back in front. But her lack of fuel forced her to slow down or risk not finishing the race.

[16]"I was disappointed because I had a chance to win the Indianapolis 500," she said. "But when I dropped back into second place, I told myself I wasn't going to be mad. I accomplished a lot." And most racing fans would agree with her.

Danica Patrick Time Line

1992
- Begins racing go-carts
- Sets a track record
- Finishes second out of 20 drivers in the overall local go-cart championship

1993
- Finishes second in overall regional go-cart championship
- Finishes fourth in overall national go-cart championship

1994
- Wins her first national go-cart championship

1995
- Wins her second national go-cart championship

1996
- Wins 39 of her 49 go-cart races
- Wins her third national go-cart championship

1998
- Attends racing school in Canada
- Moves to England to race larger cars

1999
- Finishes ninth overall in her first full season in England

2000
- Finishes second in Formula Ford Festival in England, the best finish ever for an American

2001
- Returns to the United States

2002
- Joins Bobby Rahal's racing team and begins racing in practice leagues
- Finishes seventh at her first race in Toronto
- Finishes fourth in Vancouver

2003
- Finishes in the top five at five different races
- Posts best finish, a second place in Miami

2004
- Finishes third in the overall championship

2005
- Moves up to the top level of racing
- Races in her first Indianapolis 500, finishing fourth
- Wins Rookie of the Year award

Danica Patrick Quick Facts

Born March 25, 1982

Birthplace Beloit, Wisconsin

Family Parents TJ and Bev Patrick, sister Brooke

Height 5 feet, 2 inches

Weight 100 pounds

Hobbies Working out, traveling, nice dinners, and laughing

Favorite Movies
Tommy Boy and *Dumb and Dumber*

Favorite Actors
Adam Sandler and Jim Carrey

Favorite Actress Nicole Kidman

Favorite Food Fish, veggies, and fruit

Favorite Drink Water

OUT OF MANY, ONE

U.S. Senator Barack
Obama delivers the
keynote address
at the Democratic
National Convention
in 2004.

In 2004, Barack
Obama, a state senator
from Illinois, ran as a
candidate for the United
States Senate. About four
months before the election,
Obama was invited to
give the keynote speech to
the Democratic National
Convention. The following
is an excerpt from that
speech.

¹On behalf of the great state of Illinois, crossroads of a nation, Land of Lincoln, let me express my deepest gratitude for the privilege of addressing this convention.

²Tonight is a particular honor for me because, let's face it, my presence on this stage is pretty unlikely. My father was a foreign student, born and raised in a small village in Kenya. He grew up herding goats, went to school in a tin-roof shack. His father—my grandfather—was a cook, a domestic servant to the British.

³But my grandfather had larger dreams for his son. Through hard work and perseverance my father got a scholarship to study in a magical place, America, that shown as a beacon of freedom and opportunity to so many who had come before.

⁴While studying here, my father met my mother. She was born in a town on the other side of the world, in Kansas. Her father worked on oil rigs and farms through most of the Depression. The day after Pearl Harbor my grandfather signed up for duty; joined Patton's army, marched across Europe. Back home, my grandmother raised a baby and went to work on a bomber assembly line. After the war, they studied on the G.I. Bill, bought a house through FHA and later moved west, all the way to Hawaii, in search of opportunity.

⁵And they, too, had big dreams for their daughter. A common dream, born of two continents.

⁶My parents shared not only an improbable love, they shared an abiding faith in the possibilities of this nation. They would give me an African name, Barack, or "blessed," believing that in a **tolerant** America, your name is no barrier to success. They imagined me going to the best schools in the land, even though they weren't rich, because in a generous America you don't have to be rich to achieve your potential.

⁷They're both passed away now. And yet, I know that on this night, they look down on me with great pride.

⁸And I stand here today, grateful for the diversity of my heritage, aware that my parents' dreams live on in my two precious daughters. I stand here knowing that my story is part of the larger American story, that I owe a debt to all of those who came before me, and that, in no other country on Earth, is my story even possible.

[9]Tonight, we gather to **affirm** the greatness of our nation—not because of the height of our skyscrapers, or the power of our military, or the size of our economy. Our pride is based on a very simple premise, summed up in a declaration made over two hundred years ago: "We hold these truths to be self-evident, that all men are created equal, that they are **endowed** by their Creator with certain inalienable rights, that among these are life, liberty and the pursuit of happiness."

[10]That is the true genius of America—a faith in simple dreams, an insistence on small miracles; that we can tuck in our children at night and know that they are fed and clothed and safe from harm; that we can say what we think, write what we think, without hearing a sudden knock on the door; that we can have an idea and start our own business without paying a bribe; that we can participate in the political process without fear of retribution; and that our votes will be counted—at least, most of the time.

[11]This year, in this election, we are called to reaffirm our values and our commitments, to hold them against a hard reality and see how we are measuring up to the legacy of our forbearers and the promise of future generations.

[12]And fellow Americans, Democrats, Republicans, Independents, I say to you, tonight: We have more work to do—more work to do for the workers I met in Galesburg, Illinois, who are losing their union jobs at the Maytag plant that's moving to Mexico, and now they're having to compete with their own children for jobs that pay 7 bucks an hour; more to do for the father I met who was losing his job and choking back the tears, wondering how he would pay $4,500 a month for the drugs his son needs, without the health benefits that he counted on; more to do for the young woman in East St. Louis, and thousands more like her, who has the grades, has the drive, has the will, but doesn't have the money to go to college.

[13]Now, don't get me wrong, the people I meet—in small towns and big cities and diners and office parks—they don't expect government to solve all of their problems. They know they have to work hard to get ahead—and they want to.

[14]Go into the collar counties around Chicago, and people will tell you they don't want their tax money wasted by a welfare agency or by the Pentagon.

[15]Go into any inner-city neighborhood, and folks will tell you that government alone can't teach our kids to learn; they know that parents have to teach, that children can't achieve unless we raise their expectations and turn off the television sets and eradicate the **slander** that says a black youth with a book is acting white. They know those things.

[16]People don't expect government to solve all their problems. But they sense, deep in their bones, that with just a slight change in **priorities**, we can make sure that every child in America has a decent shot at life, and that the doors of opportunity remain open to all. They know we can do better. And they want that choice. . . .

[17]Alongside our famous individualism, there's another ingredient in the American saga, a belief that we are all connected as one people.

[18]If there is a child on the south side of Chicago who can't read, that matters to me, even if it's not my child. If there is a senior citizen somewhere who can't pay for his or her prescription drugs, and having to choose between medicine and the rent, that makes my life poorer, even if it's not my grandparent. If there's an Arab American family being rounded up without benefit of an attorney or due process, that threatens my civil liberties.

[19]It is that fundamental belief—I am my brothers' keeper, I am my sisters' keeper—that makes this country work. It's what allows us to pursue our individual dreams and yet still come together as one American family.

[20]"E pluribus unum:" Out of many, one.

Connect to the Author

Barack Obama

Barack Obama was elected to the United States Senate in November 2004, less than four months after he gave this speech. Obama was born in 1961 in Hawaii. He graduated from Columbia University and then earned his law degree from Harvard, where he was the first African American to serve as editor of the *Harvard Law Review*. He worked as a civil rights lawyer, was elected to the Illinois State Senate, and then to the U.S. Senate. Obama is currently the only African American in the U.S. Senate.

From Sitcom Junkie to King of Bling

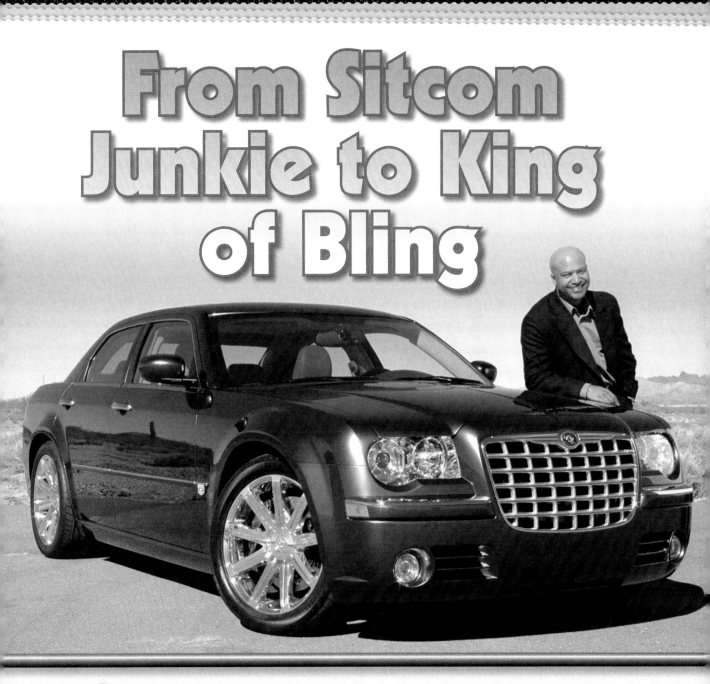

¹**R**alph hated college and dropped out before the end of his first semester. With no real plan for his life, he spent his days in front of the television in his parents' basement. For a while he got by on a steady diet of granola and reruns of the *The Dukes of Hazzard*. This is not your typical picture of a success in the making. But that's exactly what Ralph Gilles was. Within a few years, he would become one of the hottest young car designers in America.

[2]So what inspired a sitcom junkie to climb out of the basement and all the way to the top of the corporate ladder? For starters, his older brother Max lit a fire under him. Max had watched Ralph make incredible sketches of cars ever since they were kids. He hated seeing all that talent go to waste.

[3]Everyone around Ralph recognized that he had a gift. When he was just 14 years old, his aunt sent a letter to the chairman of Chrysler. "My nephew sketches cars. You guys should hire him!" she wrote. A designer at Chrysler sent her a reply suggesting that Ralph go to a design school such as the Center for Creative Studies in Detroit.

[4]Max remembered that designer's advice and got his brother an application to the school. That was just the nudge that Ralph needed. He decided to go for it, but it wasn't easy to meet the deadline for enrollment. He had just one week to create 10 sketches and turn in his paperwork! Ralph worked night and day. He just barely made the deadline.

[5]Submitting that application was the first step in Ralph's turnaround. The next thing he knew, he got an acceptance letter in the mail! Then it was up to Ralph. This time around, he thrived at school. During his years at design school, he worked hard doing what he loved—designing cars! After he graduated, several companies offered him a job. One of them was Chrysler. There was no place in the world he would rather work! Chrysler made the Dodge Charger, like the one named "General Lee" in *The Dukes of Hazzard* TV show Ralph loved so much. Chrysler also made the powerful Viper, Ralph's favorite "bad-boy" muscle car. As soon as Chrysler made an offer, Ralph took the job.

[6]At first, the job had nothing to do with creating showy body designs for muscle cars. In fact, his first assignment was to design a speedometer needle. It certainly wasn't glamorous work. But Ralph was paid well, and he felt like a success. During this time, he bought his mother a PT Cruiser and started buying and customizing race cars for fun.

[7]While working on interiors, Ralph put his best foot forward. He showed a rare talent for designing and sketching both the interiors and exteriors of cars. At the same time, he showed he was passionate about good design. He argued for features and materials that would improve the image of Chrysler cars. Soon, "higher-ups" noticed Ralph's great instincts for what made a

car look bold, aggressive, and downright cool. After just a few years at the company, Ralph was named design director of one of Chrysler's seven design teams.

[8]That's how Ralph Gilles got the dream job he has today. He guides a team of 30 designers to come up with fresh, new designs customers will love. Gilles starts by finding what works in his designers' sketches and ideas. Then he discusses changes and possibilities with his team. Finally, he gives suggestions for improvements and sends the team back to make new drawings and models.

[9]Gilles tries to capture the appeal American cars used to have. He loves the cars of the past that were showy and bold. "It's bringing back what's good about American cars," Gilles says. "American cars have to be about not just a great car, but also a great-looking car, and an artful car—a car that says more about transportation than simply getting from point A to point B."

[10]One look at the new Chrysler 300 makes it easy to see what Gilles considers "great-looking" and "artful." It was named 2004 Car of the Year in most car magazines and is as popular with the young, hip crowd as it is with the CEO set. The 300 is a luxury sedan with a long hood and low roof. Its big rounded fenders and deep body give it a "muscular" look. But its real personality is in the broad grillwork across the front of the car. It makes the car seem to bare its teeth and growl.

[11]That fierce grillwork is a strong feature of the new Dodge Charger that Gilles's team designed too. The Charger is an updated version of the *Dukes of Hazzard* muscle car. The new model is tamer, but Gilles made sure it captured the same in-your-face personality of the old Charger. "In the company, a lot of people did comment, 'Wow, this car looks like it's angry!'" he says, obviously pleased at the effect.

[12]So far, it seems that the public loves what Gilles loves. His designs have won over 30 awards, and *Time Magazine* named him the "King of Bling." The new models he has worked on are selling well and boosting Chrysler's sales. In one year the company went from over $600 million in losses to almost $2 billion in profits! That is a near-miracle at a time when American car makers are in a sales slump.

[13]Glowing reviews and strong sales give Gilles confidence that he'll get to

keep on doing what he loves. "I'm one of the few people who can say I pinch myself every day, because this is exactly what I wanted," says Gilles. "The first 10 years have been pretty, pretty cool."

[14]So what does the future hold for this young trendsetter? "I really see myself with this company, and I really have no desire at all to look elsewhere," says Gilles.

[15]That's not surprising to hear from a man who has found a job where dreams come true!

Design Achievements in Gilles's Career

Assignment	Model
Interior design	Jeep Liberty
	Viper SRT-10
Overall design	Dodge M80
	Dodge Magnum
	Chrysler 300
	Dodge Charger

WHO ARE WE?

- *How does art express your culture?*
- *How does your language connect you to a culture?*
- *What defines an American?*

from

LEARNING ENGLISH: MY NEW FOUND LAND

by Julia Alvarez

In this essay, the author describes the uneasiness and disorientation she felt when she first arrived in New York, unable to speak English. She explains how she quickly learned more and more, and she captures the feeling of triumph she felt when at last she mastered the new language.

¹**W**hen I was 10, we immigrated to New York. How astonishing, a country where everyone spoke English! These people must be smarter, I thought. Maids, waiters, taxi drivers, doormen, bums on the street, garbage-men, all spoke this difficult language. It took some time before I understood that Americans were not necessarily a smarter, superior race. It was as natural for them to learn their mother tongue as it was for a little Dominican baby to learn Spanish. . . .

²Soon it wasn't so strange that everyone was speaking in English instead of Spanish. I learned not to hear it as English, but as sense. I no longer strained to understand; I understood. I relaxed in this second language. Only when someone with a heavy Southern or British accent spoke in a movie or when the priest **droned** his sermon—only then did I experience that little catch of anxiety. I worried that I would not be able to "keep up" with the voice speaking in this second language. I would be like those people from the Bible we had studied in religion class, at the foot of an enormous tower that looked just like the skyscrapers all around me. They had been punished for their pride by being made to speak some slightly different version of the same language so that they didn't understand what anyone was saying.

³But at the foot of those towering New York skyscrapers, I began to understand more and more—not less and less—English. In sixth grade, I had one of the first of a lucky line of great teachers who began to **nurture** a love of the language, a love that had been there since childhood of listening closely to words. Sister Bernadette did not make our class **interminably** diagram sentences from a workbook or learn a catechism of grammar rules. Instead, she asked us to write little stories imagining we were snowflakes, birds, pianos, a stone in the pavement, a star in the sky. What would it feel like to be a flower with roots in the ground? If the clouds could talk, what would they say? She had an expressive, dreamy look that was accentuated by her face being framed in a wimple. Supposing, just supposing . . . My mind would take off, soaring into possibilities: a flower with roots, a star in the sky, a cloud full of sad, sad tears, a piano crying out each time its back was tapped, music only to our ears.

⁴Sister Bernadette stood at the chalkboard. Her chalk was always snapping in two because she wrote with so much energy, her whole habit shaking with the swing of her arm, her hand tap tap tapping on the board. "Here's a simple sentence: *The snow fell*." Sister Bernadette pointed with

catechism: instruction in Christianity

wimple: woman's head covering

habit: dark gown worn by nuns

her chalk, her eyebrows lifted, her wimple poked up. "But watch what happens if we put an adverb at the beginning and a prepositional phrase at the end: *Gently the snow fell on the bare hills.*"

[5]I thought about the snow. I saw how it might fall on the hills, tapping lightly on the bare branches of trees. Softly it would fall on the cold, cold fields. On toys children had left out in the cold, and on cars and on little birds and on people out late walking on the streets. Sister Bernadette filled the chalkboard with snowy print, on and on, handling and shaping and moving language, scribbling all over the board until English, those little bricks of meaning, those little fixed units and counters, became a charged, fluid mass that carried me in its great fluent waves, rolling and moving onward, to **deposit** me on the shores of the only homeland. I was no longer a foreigner with no ground to stand on. I had landed in language.

[6]I had come into my English.

Connect to the Author

Julia Alvarez

Though she was born in New York City in 1950, Julia Alvarez spent her first 10 years in the Dominican Republic. This country occupies two-thirds of an island in the Caribbean Sea. It has had a turbulent history. During Alvarez's childhood, an oppressive dictator ruled the island. Alvarez and her family had to flee in 1960 when authorities discovered her father's part in a plot to overthrow the dictator. Much of Alvarez's writing deals with the Dominican Republic and the people who live there. She draws from her experiences and the history of the island. She also writes about herself and her own feelings. "I think of myself at 10 years old, newly arrived in this country, feeling out of place, feeling that I would never belong in this world of United States of Americans who were so different from me," Alvarez once said. "Back home in the Dominican Republic, I had been an active, lively child, a bad student full of fun with plentiful friends. In New York City I was suddenly thrown back on myself . . . I found myself turning more and more to writing as the one place where I felt I belonged and could make sense of myself, my life, all that was happening to me."

How I ★ ★ ★ Learned ★ ★ ★ English

by Gregory Djanikian

The boy in this poem has just arrived in the United States. In spite of his limited English, or perhaps because of it, the boy experiences a moment of acceptance in his new country.

7It was an empty lot
Ringed by elms and fir and honeysuckle.
Bill Corson was pitching in his buckskin jacket,
Chuck Keller, fat even as a boy, was on first,
His T-shirt riding up over his gut,
Ron O'Neill, Jim, Dennis, were talking it up
In the field, a blue sky above them
Tipped with cirrus.

cirrus: thin, wispy clouds

⁸And there I was,
Just off the plane and plopped in the middle
Of Williamsport, Pa. and a neighborhood game,
Unnatural and without any moves,
My notions of baseball and America
Growing fuzzier each time I whiffed.

⁹So it was not impossible that I,
Banished to the outfield and daydreaming
Of water, or hotel in the mountains,
Would suddenly find myself in the path
Of a ball stung by Joe Barone.
I watched it closing in
Clean and untouched, **transfixed**
By its easy arc before it hit
My forehead with a thud.

¹⁰I fell back,
Dazed, clutching my brow,
Groaning, "Oh my shin, oh my shin,"
And everybody peeled away from me
And dropped from laughter, and there we were,
All of us writhing on the ground for one reason
Or another.

¹¹Someone said "shin" again,
There was a wild stamping of hands on the ground,
A kicking of feet, and the fit
Of laughter overtook me too,

And that was important, as important
As Joe Barone asking me how I was
Through his tears, picking me up
And dusting me off with hands like swatters,
And though my head felt heavy,
I played on till dusk
Missing flies and pop-ups and grounders
And calling out in desperation things like
"Yours" and "take it," but doing all right,
Tugging at my cap in just the right way,
Crouching low, my feet set,
"Hum baby" sweetly on my lips.

Connect to the Author

Gregory Djanikian

Gregory Djanikian was born in Egypt, a country in northeastern Africa. His parents were Armenian, a group of people that has suffered massacres, deportations, and other extreme abuse throughout history. Djanikian and his family came to the United States when he was 8 years old. He grew up in New York and Pennsylvania. He began writing poetry in college. His poems deal with subjects like violence, history, family, and the immigrant experience. Some are sad; others are funny. They tell stories rich with detail. "I think this is a great misconception in modern poetry that something has to be incredibly difficult to be good," Djanikian says. In addition to writing poems, Djanikian teaches poetry workshops and is in charge of the creative writing program at the University of Pennsylvania.

I Hear America Singing

Construction workers of the Northern Pacific Railroad tunneling though Stampede Pass, 1888

In this poem, Walt Whitman describes the individual voices that make up America. The songs represent the literal music each working man and woman sings. They also stand for the work itself. Whitman tells how each person, each song, each kind of work, contributes to the chorus that is America.

by Walt Whitman

I hear America singing, the **varied** carols I hear,
Those of mechanics, each one singing his, as it should be, blithe and strong,
The carpenter singing his as he measures his **plank** or **beam**,
The **mason** singing his, as he makes ready for work, or leaves off work,

The boatman singing what belongs to him in his boat, the deckhand
  singing on the steamboat deck,
The shoemaker singing as he sits on his bench, the hatter singing
  as he stands,
The woodcutter's song, the ploughboy's on his way in the morning,
  or at noon **intermission** or at sundown,
The delicious singing of the mother, or of the young wife at work, or
  of the girl sewing or washing,
Each singing what belongs to him or her and to none else,
The day what belongs to the day, at night the party of young fellows,
  robust, friendly,
Singing with open mouths their strong **melodious** songs.

robust:
strong and
healthy

Connect to the Author

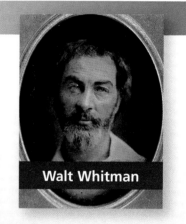

Walt Whitman

Walt Whitman is considered to be the "voice" of his age. Whitman was born in Long Island, New York, in 1819. By the age of 37, he had been fired as an editor and had failed in real estate. He showed little promise. So it was unexpected when in 1855 he came out with a self-published book of poems called *Leaves of Grass.* That book included the poem above. The poems were in a style no one had seen before. Whitman wrote poetry without meter or rhyme. Many readers found it quite unpoetic. But some, like poet and essayist Ralph Waldo Emerson, thought it was marvelous. He called it "the most extraordinary piece of wit and wisdom" America had produced. There were nine editions of the book in Whitman's lifetime. Whitman kept changing the poems—adding or rearranging lines, changing titles, adding or cutting entire poems. During the Civil War, Whitman wrote graphic and moving poems about the horrors he witnessed. In his spare time, he visited wounded soldiers. To cheer them up, he spent his small salary on little gifts for soldiers from both sides.

Through his poetry, Whitman became a symbol of the young nation. He wrote about the American experience. He championed the common person. Though he died in 1892, Whitman is still considered one of America's greatest poets.

I, Too

Langston Hughes, 1914

In this poem, Langston Hughes adds his voice to the chorus that makes up America. Hughes published this poem in 1925, at a time when African Americans were segregated and routinely discriminated against. It is a direct response to Whitman's romantic view of working-class America.

by Langston Hughes

[1] I, too, sing America.

[2] I am the darker brother.
They send me to eat in the kitchen
When company comes,
But I laugh,
And eat well,
And grow strong.

[3] Tomorrow,
I'll sit at the table
When company comes.
Nobody'll dare
Say to me,
"Eat in the kitchen,"
Then.

[4]Besides,
They'll see how beautiful I am
And be ashamed—

[5]I, too, am America.

Connect to the Author

Langston Hughes

James Langston Hughes was one of the most important figures of the Harlem Renaissance of the 1920s. During this period, musicians, artists, and writers like Hughes gathered in New York City's vast ghetto of Harlem. They explored black life and culture in ways that had never been done. Hughes wrote in many different forms, including poetry, short stories, novels, plays, and essays. Like Walt Whitman, whom he counted as a major influence, Hughes focused on working-class people. But unlike Whitman, he focused on the African American experience. Hughes was born in Joplin, Missouri, in 1902. After high school, Hughes taught English in Mexico, where his father lived. He left after a year, and briefly attended college. Because he was black, he was assigned the worst dorm room. He experienced other forms of bigotry too. He found his professors boring and often skipped class to attend shows and lectures elsewhere. Hughes left college after his freshman year and signed on as a cabin boy on a ship. He got off the ship in the Netherlands and spent a poverty-stricken year in Europe. When he returned to the United States, he worked a series of low-wage jobs and wrote poetry. He began to be recognized for his work. Some black intellectuals criticized him for his images of lower-class life. But he remained committed to recording the truth as he saw it. "I didn't know the upper class Negroes well enough to write much about them. I knew only the people I had grown up with, and they weren't people whose shoes were always shined, who had been to Harvard, or who had heard of Bach. But they seemed to me good people too."

Graffiti Is a Crime!

To the Editor:

[1]Things used to be different here in Pleasantville. When I was growing up back in the 1940s, people had respect. They had respect for other people. They had respect for the law and for teachers. But most of all, they had respect for property. Back in my day, we didn't have to have big, ugly billboards telling us to "Keep Pleasantville Pleasant." We knew better than to throw trash on the street or spray paint our names on someone else's building.

[2]Kids these days don't seem to have that kind of respect any more. Don't believe me? Think I **exaggerate** the problem? Then just take a walk down Main Street some day. Main Street used to be the sparkling pride of all Pleasantville citizens. But today the sidewalks and gutters are filled with filth, and it seems like every square inch of wall space is covered with ugly, spray-painted scrawls. Some people call this hideousness graffiti. I call it what it is—a crime. It's a crime against the **industrious** people who are trying to run businesses inside the buildings that these youngsters deface with their spray paint. It's a crime against the **prestige** of a town that used to be known across the state for its cleanliness and its public-minded citizens. And it's a crime against every citizen whose eyes get polluted by this awful vandalism.

[3]Some people say that graffiti is a form of art. They say that these vandals are just "expressing their innermost feelings" or "representing their culture for all to see." Horsefeathers! Poppycock! Graffiti is vandalism, pure and simple—nothing more, nothing less. Graffiti vandals are no more artists

than I am a flying horse. Real artists express themselves by painting on canvas, not on somebody else's building. Real artists don't have to commit crimes to represent their culture.

[4]That's why I fully support Mayor Fowler's plan to eliminate graffiti. Unlike other city leaders who throw their hands up and act helpless in the face of this menace, the mayor is trying to do something. Mayor Fowler wants to issue **instructions** to all city meter readers to wipe out graffiti in the course of their daily work. If the mayor has his way, meter readers will carry a can of paint and a paintbrush. Any time they spot graffiti, they will immediately cover it up with paint. No questions asked.

[5]The only problem with the mayor's idea is that it doesn't go far enough. We need to crack down on the juvenile delinquents who are damaging and defacing our buildings and our reputation as a city. Right now, these vandals are treated as if they have done nothing more serious than jaywalking. They get a ticket and have to pay a small fine. That's not going to stop these criminals. Rather than giving them a slap on the wrist, we should let graffiti vandals know we mean business. They should face the same punishment as someone who takes a sledgehammer and smashes a hole in a building. A little time in the city jail might make them think twice before they pull out a can of spray paint and deface someone else's property.

Sincerely,
Ernest J. Hassleblad

Is graffiti nothing more than vandalism, or is it a form of art?

283

Turn Vandals into Artists

To the Editor:

[6]I know a lot of Pleasantville citizens are angry about the graffiti that has been popping up around town lately. They say that graffiti makes our beautiful buildings ugly. They say that graffiti is no better than vandalism. In most cases, their **criticism** is valid. There is certainly a lot of ugly graffiti around town. But contrary to what some think, not all graffiti is ugly. In fact, some graffiti has a lot in common with fine art. Some graffiti, like fine art, is a personal expression that shows a great deal of thought and originality by the artist. Graffiti might not be the best way for artists to proclaim their individuality. But in some cases it's hard to miss the artistic ability of these misguided Michelangelos.

[7]I'm not saying I'm pro-graffiti. Like most citizens, I think it's wrong to paint things on walls and buildings without permission. All I'm saying is that I think there's a better solution to the problem of graffiti than Mayor Fowler's idea. Arming city workers with paintbrushes would just make a bad situation worse. Instead of city walls being covered with graffiti, they would be covered with big blotches of paint. How is that going to "Keep Pleasantville Pleasant"?

[8]My solution is to channel the creativity of graffiti artists into a project that will improve the city for us all. Most people would agree that graffiti has made the Pleasantville Public Library an eyesore. The front of the building is in good shape, but both sides and the back have been spray painted with thousands of names and symbols over the years.

[9]I propose that the city sponsor a contest. Invite graffiti artists from all three major areas of town to submit plans for painting a mural on each of the

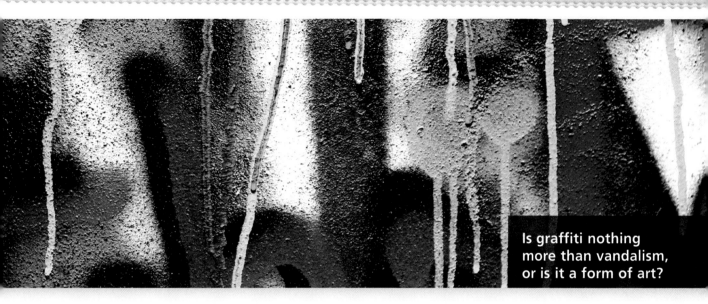

Is graffiti nothing more than vandalism, or is it a form of art?

three messed-up sides of the library. The murals should reflect some aspect of life in Pleasantville—either our history or our current culture. Then the city council could narrow the submissions to three or four for each wall and let citizens vote on their favorites. Once the winners are picked, the city can appoint a supervisor for each of the walls to make sure everything goes smoothly. Then everyone who submitted an idea would be invited to help paint the winning entries on the library walls.

[10]My solution accomplishes two things. First, it covers up the graffiti on the library while improving the appearance of the building. Second, it provides graffiti artists with **acknowledgment** of their talents while giving them a constructive way to express themselves. Some of these artists are extremely talented. With a little guidance, they could turn their talents away from destructive graffiti and toward a career in the fine arts.

[11]I'm positive that my solution will work. If you don't believe me, ask the citizens of Culver City, California. They had a similar graffiti problem five years ago. Then they invited graffiti artists to paint a mural on a run-down fire station. Not only did the program reduce graffiti, it also inspired the entire neighborhood to start sprucing up. It worked so well that the city now sponsors a mural contest every year. They raise money with bake sales and car washes to provide the winner with money for a college scholarship.

[12]Now doesn't that sound better than just throwing graffiti artists in jail?

Sincerely,
Wanda Mercurio

Phizzog

by Carl Sandburg

The title of this poem, "Phizzog," is pronounced FIZ-og. It is a shortened form of the word physiognomy *(fizzy-AHG-nuh-me), which means "a person's facial features or expression." It also refers to the study of those features. Ancient philosophers believed that the study of a person's facial features could reveal their character. Aristotle, for example, believed that people with sharp noses were easily angered and people with thick noses didn't care about other people's feelings.*

This face you got,
This here phizzog you carry around,
You never picked it out for yourself, at all, at all—did you?
This here phizzog—somebody handed it to you—am I right?
Somebody said, "Here's yours, now go see what you can do with it."
Somebody slipped it to you and it was like a package marked:
"No goods exchanged after being taken away—"
This face you got.

Connect to the Author

"Trying to write briefly about Carl Sandburg," a
friend of his once said, "is like trying to picture the
Grand Canyon in one black-and-white snapshot."
Sandburg did so much in his long life that just to list
everything he wrote would take 400 pages. During his
lifetime, Sandburg was famous as a historian, a poet,
and a musician. He was devoted to America and the
people in it. It was a love that showed in all his work,
and one that he developed at an early age. Born in
Galesburg, Illinois, in 1876, Sandburg was the son of poor immigrants. He
quit school when he was 13 years old to work as a laborer. He held many
jobs: delivery boy, fireman, housepainter, soldier, and newspaper reporter. He
devoted 13 years to writing a biography of Abraham Lincoln. The biography
was extremely well respected—and enormous. (The section about Lincoln's
war years alone is longer than all of Shakespeare's works combined.)

Sandburg gave lectures to adoring crowds. He played guitar and sang.
Above all, he wrote poems for the people, in a style that everyone could
understand. When Sandburg died in North Carolina in 1967, at the age of 89,
he had become one of America's best-known and best-loved poets.

Carl Sandburg

Television Commercial Script:
"In the Beauty Zone with Image Zone"

What teenage girl doesn't want to look like a professional model?

[1]Camera focuses on a life-size cutout of a slim, beautiful, happy Latina girl, about 15 years old. Upbeat music plays in the background.

[2]ANNOUNCER [female teenage voice]: You want to look like this. But sometimes you feel like this . . .

[3]Camera pans down the cutout. It shows an armadillo waddling from behind the cutout across the floor and out of view.

[4]ANNOUNCER: That can be an **obstacle** to happiness. There's no need to feel down about the way you look, though.

[5]The girl shown in the cutout steps from behind the cutout. She speaks to the camera. Hers is the voice of the announcer.

⁶ANNOUNCER: IMAGE ZONE has a whole **arsenal** of products to improve your looks and bring out your natural beauty. Whether you're 12 or 20, it's never too soon to start doing what you can to look your best!

⁷Camera shows an African American female. She's 30-ish and wears a physician's white coat and has a stethoscope around her neck. She is examining the face of a teenage Caucasian female. The girl is seated in a chair in the doctor's examining room.

⁸ANNOUNCER: A well-known doctor has helped the scientists at IMAGE ZONE develop the very finest in makeup and skin products for girls just like you. We know that you want the very best in teen beauty products, and IMAGE ZONE delivers. That's why our products cost a little more than others.

⁹Camera shows a close-up of a young teenage girl's face. Her skin is clear and healthy looking.

¹⁰ANNOUNCER: You've heard that beauty is skin deep? Well, that's where the experts at IMAGE ZONE begin: with your skin. The **beneficial** ingredients in "Clean & Clear" wash away daily grease and grime. That includes the subsurface stuff that most soaps can't reach.

¹¹Camera shows a plastic bottle labeled "IMAGE ZONE Clean & Clear." The same teenage girl shown in the previous shot is washing her face with the product.

¹²ANNOUNCER: Use "Clean & Clear" every morning and every night. It gets your skin deep-down clean.

¹³Camera shows the same teenage girl. She's looking in a mirror at her face. Her expression is distressed.

¹⁴ANNOUNCER: Uh-oh! Even though you keep your face clean, you can still get a pesky pimple every now and then. Don't worry. IMAGE ZONE's "Spot Remover" attacks and dries up blemishes. It's made with seaweed, green tea, and vitamins C and E!

[15]Camera shows a tube of "IMAGE ZONE Spot Remover" on a bathroom counter near the sink. The teenage girl shown in previous shots picks up the tube, opens it, and applies a dot of it to a spot on her chin.

[16]ANNOUNCER: Apply "IMAGE ZONE Spot Remover" before going to bed. The next morning, you'll be amazed at the results! "Spot Remover" is effective and fast.

[17]Camera shows same teenage girl looking in the mirror at the spot on her chin. She looks amazed. Next shot is of the announcer in the same setting as in the first scene of the commercial.

[18]ANNOUNCER: Okay. Now let's get down to business. It's a fact of life that we all want to look like the models on TV and in magazines— right? Well, who says we can't? IMAGE ZONE is here to help, with their line of makeup created especially for teens.

[19]Camera shows a brightly colored box. The top is open to reveal a tube of tinted foundation, a cylinder of mascara, and a tube of lipstick. All have the name IMAGE ZONE on them.

[20]ANNOUNCER: Looking like a fashion model is as easy as one, two, three! One—

[21]Camera shows a close-up of the tube of foundation. The name IMAGE ZONE and the numeral 1 are clearly shown on it.

[22]ANNOUNCER: —smooth on IMAGE ZONE 1. Then notice how that oily look disappears. Your skin seems to glow with a silky, natural smoothness. Two—

[23]Camera shows a close-up of the cylinder of mascara, with the name IMAGE ZONE and the numeral 2 clearly shown on it.

[24]ANNOUNCER: —brush on IMAGE ZONE 2. Watch your eyelashes lengthen and darken. All eyes will be on you when you use IMAGE ZONE 2! And three—

[25]Camera shows a close-up of a tube of lipstick with the name IMAGE ZONE and the numeral 3 on it.

[26]ANNOUNCER: IMAGE ZONE 3 lip gloss comes in three great tints. Your lips will look fuller and softer—just like a model's. That's a **guarantee**.

[27]Camera returns to a close-up shot of the announcer.

[28]ANNOUNCER: So, becoming beautiful is as simple as one, two, three with IMAGE ZONE products. Oh, yeah—the folks at IMAGE ZONE wanted me to tell you something else. They think you should accept yourself for who you are. They believe that we're all beautiful in our own way. It's just that we can use a little help, sometimes. So there's no need to feel like this—

[29]Camera shows the announcer reaching down, although it doesn't show what she's picking up—just a shot of her upper body. Then the shot reveals that she has picked up the armadillo, which she holds in both hands.

[30]ANNOUNCER: —when you can look like this!

[31]The announcer walks over to her identical cutout. She stands next to it, tilting her head toward it with the word "this." Then she smiles at the camera. [time: 1:00 minute]

291

Wheatsville Daily News   SOUND OFF   March 23

Immigrants in America: *Wheatsville Sounds Off*

The Melting Pot Works

[1]If you're like me, you've noticed that migrant workers are changing the face of Wheatsville these days. Some of you are not too happy about the newcomers because they haven't yet learned our customs and language. But I think we should all make these new arrivals welcome. We should help them become true Americans. After all, immigrants are part of our heritage.

[2]Being a nation of immigrants is one thing that has made America great. Our founding fathers came here from England. Throughout our history, America has been a safe haven for people in trouble. Thousands came to escape starvation during Ireland's potato famine. When times got hard in the rest of Europe, people from all over the continent came to find jobs in America's cities. Chinese workers struggling to make a living crossed the ocean to join the Gold Rush in America. Jews fled from the Nazis and found safety here. These early groups came, worked hard, and embraced American life. I think that is what today's immigrants need to do too. Like those early groups, immigrants today come from countries with poor economies or unfair political systems. In this country, they can leave their difficult past behind and learn to live the American way.

[3]There is plenty of proof that immigrants can fit in and learn to be great Americans. Albert Einstein, a German immigrant, was perhaps the greatest scientist ever. Madeleine Albright, who came from the Czech Republic, became our Secretary of State. An immigrant from Chile, Isabel Allende, is a world famous writer. Fernando Valenzuela came from Mexico to become a great major league pitcher. And I'm sure many of you will agree that Arnold Schwarzenegger did us a favor by coming from Austria to star in American action movies! You can probably think of many more examples, too. That's because immigrants have made contributions in almost every field. Isn't that reason enough to

welcome them and help them adjust to American life?

[4]Instead of resenting immigrants, we should become their teachers. We should go out of our way to talk to them and help them learn the language. We should share our recipes, our music, and our celebrations. As they learn about these things, immigrants can slowly become true Americans, just as immigrants have been doing for more than 200 years.

[5]Farmers around here set a great example for how to help immigrants. I'm sure you know what I mean because you, too, see local farmers going the extra mile. They hire whole families of migrant workers and often help them find housing. They teach workers our way of farming and help them learn English on the job. The rest of us can follow their example by making immigrants welcome at community events, such as parades and the county fair. We can invite them to church services and potluck dinners. We can encourage them to sign up their children for scout groups and Little League. I believe that the more we help immigrants participate in our community, the faster they will blend in and feel a part of it. They can truly become our neighbors and friends.

[6]Immigrants need time, along with our help and understanding, to learn how to be Americans. That's what they have come here to do. If we welcome them and share our language and customs, I'm sure that migrant workers in our area will become good citizens of Wheatsville and true Americans.

Trade the Melting Pot for a Salad Bowl

[7]America should quit trying to be a melting pot. People only want to blend newcomers into one American culture so that everything "foreign" will disappear. When they say that we must become alike to be American, they really mean, "Everyone must become like me because my way is best." Rather than a melting pot, America should be a salad bowl filled with many textures and flavors. In a salad, separate ingredients are mixed together without losing their distinct colors and flavors. In that same way, we should "mix" immigrants into America while allowing them to preserve their heritage.

[8]While a melting pot melts away differences that cause conflict, it also melts away differences that make America better. In countries with a

single culture, people think alike. They have fewer disputes over how to govern, what laws are fair, and what rights people should have. That is far more convenient than having many cultures and viewpoints. But putting up with the inconvenience of differing cultures yields a big payoff. That payoff is diversity. Diversity helps keep Americans open to new ideas. I believe it is that openness that makes America a leader in the arts, in invention, and in research. Tolerance of diversity also attracts great thinkers from other countries. They are eager to study and work in America, where they can dare to express new ideas. America can only keep that "think tank" appeal if it is a place that values the contributions of all kinds of people and cultures.

[9]Another problem with the "melting pot" is that it is disrespectful. Immigrants shouldn't have to give up their native culture in order to fit in. This kind of "blending" destroys people's self-respect along with valuable traditions. I know this from experience. My family came to America when I was very young. We were excited about living in a land that offered so much opportunity. But when I went to school, I found that my opportunities were limited. The only way I could understand

the teacher was to ask for help from other students who spoke Spanish. When I did, my teacher made me stand up for a public scolding. She told me I would never learn English unless I quit speaking Spanish. I was humiliated for simply being who I was. After that, I sat silently, wasting time in a classroom where I could not use the beautiful language I knew. Like so many immigrants, I was denied access until I could learn English. I was made to feel irrelevant and invisible. The worst thing was that it made me ashamed that my culture and my family were different. If only that teacher had been able to respect my culture instead of expecting it to "melt" away, I could have asked questions and taken part while I learned English!

[10]It is time for Americans to do more than allow immigrants to "melt" into the culture. They must recognize that having many cultures is part of what makes America great. Immigrants like myself who have blended in and found a place here can still find a better life. That life is one in which we are free to be proud of our culture and proud to be ourselves. Give us this, America, and we will give you the best that we have to offer.

Vocabulary

A **absolutely**   totally

access   the ability or right to enter a place or use something

accumulate   to gather a little at a time

accurate   correct or right

achieve   to get something you have worked for

acknowledgment   credit for achievement; recognition of someone's rights or authority

actual   existing in real life; not false

affect   to cause a change in

affirm   to state that something is true

aggressively   with energy and strength of mind

agree   to have the same opinion

alliance   a union of people or groups

analyze   to carefully study each part of something

ancestor   one from whom a person is descended

annual   happening every year

anticipate   to wait for or expect

apparel   clothing

application   a written request for a job

array   a large number

arsenal   a collection of things, often weapons, that will be used to accomplish a purpose

artificial   not natural; something made by humans

associate   to connect or combine

assurance   a feeling of certainty; confidence

astronaut   someone trained to travel and work in space

attached   fastened to something

audio   of or related to sound

	authentic	real, not fake
	authorize	to give official permission
	available	ready to be used
B	**balmy**	warm and pleasant
	banish	to kick out or make stay away
	barren	with no trees or other plants growing
	basis	a support or base
	beam	a long, sturdy piece of lumber that is very thick and is often used to support a roof
	beneficial	of or related to benefits; helpful
	biofuel	fuel produced from living matter, such as wood and corn
	bloat	to swell
	bombard	attack in a determined way
	boredom	the feeling of being bored
	boycott	the refusal to buy something as a form of protest
	brilliant	very clever
	budget	a financial plan
	bulky	something that takes up a lot of space
C	**calculate**	to figure out using math
	calorie	a unit for measuring food to produce energy in the body
	cancer	an aggressive growth of cells
	capacity	the largest amount something can hold
	casualty	person who is hurt or killed
	celebrate	to have a party or other such activity to honor a special occasion
	challenge	something difficult to do
	choice	a number of things from which to pick
	claim	to say that something is yours
	classify	to put in groups
	clog	to block
	clot	thickened clump
	confidence	feeling sure of yourself

	confidential	meant to be kept private or secret
	consequence	effect or result of certain actions
	conspicuous	easily seen or noticed
	consumer	someone who buys and uses goods or services
	contradict	state the opposite of something
	correspondence	letters that are sent or received
	criticism	finding fault or pointing out a weakness
D	daze	to stun or shock because of a blow
	debate	a discussion in which people take sides on an issue
	decade	a period of 10 years
	decay	rot; break down naturally
	decline	to become weaker or fewer
	decompress	to relax; to relieve pressure
	demonstrate	to show how to do something
	dense	packed close together
	deposit	to put something in a certain place
	deprive	to keep from having or enjoying something
	deserted	empty
	desolate	bare and deserted
	destination	the place to which someone or something is going
	detect	to discover, figure out, or notice
	devise	to invent or come up with a plan
	difficult	hard to do or understand
	digest	to break down the food in the body
	digital	created using a code of digits such as those used in computer programs
	disagreeable	unpleasant
	discipline	self-control
	disorder	a problem in the mind or body
	displace	to remove from a usual or common place
	distinct	not connected

	document	an official paper
	doubtful	unsure about something
	download	to copy a file from the Internet onto a private computer
	drone	to talk in a boring way
E	**ease**	to make something less difficult or painful
	economy	system of making, selling, and buying goods and services
	elevate	to raise or lift
	eligible	having the needed skills or requirements
	encourage	to urge others to do something
	endeavor	to make an effort to try something
	endow	to provide or furnish
	enforce	carry out; make happen
	enlist	get the help of
	entire	whole; complete
	entitle	to give someone the right to something
	epidemic	an outbreak of disease that spreads quickly and affects many people
	equipment	tools used for a certain purpose
	estimate	to roughly calculate
	eternity	forever
	eventually	finally, after a series of events
	evidence	proof; things studied for the purpose of learning something
	exaggerate	to make something seem larger or greater than it really is
	expand	to increase in size
	extract	to pull out or draw out
	extreme	far past normal
	extremely	very much; in a way that is far beyond normal
F	**fabric**	cloth
	facility	a place where an action or operation is completed
	factor	something that influences the result
	falter	to become unsteady; to begin to fall apart

	fiery	burning; full of fire
	fitness	state of being fit or in good health
	fossil	remains of an animal or plant preserved in rock
	fragile	easily broken or damaged
	fragrant	having a sweet or pleasant odor
G–I	**gadget**	a small, clever invention
	geoscientist	a scientist who studies how Earth's natural systems relate to one another
	goal	something you aim for
	guarantee	a promise that something will happen or be done
	hemisphere	a division of the world into halves
	historical	of or related to history
	humid	moist or damp
	identity	who a person is as proved by name, features, and legal documents
	illegally	in a way that is against the law
	image	a picture or a mental idea
	impact	a strong effect or influence
	impatient	not patient; not willing to wait
	implement	to put into place
	import	to carry in from another country
	impossible	not possible; could not be true
	inconvenience	something that makes things difficult or uncomfortable
	industrious	hard working; driven to get things done
	infinite	going on forever; without an end
	influential	having strong influence or power
	inhabited	lived in
	inherit	to receive from one's parents
	institution	an organization, or group, formed to serve a religious, educational, or charitable purpose
	instruction	an explanation of how to do something
	interminably	endlessly

	intermission	a pause or break
	international	involving different countries
	interview	a meeting in which an employer asks a job seeker questions to see if he or she is right for the job
	invisible	not visible; cannot be seen with the eyes
	irresistible	impossible to say no to
	isolate	to set apart
K–M	**kidnap**	to take someone by force and hold him or her prisoner
	landscape	natural scenery in an area
	layer	a single thickness of something that lies over or under something else
	liable	likely
	magnitude	the size or strength of something
	mason	a worker who builds with stone
	meager	barely enough
	melodious	having a pleasant melody or musical sound
	mentor	a teacher or guide
	method	a way of doing something
	microsurgery	surgery performed while looking through a microscope
	migrant	a person who moves from place to place to get work
	miniature	very small
	minimum	as few or as small as can be
	miserable	very uncomfortable
	misery	great suffering or unhappiness
	misuse	to use in the wrong way
N–O	**network**	a group of people or things that are connected in some way
	nonresident	a person who does not live permanently in a place
	nurture	to care for and help grow
	objective	the goal of an action
	obstacle	something that gets in the way or stops progress

occur	happen; take place	
opportunity	a good time or chance to do something	
orbit	the path one object takes as it travels around another object in space	
P paltry	very small	
particle	a small piece or part of something	
patent	a legal document giving a person or group the right to make, use, or sell a certain invention	
pave	to cover with a hard material	
penalty	a loss of money or rights which is brought on by some action	
penetrate	pass into	
permit	a document or paper that gives official permission to do something (noun); to allow (verb)	
persist	to continue with purpose	
persistent	continuing with purpose	
phonetically	in a way that matches letters to sounds	
plank	a long, flat board	
policy	rules that guide a particular business or group	
popular	commonly approved of or liked	
portable	able to be carried or moved from place to place	
portion	a part of something	
portray	to describe or represent	
possess	to control or take over	
postpone	to put off	
potent	powerful	
potential	possibility; talent not yet used	
precaution	an action taken in advance to prevent harm	
precision	accuracy; exactness in fine details	
prefer	to like one more than another	
premises	grounds or locations	
prescribe	to write instructions to a drug store for a medicine	

	preserve	to save or protect
	pressure	the force or weight against something; application of influence or intimidation
	prestige	respect or influence
	priority	something given special attention; a main focus
	procedure	a series of steps
	production	the act of making something
	program	a plan for doing something
	prohibit	to forbid or prevent
	prominent	important or outstanding; standing out or easily noticed
	prompt	to move to action
	prone	tending to do something
	proportion	a balanced relationship between sizes
	protrude	to stick out
R	**range**	the space or distance covered
	recent	not that long ago
	reception	the receiving of broadcast signals
	recycle	to use again
	reliable	dependable or able to be trusted
	remnant	something that is left over
	renew	to begin something again
	repetition	doing something again and again
	resist	to stand firm against something
	responsibility	something a person must take care of
	restraint	using control; holding back
	revenue	money that is made; income
	ritual	a set way of doing something
	rocky	having or consisting of rocks
S	**sanitize**	to clean thoroughly
	scorched	burnt
	select	to choose from among several

sensor	a device that shows changes in light, heat, or motion
site	location; place where something is found
skeleton	the bones that make up the body
slander	a critical and usually false statement
slavery	one person being "owned" by another
sliver	a small, narrow piece of something
somber	serious; gloomy
source	thing, place, or person from which something comes
sparse	few and scattered
specific	clearly described or explained
speculate	to make a guess
sterilize	to kill all living microorganisms
strand	to leave somebody in an unfamiliar place
structure	something built with many parts
subscription	a contract to receive a certain number of issues of a magazine or newspaper
subtle	faint and not easy to notice
symmetrical	each part having the same form or shape
T **technology**	the use of scientific knowledge to invent or build things
tedious	boring
tendency	a behavior or attitude that leans toward a particular direction
texture	how rough or smooth something is
theory	an idea about something
thinness	the state of having little body fat
throughout	in, to, or during every part of
tolerant	allowing to exist; not wanting to limit
transfix	to hold frozen in place by shock or surprise
transform	to change completely
trek	to hike or travel
tremendous	powerful
trend	a general course or direction

	typical	normal or usual
U–W	**unanimous**	having one voice; being without disagreement
	unbearable	more than a person can stand
	underneath	below another thing
	unleased	let loose
	valuable	worth a great deal
	varied	of many kinds
	variety	a collection of different kinds
	various	of different kinds
	vast	covering a huge area
	vehicle	something that carries people or goods from one place to another
	vitamin	a substance you need to stay healthy; a necessary element of nutrition
	welfare	the state of being well
	windpipe	breathing tube connecting the throat and the lungs